PETER LOMBARD

GREAT MEDIEVAL THINKERS

Series Editor
Brian Davies
Blackfriars, University of Oxford,
and Fordham University

DUNS SCOTUS
Richard Cross

BERNARD OF CLAIRVAUX
Gillian R. Evans

JOHN SCOTTUS ERIUGENA
Deirdre Carabine

ROBERT GROSSETESTE
James McEvoy

BOETHIUS
John Marenbon

PETER LOMBARD
Philipp W. Rosemann

PETER LOMBARD

Philipp W. Rosemann

OXFORD
UNIVERSITY PRESS

2004

OXFORD

UNIVERSITY PRESS

Oxford   New York
Auckland   Bangkok   Buenos Aires   Cape Town   Chennai
Dar es Salaam   Delhi   Hong Kong   Istanbul   Karachi   Kolkata
Kuala Lumpur   Madrid   Melbourne   Mexico City   Mumbai   Nairobi
São Paulo   Shanghai   Taipei   Tokyo   Toronto

Copyright © 2004 by Oxford University Press, Inc.

Published by Oxford University Press, Inc.
198 Madison Avenue, New York, New York 10016

www.oup.com

Oxford is a registered trademark of Oxford University Press

Library of Congress Cataloging-in-Publication Data
Rosemann, Philipp.
Peter Lombard / Philipp W. Rosemann.
p.   cm.—(Great medieval thinkers)
Includes bibliographical references and index.
ISBN 0-19-515544-0; 0-19-515545-9 (pbk.)
1. Peter Lombard, Bishop of Paris, ca. 1100–1160.   2. Peter Lombard,
Bishop of Paris, ca. 1100–1160. Sententiarum libri IV.   3. Theology,
Doctrinal—History—Middle Ages, 600–1500.   I. Title.   II. Series.
BX1749.P4 R67 2003
230'.2'092—dc21   2003005370

1 3 5 7 9 8 6 4 2

Printed in the United States of America
on acid-free paper

One should not accept too lazily, right inside [the sphere of] theological speculation, a certain schema of progress that all of the forces of the century contributed yesterday to impose upon us (and it is not certain, some appearances notwithstanding, that they do not continue doing so today). In reacting against the "modern" self-importance which makes our contemporaries believe that they have more wits than their fathers, for the sole reason that they were born after them, we believe that we are returning to a more traditional assessment, from which not only the patristic era and the high Middle Ages, but the following centuries as well, must benefit.

—Henri de Lubac, S.J.,
Corpus mysticum

SERIES FOREWORD

Many people would be surprised to be told that there *were* any great medieval thinkers. If a *great* thinker is one from whom we can learn today, and if "medieval" serves as an adjective for describing anything that existed from (roughly) the years 600 to 1500 A.D., then, so it is often supposed, medieval thinkers cannot be called "great."

Why not? One answer often given appeals to the ways in which medieval authors with a taste for argument and speculation tend to invoke authorities, especially religious ones. Such invocation of authority is not the stuff of which great thought is made—so it is often said today. It is also frequently said that greatness is not to be found in the thinking of those who lived before the rise of modern science, not to mention that of modern philosophy and theology. Today's students of science are hardly ever referred to literature earlier than the seventeenth century. Modern students of philosophy are often taught nothing about the history of ideas between Aristotle (384–322 B.C.) and Descartes (1596–1650). Modern students of theology are often encouraged to believe that sound theological thinking is a product of the nineteenth century.

Yet the origins of modern science lie in the conviction that the world is open to rational investigation and is orderly rather than chaotic—a conviction that came fully to birth, and was systematically explored and developed, during the Middle Ages. And it is in medieval thinking that we find some of the most sophisticated and rigorous discussions in the areas of philosophy and theology ever offered for human consumption—not surprising, perhaps, if we note that medieval philosophers and theologians, like their contemporary counterparts, were mostly university teachers who participated in an ongoing, worldwide debate, part of a large community of teachers and students with whom they were regularly involved, and were not (like many seventeenth-, eighteenth-, and even nineteenth-century philosophers and theologians) people working in relative isolation. As for the question of appeal to authority: it is certainly true that many medieval thinkers believed in authority (especially religious authority) as a serious court of appeal, and it is true that most people today would say that they cannot do this. But as many contemporary philosophers are increasingly reminding us, authority is as much an ingredient in our thinking as it was for medieval thinkers (albeit that, because of differences between thinkers, one might reasonably say that there is no such thing as "medieval thought"), for most of what we take ourselves to know derives from the trust we have placed in our various teachers, colleagues, friends, and general contacts. When it comes to reliance on authority, the main difference between us and medieval thinkers lies in the fact that their reliance on authority (insofar as they had it) was often more focused and explicitly acknowledged than it is for us. It does not lie in the fact that it was uncritical and naive in a way that our reliance on authority is not.

In recent years, such truths have come to be increasingly recognized at what we might call the academic level. No longer disposed to think of the Middle Ages as "dark" (meaning "lacking in intellectual richness"), many university departments and many publishers of books and journals now devote a lot of energy to the study of medieval thinking. And they do so, not simply on the assumption that it is historically important, but also in the light of the increasingly developing insight that it is full of things with which to dialogue and from which to learn. Following a long period in which medieval thinking was thought to be of only antiquarian interest, we are now witnessing its revival as a contemporary voice—one to converse with, one from which we might learn.

The Great Medieval Thinkers series reflects and is part of this exciting revival. Written by distinguished experts, these volumes aim to provide substantial introductions to a range of medieval authors, who are as worth reading today as they were when they wrote. Students of medieval

literature (for example, the writings of Chaucer) are currently well sup-
plied (if not oversupplied) with secondary works to aid them when reading the objects of their concern. But those with an interest in medieval
philosophy and theology are by no means so fortunate when it comes to
reliable and accessible volumes to help them. The Great Medieval Thinkers series therefore aspires to remedy that deficiency by concentrating on
medieval philosophers and theologians and by offering solid overviews
of their lives and thought coupled with contemporary reflection on what
they had to say. Each entry in the series will provide a valuable treatment
of a single thinker. Taken together, the series will constitute a rich and
distinguished history and discussion of medieval philosophy and theology.
With one eye on college and university students and the other eye on
the general reader, the authors in the series will clearly and accessibly
present each thinker's perspective for those unfamiliar with the concepts.
But each contributor to the series also intends to inform, engage, and
generally entertain even those with specialist knowledge in the area of
medieval thinking. So, as well as surveying and introducing, the volumes
in the series seek to advance the state of medieval studies both at the
historical and the speculative level.

Since few of his writings have been translated, Peter Lombard has
not been much studied for a very long time except by those with serious,
professional interests in medieval scholarship. Yet he had a major intellectual influence from the thirteenth to the sixteenth century. His best-
known work, the *Sententiae in IV libris distinctae* (commonly known as
the *Sentences*), became the standard textbook for students and teachers of
theology in the years following the Fourth Lateran Council (1215). Medieval theologians were routinely required to lecture on it, and some of
the greatest of them wrote commentaries on it. Hence, for example, we
have commentaries on the *Sentences* from Alexander of Hales (c. 1186–
1245), St. Bonaventure (c. 1217–1274), St. Thomas Aquinas (c. 1225–1274),
Duns Scotus (c. 1266–1308), William of Ockham (c. 1285–1347), and Martin Luther (1483–1546). Anyone who wants to understand what medieval
theology was all about certainly needs to know about Peter Lombard.

Despite this long history of study, the verdicts on whether he was a
great medieval thinker have differed, as Philipp Rosemann makes clear
in what follows. As Rosemann also explains, however, Peter Lombard is
more than the sum of his commentators. He was an original thinker. His
historical significance is unquestionable. But, as Rosemann skillfully in-

dicates, Lombard is of more than merely historical interest. All contemporary students and teachers of medieval thinking know of Lombard by name, although few of them could explain what he actually said and why it might matter. In this book, however, they will find expert help as they seek to put a mind to a name. In it they will find an ideal introduction to a currently neglected but very significant figure.

Brian Davies

ACKNOWLEDGMENTS

My principal debt in composing this book is to the University of Dallas, where I have over the past six years taught courses in medieval philosophy, Scholastic tradition, and related topics. For the fall of 2001, the university reduced my teaching load to one course, allowing me to begin preparations for this book.

The William A. Blakley Library of the University of Dallas houses extensive collections in the fields of medieval philosophy and theology, collections without which my work on Peter Lombard would not have been possible. I am grateful for the excellent collaboration with a team of dedicated librarians. Ms. Alice Puro, head of interlibrary loans, has been diligent and efficient in obtaining literature that was unavailable in the university's own library.

I have received much encouragement from Professor James McEvoy of the National University of Ireland, Maynooth, who generously agreed to read my chapters and has offered many suggestions for improvements. Some of these suggestions have saved me from mistakes. Such errors as remain are, of course, my sole responsibility. Professor Bruce C. Brasington (West Texas A&M University), Madame Caroline Heid (Institut de Recherche et d'Histoire des Textes, Paris), Professor Constant J. Mews (Monash University, Melbourne), and my colleague at the University of Dallas Professor Francis R. Swietek have provided helpful advice on particular aspects of the project. I am grateful as well to Monsieur Pascal Jacquinot of the Médiathèque de l'agglomération troyenne (Troyes, France) for making available a digital file of the illustration used in the frontispiece. Boydell Publishers of Woodbridge, Suffolk (England), have granted me permission to reproduce some drawings from Christopher de Hamel's work, *Glossed Books of the Bible and the Origins of the Paris Booktrade*.

Finally, I wish to acknowledge Professor Brian Davies, O.P., who commissioned me to write this volume for the series he edits.

CONTENTS

ABBREVIATIONS

Brady, *Prolegomena*	Magistri Petri Lombardi *Sententiae in IV libris distinctae*, ed. Ignatius Brady, O.F.M., vol. 1, part 1, Spicilegium Bonaventurianum 4 (Grottaferrata: Editiones Collegii S. Bonaventurae Ad Claras Aquas, 1971).
Colish, *Peter Lombard*	Marcia L. Colish, *Peter Lombard*, 2 vols., Brill's Studies in Intellectual History 41 (Leiden/New York/Cologne: Brill, 1994).
Miscellanea lombardiana	*Miscellanea lombardiana* (Novara: Istituto geografico de Agostini, 1957).
PL	*Patrologia latina, cursus completus*, 221 vols., ed. J.-P. Migne (Paris: Migne, 1844–1865).
Sentences	Magistri Petri Lombardi *Sententiae in IV libris distinctae*, ed. Ignatius Brady, O.F.M., 2 vols., Spicilegium Bonaventurianum 4–5 (Grottaferrata: Editiones Collegii S. Bonaventurae Ad Claras Aquas, 1971–1981). Vol. 1, part 2 contains books 1 and 2; vol. 2 contains books 3 and 4. All translations from the *Sen-*

tences are my own. Following the practice of the edition, I use **bold** characters to indicate rubrics. Marginal rubrics are marked with an additional asterisk (*).

Note: All English translations from Scripture follow the Douay-Rheims version, which has been chosen for its closeness to the Vulgate: *The Holy Bible, translated from the Latin Vulgate . . . the Whole Revised and Diligently Compared with the Latin Vulgate by Bishop Richard Challoner* (Baltimore, Md.: John Murphy, 1889; reprint, Rockford, Ill.: TAN Books, 2000).

PETER LOMBARD

Peter Lombard in an illumination from one of the earliest manuscripts of the *Book of Sentences* (MS. *Troyes, Bibliothèque municipale 900*, fol. 1). © Pascal Jacquinot, Médiathèque de l'agglomération troyenne, Troyes, France.

Introduction

A GREAT MEDIEVAL THINKER?

Peter Lombard, who was born between 1095 and 1100 in the region of Novara in Lombardy and died in 1160 as bishop of Paris, is the author of a celebrated work with the title, *Sententiae in quatuor IV libris distinctae*. For several centuries, these *Sentences Divided into Four Books* served as the standard theological textbook in the Christian West. Only in the sixteenth century were they gradually replaced by Thomas Aquinas's *Summa theologiae*.

The *Sentences* shaped the minds of generations of theologians during one of the most formative periods in the history of Christian doctrine. Indeed, since in the medieval university it was part of the duties of every aspiring master of theology to lecture on the *Sentences*, there is no piece of Christian literature that has been commented upon more frequently—except for Scripture itself.[1] A compilation of commentaries on the *Book of Sentences* that appeared more than fifty years ago (and has since been added to) already listed 1,407 items.[2] Toward the end of the *Sentences'* long career, at the beginning of the sixteenth century, the young Martin Luther was one of the last great theologians to lecture on the work. He left behind a series of detailed glosses that have become the object of intense study.[3] As commentator on the *Sentences*, the reformer was preceded by thinkers such as Alexander of Hales, Bonaventure, Thomas Aquinas, Duns Scotus, Ockham, Marsilius of Inghen, and Gabriel Biel—

to mention but a few of the most famous. As a consequence of this unique situation, it would be possible to write the history of much of later medieval and early modern thought as a history of commentaries on the *Book of Sentences*. In her magisterial study of Peter Lombard, the intellectual historian Marcia L. Colish observes: "I was struck by the fact that medievalists would be able to survey and map the *terra incognita* that remains in our knowledge of much of the history of speculative thought from the middle of the twelfth century to the end of the period if the *Sentence*[*s*] commentaries of all the scholastics known to have made them could be studied in chronological order and in a comparative way."[4]

The *Book of Sentences* not only constituted the point of departure for much of theological reflection from the time of the first universities through the Council of Trent; it was also the point of arrival for the development of the Christian thought that preceded it.[5] For that was the nature of the sentence collection as a literary genre: to gather together the most important scriptural and patristic quotations—the *sententiae*—on crucial theological topics; to arrange these topics in a systematic order; and to synthesize, as far as possible, the positions represented by the quotations, while bearing in mind contemporary theological debates. A good sentence collection—and Peter Lombard's is an outstanding one—would thus represent the state of the art in theology.

The Sentences: A Work of Undeserved Fame?

Peter Lombard's contemporaries chose the *Book of Sentences*, among a number of similar works, as the best account of theological research in its day. What is more, long after their author's death, several generations of thinkers continued to consider the *Sentences* a valuable, or at least viable, *point de départ* for their own reflections. Against this background, it is not easy to understand the modern judgment on the standard theological manual of the Scholastics, for this judgment has been overwhelmingly negative. It may not surprise us that many Reformation Protestants distanced themselves from this epitome of Scholasticism or that Enlightenment thinkers did not find much to their liking in a collection of authoritative quotations.[6] But why does Joseph de Ghellinck, one of the pioneers of modern research on Peter Lombard and not at all an unsympathetic commentator, call the *Book of Sentences* "a work whose celebrity surpasses its value"?[7] De Ghellinck is not in bad company with his judgment. In his *History of Scholastic Method*, Martin Grabmann, one of the most influential medievalists of the twentieth century, compares the *Sentences* with a roughly contemporary work of systematic theology, Hugh of St. Victor's *De sacramentis christianae fidei*. He arrives at the following conclusion:

> Hugh's chef d'oeuvre, *De sacramentis christianae fidei*, could also light the way for our Schoolman, as an ideal of large-scale systematicity. Peter Lombard has not reached this ideal. Due to its twofold division into *opera conditionis et restaurationis* and its broad unified point of view stemming from the person and work of Christ, Hugh's work has a considerably better structure and represents, right to the level of detail, an organic view and digestion of ideas from Scripture and the Fathers; it possesses to a larger extent the appeal and power of the personal, whereas for long stretches Peter Lombard does not rise above an external classification of statements from Scripture and the Fathers. On the level of detail, too, through the constant attempt at reconciling contradictory authorities, he does not sufficiently bring out the architectonic principles of his work.[8]

With this negative assessment, Grabmann has no other way to explain the success of the *Sentences* than through "a happy coincidence of historical accidents or, if one wants to put it that way, chance events."[9]

Significantly, only one scholar marked the seventh centenary of Peter Lombard's death, in 1960. In that year, Louvain moralist Philippe Delhaye devoted the annual Albert the Great lecture, which he was invited to deliver at the now defunct Institut d'études médiévales in Montreal, to "Peter Lombard: His life, works, and ethics."[10] While acknowledging the historical influence of Peter Lombard's work—"Peter Lombard is the author who has most profoundly marked medieval theology and thought," Delhaye writes[11]—the author is quick to dismiss the Lombard's achievement as a thinker: "his epoch knew more profound theologians ... [and] better informed philosophers."[12]

It is only recently, through the groundbreaking study by Marcia L. Colish from which I have already quoted, that the dominant view of the *Sentences* as a work of modest intrinsic merit has come to be challenged. Colish, whose research was inspired by the "paradoxical situation"[13] of the gap between the Lombard's former fame and his contemporary underrating, dismisses the negative assessment of the *Sentences* as an anachronistic caricature. In her *Peter Lombard*, she explains why exactly "a young scholar who arrive[d] in Paris in the 1140s or 1150s, seeking the instruction that would enable him to become a master of theology in his own right," would have found the *Sentences* "so clearly superior" to the essays in systematic theology of the other masters.[14] Colish answers this question by means of a painstaking comparison, over more than 800 pages, between Peter Lombard's teachings and those of his contemporaries. In this way, she manages to draw a picture of the Lombard and his achievement that corresponds more closely to historical fact, rather than resorting to the unsatisfactory strategy of attributing the high esteem in which he was held to mere chance. Unfortunately, in attempting to establish Peter Lombard's superiority by comparison with his contemporaries, Colish is sometimes carried away by her enthusiasm. Thus, she has a tendency to attribute to the Lombard positions of greater sophistication than those he actually held. Occasionally, she misinterprets him altogether. And in an astonishing gesture of anachronism, she laments the absence of a synthetic treatment of ethics in the *Sentences*, subsequently gathering together arguments advanced in different books of the work to reflect later ideals of what shape a successful ethics should take.[15] In the course of this book, I will occasionally point out such flaws in Colish's reading of the Lombard—flaws that in no way diminish Colish's accomplishment in single-handedly reviving and giving a fresh direction to Lombard studies.

A Great Medieval Thinker

Colish's study has already given rise to new interest in Peter Lombard and the *Book of Sentences*.[16] It is unlikely, however, that the *Sentences'* status as "one of the least read of the world's great books"[17] will change fundamentally. Certainly, an English translation would render the work accessible to an audience beyond the narrow circles of medievalists to which acquaintance with it is currently confined. Yet, the *Sentences* are too strange, too "different" a piece of writing ever to become a bestseller. The books force us to rethink our conception of what a great work, a great author, and a great thinker are. The *Sentences* are not like Augustine's *Confessions*—a deeply speculative work by a Christian thinker who deploys all the devices of late Roman rhetoric to move our hearts closer to God through a gripping narrative of the struggles of his spiritual life. The *Book of Sentences* is comparable more to Aquinas's *Summa theologiae*—a work of rigorous, highly repetitive structure that is composed in the dry technical jargon of another age. What distinguishes the *Sentences* from the *Summa*, however, is that the latter contains texts that clearly testify to the author's ability to rise above his sources and thus to produce "original" and "personal" syntheses. These texts thus fulfill the conditions of what we are prepared to recognize as great thought. Peter Lombard's case is different. For reasons that are related to the methodological development of Christian thought in the Middle Ages (which we are going to examine momentarily), the originality and personal stamp of the Lombard's theological vision are more difficult to discern. To the eye of the untrained reader, the *Sentences* could appear as nothing but a string of quotations from Scripture and the Fathers, precariously held together by a few connecting words. What counts, however, is the selection of the quotations, their arrangement into a coherent theological system "with a place for everything and everything in its place,"[18] and the attempt to distill doctrine out of the often discordant voices of the tradition. This is where Peter Lombard's achievement lies. In order to appreciate his genius, it is necessary to provide a brief outline of the development of the Christian tradition which, in a certain sense, culminates in his work.

FROM STORY TO SYSTEM

Traditions develop around texts that have acquired such authoritative status as to become foundational.[1] A tradition, then, is in a sense nothing but the history of the interpretation of a foundational text, or a set of foundational texts. In ancient Greece, the tradition developed around Homer; in Judaism, it developed around the Torah; in Christianity, around the Bible; in Islam, around the Qur'an. The political tradition of modern America is, in many ways, centered on the Constitution.

Many of these foundational texts, especially religious ones, seem to share a significant characteristic. They possess a narrative structure, as opposed to presenting a rational argument. Thus, Homer tells us the story of Ulysses; the Old Testament relates the story of the people of Israel; and the New Testament offers us four versions of the life of Jesus Christ. To be sure, the Bible's narrative form does not exclude that it also comprises elements of teaching, or doctrine. The Old Testament contains the Ten Commandments, while the Gospels, in particular the Gospel according to John, are not a transcript of Jesus' sayings, but already represent a first stage of reflection on the Savior. Nonetheless, neither Testament constitutes anything like a theological "system" or synthesis. The Bible is not a catechism, *summa*, or sentence collection.

The Christian Tradition from Story
to System: Scriptural Roots

The Bible does, however, contain the germs of such properly theological projects. It has been said, and aptly so, that "the theological philosophy of the Middle Ages begins in the first century with St. Paul."[2] Although in the First Letter to the Corinthians, Paul emphasizes that Christian thought is not in a relationship of simple continuity with the wisdom of the Greeks, because "the foolishness of God is wiser than men" (1 Cor 1:25), he is far from rejecting the idea of an intellectual penetration of the faith—even if that means using the traditions of the Greeks. In the Letter to the Hebrews, Paul (if indeed Paul is the author of Hebrews) offers the classical definition of faith (Heb 11:1): a definition, not a story or a simile. In the Letter to Titus, he explains that a bishop should "be able to exhort in sound doctrine (ἐν τῇ διδασκαλίᾳ τῇ ὑγιαινούσῃ), and to convince the gainsayers" (Ti 1:9). In other words, the faith needs to be able to defend itself intellectually. Similarly, in the Second Letter to the Corinthians, the apostle speaks of the importance of "destroying counsels, and every height that exalteth itself against the knowledge of God (κατὰ τῆς γνώσεως τοῦ θεοῦ)" (2 Cor 10:4). Peter agrees: "But sanctify the Lord Christ in your hearts, being ready always to satisfy every one that asketh you a reason (λόγον) of the hope which is in you" (1 Pt 3: 15). From scriptural passages such as these, it is clear that Greek *logos* was not, as some have argued, grafted externally onto the faith by intellectuals several generations removed from Jesus. No, the apostles themselves were the first theologians—theologians, by the way, who were not afraid of availing themselves of Greek traditions in their work of "exhorting and convincing the gainsayers," as it appears from Paul's references to the Greeks' own prophets and poets (see Ti 1:12 and Acts 17: 28).[3]

Thus the New Testament, despite its preponderantly narrative character, not only carries the germs of theological reflection within itself, but even hints at the proper attitude that such a reflection should take toward non-Christian sources—one could call it an attitude of Christian discernment. Christianity is not the same as secular wisdom; indeed the foolishness of the cross subverts natural reason. Nevertheless, the faith should adopt, and adapt, such elements of secular wisdom as may help it to arrive at a greater knowledge of God.

Apart from this guarded openness toward reflection on the faith that is aided by non-Christian sources, there is a second element in Scripture that was to become crucial in the development of the Christian intellectual tradition. Since Christianity is based on a set of texts believed to be divinely inspired, proper understanding and interpretation of these texts is of paramount importance for the Christian believer—not only for the discovery of the truth, but for salvation itself. These texts, however, are not without internal tensions; most importantly, perhaps, there are significant differences between the religious messages of the Old and the New Testament. In the field of morality, for example, the Old Testament condones divorce (see Dt 24:1); the New does not (see Mt 5:32). The Old Testament stipulates "an eye for an eye" (Ex 21:24), whereas Jesus preaches love of one's enemy (see Mt 5:44). In its own self-understanding, then, the Christian message supersedes the Old Law. Yet this supersession does not, and cannot, mean simple abolishment. Rather, throughout the Gospels, the New Law is presented as a "fulfillment" of the Old Law: "I am not come to destroy, but to fulfill ($\pi\lambda\eta\rho\tilde{\omega}\sigma\alpha\iota$)," Jesus says (Mt 5: 17). The notion of fulfillment implies a rather subtle relationship of identity and difference. The Old Law is sublated—*aufgehoben*, as Hegel might say—in the New, such that it is all at once lifted up to a higher level, preserved at that level, and canceled out in its previous form. The cancellation, however, must not be understood as detracting in any way from the integrity of the Old Law. After all, Jesus declares that "till heaven and earth pass, one jot, or one tittle shall not pass of the law" (Mt 5:18). This can only mean that the New Law is to be understood as a radicalization of the Old; far from doing away with it, it goes beyond it, boiling it down to its essence. "Not the *law* is repealed," Swedish theologian Henrik Ljungman writes in his study of Matthew 5:17, "but the *limitation* of the law for the sake of sin is repealed and eliminated."[4] The New Testament fulfills the Old by reducing the multiplicity of ethical rules and regulations that the latter contains to their essential spirit: "For all the law is fulfilled ($\pi\epsilon\pi\lambda\eta\rho\omega\tau\alpha\iota$) in one word: *Thou shalt love thy neighbor as thyself*" (Gal 5:14).

The notion of fulfillment constitutes Christianity as a tradition that carries another one—Judaism—already within itself, in a form such that the "other" retains its full significance while nonetheless, at least from the Christian point of view, having been sublated. In recognizing the "existing spiritual and moral capital"[5] of Judaism, Matthew 5:17 epitomizes the Christian attitude toward non-Christian traditions that we already encountered in discussing St. Paul. But Matthew 5:17 is of more fundamental significance, for it concerns the relationship of Christianity not to a tradition that is relatively external to it, such as pagan antiquity, but rather to a tradition that is, even from the Christian viewpoint, founded on divine revelation, as such always remaining authoritative and foundational. Following Protestant theologian Adolf von Harnack, one could say that it is Christianity's internal constitution that has taught it the value of synthesis.[6]

To sum up, the New Testament, while fundamentally narrative in structure, encourages theological reflection, that is to say, the penetration of the faith by means of reason (λόγος). First and foremost, such theological reflection faces the task of demonstrating the unity of God's revelation in the Old and New Testaments. This is a task of reconciling, and synthesizing, two sets of divinely inspired texts. The use of non-Christian concepts and ideas is portrayed as legitimate, so long as no attempt is made to reduce the foolishness of the cross to mere natural reason—and, of course, so long as these concepts and ideas can themselves be reconciled and synthesized with the Christian tradition. In these three elements—intellectual penetration of the faith, systematization of the texts upon which it is based, and dialogue with non-Christian thought—we already find the seeds of what Martin Grabmann has called the Scholastic method.[7]

The Latin Fathers

The transformation of the Christian faith into a doctrine began in early patristic times. Christian intellectuals, the Church Fathers, attempted to gather together specific themes from the story of Jesus and distill them into (relatively small) units of teaching. Thus, Tertullian (c. 160–after 220) reflects upon the relationships among God the Father, the Son, and the Spirit—all of whom are of course mentioned in the New Testament, but in different passages and without terminological precision. Tertullian decides to term this relationship *Trinitas*, "Trinity," which he defines as three "persons" in one "substance."[8] Tertullian is evidently engaged in a project of bringing reason to bear upon the data of the faith, and this reason is ultimately the reason of the philosophers—as is particularly clear in the term *substantia*. Nonetheless, Tertullian remains acutely aware of the distance that separates the faith from the wisdom of the Greeks. His outburst against "Athens" in his treatise *Prescription against Heretics* has become famous: "What has Athens to do with Jerusalem? What the Academy with the Church? What heretics with Christians? . . . Away with those who have professed a Stoic and Platonic and dialectical Christianity! We need no curiosity after Christ Jesus, no inquiry after the Gospel."[9]

Tertullian's apparent inconsistency in both affirming the value of pagan rationality and rejecting it rather forcefully is best interpreted as a struggle for a new, authentically Christian form of thinking, one that employs reason to come to a proper understanding of the story of Jesus while never forgetting that mere human thought falls short of the mystery of God. One sees the two unreconciled sides of this struggle when comparing statements such as "What aspect of the divine would not be rational? [*Quid enim diuinum non rationale?*]"[10] with other passages that affirm the absolute irreducibility of the faith to reason, indeed the rational impossibility of the faith. Of the Resurrection, for instance, Tertullian writes that "it is certain, because it is impossible [*certum est, quia impossibile*]."[11]

In Augustine (354–430), the greatest Church Father of the Latin West, the relationship between reason and revelation, together with the role of the former in the elucidation of the latter, is already articulated with considerable precision. Augustine's *On Christian Teaching* is a treatise that sets out to define the program of a Christian education. Throughout the medieval period, it was among the bishop of Hippo's most influential works. The book is firmly centered on the problem of scriptural exegesis, but many other branches of learning are grouped around this center, turning out to be necessary for the interpretation of the sacred texts. In book 1, Augustine develops the distinction between things and signs that was to become Peter Lombard's guidepost in composing the *Book of Sentences*. Scripture contains both things and signs—or, rather, things that do not signify anything else and things that do (and therefore function as signs, all signs being things). In other words, sometimes in Scripture a stone is just a stone, while on other occasions it might carry a metaphorical meaning. Things are either to be enjoyed for their own sake, or to be used, or both at the same time.[12] We may take Augustine to mean

that the things to be enjoyed do not point beyond themselves, by functioning as signs of something else, whereas things to be used do refer us
to some higher good. It makes sense, then, that Augustine presents the
Trinity as the ultimate thing. The proper response to it is love, which
Augustine calls "the fulfillment and end of the law and all the divine
scriptures"[13]: "So anyone who thinks that he has understood the divine
scriptures or any part of them, but cannot by his understanding build up
this double love of God and neighbor, has not yet succeeded in understanding them."[14]

Love, therefore, is the very core of Scripture and the Christian life,
the principle of unity that holds them together. Augustine devotes the
remainder of book 1 to its analysis, in the process going through all the
main elements of the faith. Grabmann considers chapters 9 through 19
of this book "a brief system of theology."[15]

Books 2 and 3 deal with signs, which, by their very nature, require
interpretation. In the human realm, words are the most dominant kinds
of signs. In Scripture, God has used human words in order to communicate his message. The correct interpretation of this message necessitates
knowledge: first of all, knowledge of the whole of Scripture, since its
texts cast light upon each other. Secular learning, however, is equally
indispensable, not only because accurate interpretation of a text may require recourse to the original language in which it was written,[16] but also
because the words of Scripture touch on many subjects, ranging from
biology and petrology to arithmetic, music, history, astronomy, medicine,
agriculture, and navigation, not excluding dancing, running, and even
wrestling! Logic plays a particularly important role in scriptural exegesis,
because it "permeates the whole body of scripture, rather like a network
of muscles."[17] It is not possible, then, to comprehend the Word of God
without knowing the rules of right reasoning. This last consideration
leads Augustine to the following justification of the study of pagan philosophers:

> Any statements by those who are called philosophers, especially the
> Platonists, which happen to be true and consistent with our faith
> should not cause alarm, but be claimed for our own use, as it were
> from owners who have no right to them. Like the treasures of the
> ancient Egyptians, who possessed not only idols and heavy burdens
> which the people of Israel hated and shunned but also vessels and

ornaments of silver and gold, and clothes, which on leaving Egypt the people of Israel, in order to make better use of them, surreptitiously claimed for themselves (they did this not on their own authority but at Gods command, and the Egyptians in their ignorance actually gave them the things of which they had made poor use)—similarly all the branches of pagan learning [*doctrinae omnes gentilium*] contain not only false and superstitious fantasies and burdensome studies that involve unnecessary effort, which each one of us must loathe and avoid as under Christ's guidance we abandon the company of pagans, but also studies for liberated minds which are more appropriate to the service of the truth, and some very useful moral instruction, as well as the various truths about monotheism to be found in their writers. These treasures—like the silver and gold, which they did not create but dug, as it were, from the mines of providence, which is everywhere—which were used wickedly and harmfully in the service of demons must be removed by Christians, as they separate themselves in spirit from the wretched company of pagans, and applied to their true function, that of preaching the gospel. . . . This is exactly what many good and faithful Christians have done. We can see, can we not, the amount of gold, silver, and clothing with which Cyprian, that most attractive writer and most blessed martyr, was laden when he left Egypt; is not the same true of Lactantius, and Victorinus, of Optatus, and Hilary, to say nothing of people still alive, and countless Greek scholars? This is what had been done earlier by Moses himself, that most faithful servant of God, of whom it is written that he was trained in "all the wisdom of the Egyptians." . . . As students of the divine scriptures, equipped in this way, begin to approach the task of studying them in detail, they must ponder incessantly this phrase of the apostle Paul: "knowledge puffs up, but love builds up."[18]

The strategy that Augustine employs in order to justify the application of pagan knowledge, and in particular of philosophy, to the study of Scripture is complex and fascinating. He invokes biblical precedent—the Israelites' use of Egyptian goods on one side (see Ex 3:21–22, 11:2, and 12:35–36), and Moses' training in "all the wisdom of the Egyptians" on the other (see Acts 7:22)—as well as the authority of such predecessors as Victorinus, Hilary of Poitiers, and Ambrose (no doubt one of the "people still alive"). Augustine is suggesting that the appropriation of pagan learning is done "at God's command," just as the actions of the

Israelites in Egypt occurred under God's immediate guidance. At the end of the passage, he explicitly recenters all profane learning on Scripture, cautioning his reader, moreover, that all knowledge must be pursued in the spirit of Christian love. Book 3 of *On Christian Teaching* enters into the details of scriptural exegesis, and book 4 is a treatise on Christian rhetoric, or homiletics. There is no need to discuss them in the present context.

We are now in a position to understand Augustine's conception of Christian knowledge. Just as "all the law is fulfilled in one word: *Thou shalt love thy neighbor as thyself*" (Gal 5:14), so love is the center of Christian wisdom. Love, therefore, is the principle of unity both of the sacred texts themselves and of the Christian knowledge that develops as a result of their interpretation. As long as it is animated by the spirit of love, this interpretation may avail itself of all the branches of non-Christian learning.

Augustine implemented this program in his many theological writings, placing pagan learning—and in particular the Neoplatonic philosophy in which he was so deeply steeped—at the service of the intellectual penetration of the faith. In this way, he contributed to its further systematization, attempting to distill doctrine from the texts of Scripture. *On the Trinity* is the paramount example of Augustine's work as a systematic theological thinker.

It is interesting to see that the struggle for a new, authentically Christian form of thinking to which Augustine made such a crucial contribution went hand in hand with the quest for an appropriate literary form. In order to be elucidated and systematized through critical reflection, the narrative of Scripture had to be translated into logically structured arguments; but how could such arguments be presented? Augustine experimented with a number of different literary genres: the treatise, the dialogue,[19] the letter, and even autobiography. The *Confessions*, an account of Augustine's life leading to his conversion, is perhaps his most comprehensive work, though it is by no means a systematic treatment of the whole of theology. In the *Confessions*, the bishop of Hippo weaves reflections on love, providence, evil, friendship, memory, time, creation, exegesis, and many other topics into the form of a prayer that draws heavily on Neoplatonic themes. The narrative follows the chronology of his own life.

The Greek Fathers

In the attempt to give theology a systematic shape in comprehensive, logically structured accounts, the Greek Church Fathers were more advanced than the Latin tradition. Yet in this quick survey, which serves only the purpose of providing some background to place Peter Lombard in the Western Christian tradition, our treatment will have to be short. The "first systematic exposition of theology," as Grabmann calls it in his *History of Scholastic Method*,[20] was Origen's work *On First Principles*. The *Peri archōn*,[21] which was composed before 231, covers the entire field of Christian theology, starting with God, the Trinity, and the angels and proceeding logically to the material creation, man, free choice, sin, and redemption. It ends with a discussion of Scripture. Since Origen's speculations, particularly on the Trinity and Christological issues, came to be regarded as unorthodox after the Council of Chalcedon (451) had pronounced itself on these matters, *On First Principles* was subsequently lost, having to be reconstructed from secondhand quotations. The work exercised a limited influence on the Latin Middle Ages through Jerome (347–419) and through a translation by Tyrannius Rufinus (c. 345–410/11). John of Damascus's *Source of Knowledge*, on the other hand, was enormously influential, not only in Greek Orthodoxy—for which it became a standard textbook—but also in the Latin West. The *Pēgē gnōseōs* is of a compilatory character, drawing together elements from the preceding theological tradition, which it presents in Aristotelian language. Put together in the first half of the eighth century, it already reads like one of the later Western sentence collections. De Ghellinck considers it the Eastern equivalent of the *Book of Sentences*.[22] The work falls into three parts. The first is propaedeutic, offering an introduction to Aristotelian logic insofar as it is relevant to theology. The second constitutes a catalog of one hundred heresies, derived from Epiphanius. In the third, and main, part John creates a complete system of dogmatics in the form of a compilation of earlier Greek Fathers.[23] Among other sources, he cites Athanasius, Gregory of Nazianzus, Gregory of Nyssa, Basil, Chrysostom, Epiphanius, Cyril of Alexandria, the Pseudo-Dionysius, Leontius, and Maximus Confessor. John's system of theology treats first of God and the Trinity, moving on to creation, the angels and man, the Incarnation, the sacraments, evil, and finally eschatology. When, around 1150, two Latin versions of the third part of the *Pēgē gnōseōs* became available—first a partial one by Cerbanus, a Cistercian of the monastery of St. Mary of Pásztó in Hungary, and then a complete one by Burgundio of Pisa[24]— they made an immediate impact upon the contemporary theological scene. Both through its systematicity and through the wealth of fresh theological material that it placed at the disposal of Latin theologians, the work had a major effect on the development of Western theology. One of the first Scholastic authors to have access to the new translations was none other than Peter Lombard.

Latin Theology after Augustine

In the Latin West, efforts to synthesize and systematize the writings of the Church Fathers started immediately after Augustine's death, though on a more modest scale than in the Greek world. The first sentence collection in the West, which became the prototype of the literary genre to which the *Book of Sentences* belongs, was due to Prosper of Aquitaine (c. 390–463), a correspondent of the bishop of Hippo and ardent defender of his teachings on grace, predestination, and free will. Toward the end of his life, Prosper composed the *Liber sententiarum Sancti Augustini*, or "Book of Sentences of Saint Augustine."[25] The Latin word *sententia* signifies an opinion expressed by an authoritative writer;[26] *sentence*, by the way, used to carry a similar sense in English.[27] Interestingly, *sententia* also means the deeper—as opposed to merely grammatical or literal—sense of Scripture, which indicates the origin of the authoritative statements of the Fathers in scriptural interpretation. Prosper's *Liber sententiarum* comprises 392 "sentences" from Augustine's writings, constituting an elementary résumé of his theology. However, they are not arranged in any methodical order.

Another, perhaps more important predecessor of Peter Lombard's work deserves to be mentioned here. Isidore of Seville (c. 560–636) not only authored the *Etymologies*, a book part glossary, part encyclopedia that continued to be one of the most important works of reference in the West right into the high Middle Ages.[28] Drawing heavily on Scripture, Augustine, and Gregory the Great, he also compiled *Sententiae* in three books devoted to dogmatics (book 1) and ethics (books 2 and 3).[29] The arrangement of topics in book 1 foreshadows the systematic order of later, much more advanced manuals of theology. Isidore first treats of the properties and knowability of God, as well as His eternity. From there, he proceeds to a discussion of creation, evil, the angels, and man. This part is followed by a section devoted to Christ and the Holy Spirit, which in turn leads to a consideration of the Church, heresies, and pagans, as well as the relationship between the Old and the New Testaments. Toward the end of book 1, we find reflections on the Apostles' Creed, prayer, some of the sacraments, and Last Things. Like his *Etymologies*, Isidore's *Sentences* were one of the most frequently read books of the medieval period.[30]

In these first sentence collections, we witness a major step in the movement "from story to system" whose outlines we are sketching here. We have seen that the Christian intellectual tradition is ultimately rooted in Scripture, which already contains certain hints as to the principal strategies to be employed in reflecting upon the faith—strategies such as the reconciliation and synthesis of texts ("I am come not to abolish but to fulfill"), as well as critical discernment in the use of non-Christian ideas and concepts. The Church Fathers, taking up this programmatic advice, began the transformation of the story of Jesus into a theological system. In so doing, they drew the world of pagan learning into the sphere of Christian reflection, creating a kind of intersection between the two. Augustine's *On Christian Teaching* is an explicit statement of the parameters governing this dialogue. The writings of the Church Fathers, however, give rise to a task similar to the original problem of the concordance of the two Testaments. For, in their pronouncements on doctrinal issues, the Fathers do not always speak with one voice. Indeed, even a single Church Father, such as Augustine writing on predestination and free will, does not always seem unambiguous in his positions. Hence the need to collect and compare the Fathers' sentences on given theological topics. In addition, the sentence collections constitute an important move toward the constitution of systematically arranged, comprehensive accounts of theological knowledge.

A word needs to be said here about Boethius (c. 480–524), who undertook the ambitious project of translating the entirety of Plato's and Aristotle's works into Latin and elucidating them by means of commentaries.[31] This project became necessary once educated Romans (such as even the great Augustine) no longer knew Greek, thus being cut off from the Greek literary and intellectual tradition. Unfortunately, Boethius, who worked in the service of the Ostrogothic king Theodoric, was accused of treason and subsequently executed. This tragic accident of history cut his project short, so that he completed translations of only two of Aristotle's logical writings, the *Categories* and *On Interpretation*, together with a Latin version of Porphyry's introduction, the *Isagoge*. Although the bulk of the Aristotelian heritage was thus to remain inaccessible to the Latin-speaking world until the twelfth century, Boethius's translations ensured the availability of fundamental concepts of Aristotelian thought to Western theologians. Apart from a number of other works on logic, Boethius also authored a series of important treatises on theological issues, the *opuscula sacra*,[32] in which he endeavored to elucidate elements of the faith—such as the Trinity and the Incarnation—by means of philosophical strategies. However, Boethius did not attempt to create a comprehensive system of theology.

John Scottus Eriugena

In the *History of Scholastic Method*, Martin Grabmann frequently emphasizes the importance of the influx of new material for the development of patristic and medieval thought.[33] Indeed, the student of the Christian intellectual tradition observes that it is driven by two forces: the *intrinsic* necessity of clarifying the faith and providing as coherent an account of it as possible, and the *extrinsic* challenges that periodically force Christian thinkers to reexamine their tradition in light of foreign sources. The work of John Scottus Eriugena (c. 800–c. 870) marks the point where the Latin West comes, for the first time, into contact with the theological traditions of the Eastern Church. This encounter, made possible by Eriugena's knowledge of Greek—an ability that remained surprisingly rare among Latin thinkers throughout the medieval period—occasioned the most daring speculative system of Christian thought in the earlier Middle Ages: the *Periphyseon*, also entitled *De divisione naturae* (*On the Division of Nature*).[34] The unprecedented scope of the work becomes apparent from its very first page, where Eriugena announces nothing less than an investigation of "nature," defined as "the general name . . . for all things, for those that are and those that are not."[35] The puzzling reference to "things that are not" as part of nature already indicates the extent of Eriugena's debt to the negative theology of the East. In fact, he also prepared a translation of the writings of the Pseudo-Dionysius, a mysterious Syrian monk posing as Dionysius the Areopagite (see Acts 17:34) who enjoyed subapostolic authority among medieval theologians. In the tradition of negative theology, God is considered to lie beyond the realm of being. A major task Eriugena addresses in the *Periphyseon* consists in the attempt to incorporate the insights of negative theology into the Western tradition. Almost the whole of book 1 is devoted to a discussion of the Aristotelian categories, which ever since Boethius figured so prominently in the Christian thought of the West. Eriugena faces the challenge of having to rethink the entire theory of the categories in light of his new "Eastern" insights, specifying, in particular, what their relationship is to the superexistent, ineffable Divine. The dialogue between the East and the West finds expression in the literary form itself of the *Periphyseon*, for it is written as a conversation between a teacher and a student; the teacher, significantly, represents Eastern thought, whereas the student often formulates concerns and objections that are based upon his familiarity with the Latin Fathers, especially Augustine.

Yet the overall structure of the *Division of Nature* is not dictated by the narration of the conversation between Nutritor and Alumnus. Indeed, the dialogue is clearly contrived. "Set an end to the book," the student remarks at the end of book 1.[36] Rather, Eriugena brings a purely rational criterion to bear on the division of his material: the famous fourfold division of nature into (1) that which creates and is not created, (2) that which is created and also creates, (3) that which is created and does not create, and (4) that which neither creates nor is created.[37] On first sight, this division might seem excessively formal and logical. For Eriugena, however, it corresponds to the very rhythm of nature. For nature is created by God (1) through the ideas of creaturely beings that are contained in the Word (2); once created, these creaturely beings (3) return to their Creator, who is also their final cause (4). Dialectic or philosophy, then, is more than a logical tool; it captures the heartbeat of everything that is and that is not. The question has been asked as to whether Eriugena's confidence in philosophy was excessive. At times, he seems to be reducing all authority to reason.[38] On the other hand, he affirms that "the authority of Holy Scripture must in all things be followed,"[39] and the *Periphyseon* is full of long quotations of authoritative writers. As a matter of fact, the structure of the work is far less "rational" than it might appear on the face of it. Large parts of books 3 and 4 are devoted to a commentary on the first six days; that is to say, the text follows an order that is scriptural. Has Eriugena's struggle for the appropriate literary form for his Christian synthesis failed, then? It is difficult to say, for after all, negative theology denounces the excessive claims of reason to be able to account for all of reality. In this light, some stammering might be quite appropriate.

The Eleventh Century

Whereas the tenth century was one of intellectual decline, the eleventh made substantial progress in the movement toward greater systematicity in theological reasoning. We have already seen that, since Prosper of Aquitaine, the Western tradition knew and practiced methods of compiling authoritative statements to create larger surveys of theological material. Unavoidably, such compilations had the effect of drawing attention to dissonances in the authorities' opinions on certain issues. But how could such dissonances be overcome? Was it admissible to side with one Father against another? Medieval thinkers did not share our modern rigorous distinction between the inspired texts of Scripture, on the one hand, and the merely human words of postapostolic Christian writers. Hugh of St. Victor, in the twelfth century, is not at all untypical in declaring the Fathers and doctors of the Church to be a "third order" of the New Testament, after the Gospels and the apostolic material.[40] In the same way, therefore, in which the Old Testament could not simply be dismissed in favor of the New (and was hence interpreted figuratively),[41] it was necessary to create a tradition that would, as much as possible, be able to draw on a consensus of authorities. Up to the eleventh century, however, no methodology was available to achieve such a consensus. The canonists were to change that, by creating a new legal method that has been labeled "dialectical jurisprudence."[42]

Bernold of Constance (c. 1050–1100) is the author of, among other works, a collection of treatises entitled *De excommunicatis vitandis, de reconciliatione lapsorum et de fontibus iuris ecclesiastici* ("On Avoiding Excommunicated People, the Reconciliation of Sins, and the Sources of Ecclesiastical Law").[43] The letter and first two opuscules published under this title gather together canons of councils, papal decisions, and patristic statements dealing with the respective subjects of excommunication, penance, and heresy; the last (and longest) opuscule, "On the Sources of

Ecclesiastical Law," is of a more theoretical orientation. It discusses the three authoritative sources of canon law, namely, the apostles, the popes, and finally, ecumenical councils and provincial synods. In the second half of this treatise, Bernold, in analyzing an example, notes some diversity of opinion in the authoritative material. But he remains unperturbed: "We shall easily reconcile the diversity of these 'sentences,' " he writes.[44] His assertion is followed by a number of rules that Bernold suggests should be applied when authorities contradict each other. First, consideration of the complete text (rather than an excerpted version) and its context, careful collation, and comparison will help to shed light upon individual sentences, thus resolving contradictions that are merely apparent. Moreover, often it will prove useful to consider the historical circumstances—time, place, and people—in which a certain pronouncement occurred; it may turn out to apply specifically to a particular situation. Similarly, the causes that have occasioned an opinion need to be taken into consideration. Finally, it may be the case that some decrees and canons were instituted for a limited time only, whereas others were meant to be of unlimited validity. In another treatise, Bernold cautions that sometimes seemingly authoritative sentences may have been falsely attributed to a Church Father.[45]

The *Decretum* and *Panormia*, which were far more influential than Bernold of Constance's work, contain similar ideas in their prologue. Yet Ivo of Chartres (c. 1040–1115), the great canonist to whom authorship of the two works is usually attributed, does not formulate explicit rules. The *Panormia* is derived from the *Decretum*, which is why the two compilations share one preface. Both are comprehensive collections of canonical material; the *Panormia*, in particular, was widely diffused in medieval and even early modern times, serving later canonists and theologians as a source of quotations. It has been shown that Abelard and, through him, Peter Lombard depended heavily on the *Decretum* and the *Panormia*.[46] In his preface,[47] which also circulated independently under the title "On the Consonance of Canons" (*De consonantia canonum*), Ivo stresses that he intends to create a unified body (*unum corpus*) of doctrine and law, arranged methodically for easy consultation. He even appends a table of contents to the preface. Toward the beginning of the prologue, Ivo admonishes his readers not to dismiss canons that may appear contradictory. In particular, some rules may apply from the point of view of strict justice, while others may have been formulated in a spirit of leniency and compassion. The two are not mutually exclusive. Ivo's theory of dispensation was to become central to canon law.

It is not without significance that rules for the methodical harmonization of authoritative texts were first formulated by canonists. Canon law governs the religious life of the Church in a much more immediate manner than philosophico-theological speculation. For the care of souls, it is crucial to know, for example, what is required to administer the sacraments validly; it is a less pressing concern, by contrast, to resolve all the subtle problems of Trinitarian theology. This consideration explains why the need for the systematic codification of authorities was felt first in the practical domain. The techniques initially developed by canonists were then, only subsequently, brought to bear upon theological matters. Joseph de Ghellinck has impressively shown that theological systematization remained indebted to canon law far into the twelfth century, with regard to both the authoritative texts it employed and the methods it used to reconcile them.[48] But let us return to the field of theology itself and its further development in the eleventh century.

Martin Grabmann dubs Anselm of Canterbury (1033–1109) the "Father of Scholasticism,"[49] but with what right? At first sight, Anselm has very little in common with the intellectual movement whose outlines we have been tracing in the last few pages, and which was to come to a natural, though provisional, conclusion in Peter Lombard's *Book of Sentences*. In his major works, the *Monologion*, *Proslogion*, and *Cur Deus Homo* ("Why Did God Become Man?"), Anselm is not engaged in a project of reconciling authorities. He does not cite any. His penetration and interpretation of the faith seem to rely exclusively on the powers of reason. It is not surprising, then, that Anselm has been suspected of rationalism. But such a suspicion rests on a misunderstanding.

In a letter to his teacher Lanfranc, Anselm claims that in the *Monologion* it was his intention to "assert nothing that [he] saw could not be immediately defended from either canonical statements or the words of the blessed Augustine."[50] Something very similar could be said of the *Proslogion*,[51] which contains the so-called ontological argument, a piece of reasoning that has fascinated commentators from the entire philosophical spectrum for almost a millennium. Anselm found the definition of the word *God* as "that than which nothing greater can be thought" almost literally in Augustine's *On Christian Teaching*.[52] This does not mean that his argument is devoid of all originality. On the contrary; Anselm's brilliant insight lies in the realization that this definition, once accepted, amounts to an admission that God must indeed exist. For if "that than which nothing greater can be thought" did not exist, then this same entity considered *as* existing would be greater than it—an obvious contradiction. However, in order to understand the true import of this proof, we must remember that the *Proslogion* has the form of a meditative prayer, just like Augustine's *Confessions*. Like Augustine, Anselm is engaged in a spiritual quest for God, whose presence in human nature has been obscured as a consequence of the Fall. Nonetheless, God, the utterly transcendent and ineffable God, remains present at the heart of the human being, who is created in his image and likeness. To lead the reader to this realization—namely, that the transcendent God is the immanent God, or that the human being, as created in the image and likeness of God, carries transcendence within itself—is the point both of the *Confessions* and of the ontological argument.

In other words, Anselm is not a rationalist, developing as he does his ideas in intimate dialogue with the tradition, in a meditative context where reason presupposes faith. In chapter 1 of the *Proslogion*, he captures this primacy of faith in the pithy phrase *credo ut intelligam*: "I do not seek to understand that I may believe, but I believe in order to understand." It remains undeniable, however, that Anselm's indebtedness to the tradition is of a different character than what we see in the work of a Prosper of Aquitaine or an Ivo of Chartres. Anselm's debt to Augustine, in particular, does not manifest itself in long series of quotations. Rather, the archbishop of Canterbury reappropriates the tradition by penetrating right to its roots and rethinking it fundamentally. One could say that he is the dialectical opposite of the sentence collections, *florilegia*, and *catenae*, which gather together strings of quotations in a more or less extrinsic fashion. To bring these quotations into a unity, it is possible to apply rules of reconciliation to isolated instances, proceeding step by step toward a greater whole. This method results in a systematicity that arises from methodical arrangement. Or one can attempt to grasp the living core of the thought, the tradition, and the faith that have generated the quotations, together with their contradictions. This speculative approach yields a system that is the result of organic growth.[53] "The importance of Anselm consists in the fact that he led [the tradition] from the formulae of Augustine back to his spirit and way of thought."[54] Such contemplative genius—not only methods of textual synthesis—was also a necessary element in the journey of the faith from story to system.

The Century of Peter Lombard

If one had to choose one word to characterize the difference between Christian thought in the eleventh and the twelfth centuries,[55] it would perhaps be *professionalization*.[56] We should neither exaggerate nor belittle the importance of this development. We should not exaggerate it because, as we have seen, the emergence of theology as a set of skillfully constructed doctrines has a prehistory that can, ultimately, be traced to Scripture itself.[57] But we should not underestimate the implications of professionalization either. In the twelfth century, theology became a subject largely taught by masters in their own schools. These masters were *professional* theologians in the sense that they devoted their lives to the study and teaching of sacred doctrine. The master was neither a bishop, charged with responsibility for the pastoral care of souls, nor yet a monk, dedicated to contemplation. Thus dissociated from its former roots in the life of the Church, the intellectual penetration of the faith assumed a new, more autonomous role. Marie-Dominique Chenu writes:

> The place of the masters in the church became increasingly difficult to determine as they organized theology into a science with its own rules, constructed within the faith and its premises to be sure, but according to criteria stemming from the intelligible nature of the subjects they were examining, and not according to the needs and opportunities of pastoral responsibility or of subjective, pious intentions. There would now necessarily be "theological" errors, whereas hitherto the term heresy simply denoted any lapses from orthodox faith.... In the second half of the twelfth century, reason and its various disciplines no longer furnished simply the tools for studying the sacred text (*sacra pagina*). Reason, by introducing "well ordered arrangement" (*artificioso successu*), somehow entered into the structuring of the faith itself, as Alain of Lille suggested in his *Ars fidei*.[58]

The masters required efficient tools to facilitate their research, as well as textbooks for their teaching. The *Glossa ordinaria* is the quintessential example of the first category, whereas improved versions of the old literary genre of the sentence collection were developed to serve as textbooks.

The literary history of the *Glossa ordinaria*, the "standard gloss" on the Bible, is extraordinarily complex and still largely a mystery. There is no modern edition of the work which, in the words of Margaret Gibson, was used as "the definitive reference edition of the Bible"[59] from around 1150 until as late as the eighteenth century.[60] The Gloss comprises a text of the Bible complete with marginal and interlinear notes derived from a large number of patristic and medieval authorities. Its sources differ for individual books, often remaining unnamed. They range from Church Fathers such as Origen (in the translation by Rufinus), Ambrose, Jerome, Augustine, and Gregory the Great through Cassiodorus and Bede to Carolingian writers like Alcuin, Rabanus Maurus, Walafrid Strabo, Eriugena, Paschasius Radbertus, and the masters of Auxerre; later medieval authors such as Berengar of Tours and Lanfranc are also represented.[61] The Gloss thus brings together the fruits of one thousand years of scriptural interpretation. It does so not in an unwieldy library of dozens of complete volumes, but rather in the form of brief extracts handily associated, for quick reference, with individual words or verses.

It is true that glossed books of the Bible had been in circulation since Carolingian times. There was, however, no uniform standard for the selection of sources and their physical arrangement on the page. The twelfth century saw the codification of the Gloss, whose text would hitherto remain "surprisingly stable,"[62] despite the considerable complexity of its layout. No single master was responsible for the final redaction of the Gloss covering the entirety of Scripture. Anselm of Laon († 1117) and his circle, including his brother Ralph and pupil Gilbert of Auxerre, are usually credited with the creation of the *Parva Glosatura*, a "smaller" version of the Gloss that was subsequently expanded upon by Gilbert de la Porrée (another student of Anselm's). The Gloss reached its most developed state through Peter Lombard, whose *Magna Glosatura* offered a revised, continuous, and more sophisticated commentary on the Psalms and Pauline epistles. We will have the opportunity to consider Peter Lombard's work on the Gloss in more detail in the next chapter. The Lombard's use of the Gloss as a work of reference in his biblical lectures contributed significantly to its general acceptance in Scholastic circles.

We now turn from the Gloss to the textbooks, another tool the twelfth-century masters fashioned for their professional work. The text-books were meant to address two central tasks. On the one hand, they introduced the student to the methodology of theological thinking, especially to the strategies involved in the successful handling of authorities. On the other hand, they had to unfold before the eyes of the young theologian the whole theological curriculum, presented in as coherent and well-organized a manner as possible.[63] The generation of theologians immediately preceding Peter Lombard experimented with a number of different schemata for the structuring of the theological material.[64] Here, we shall examine two of the most influential of these schemata: the Hugonian and the Abelardian, with both of which Peter Lombard was intimately acquainted.

Peter arrived in Paris to study with Hugh of St. Victor (1096–1141) just as the latter was completing his chef d'oeuvre, *De sacramentis christianae fidei*, "On the Sacraments of the Christian Faith." This "first large, complete system of dogmatics in the period of early Scholasticism"[65]—as Grabmann characterizes it—is divided into two books. The first of them covers the origin of the world up to the Incarnation, while the second extends from the Incarnation to the end of the world, including Last Things. Hugh himself presents the rationale of his work in the following way:

> The material of all the divine Scriptures is the works of man's restoration [*opera restaurationis humanae*]. For there are two works in which everything that is, is contained. The first is the work of foundation [*opus conditionis*]. The second is the work of restoration [*opus restaurationis*]. The work of foundation is that through which it was made to pass that those things that were not, came to be. The work of restoration is that through which it was made to pass that those things that were lost, were made better. Thus, the work of foundation is the creation of the world with all its elements. The work of restoration is the Incarnation of the Word with all its sacraments, either those that have existed since the beginning of the world, or those that ensue right to the end of the world.[66]

It is clear, then, that the principle Hugh uses to structure his theological material is historical, or chronological: *De sacramentis* proceeds from the beginning of the world, through the Incarnation, to the end of time. More importantly, however, its structuring principle is scriptural, as Scripture itself opens with the narration of creation and ends with the

Apocalypse.[67] In other words, in Hugh's *De sacramentis* we are dealing with a theological system that has not yet made the transition from an essentially narrative order to the stage where, to use Chenu's words, "reason has entered into the structuring of the faith itself." Hugh's work is still relatively traditional and conservative, an impression that is confirmed by the fact that, in an almost Anselmian manner, he rarely identifies and quotes the authorities on which his arguments depend. Neither does he juxtapose conflicting quotations, proceeding to reconcile them. The absence both of explicit references and of dialectical method had to impinge upon the usefulness of *De sacramentis* as a textbook for students, who needed to learn how to sift through the tradition and its discordant voices.[68]

Admittedly, Hugh of St. Victor was not the typical twelfth-century master Chenu had in mind in the passage we quoted earlier. Although the school of St. Victor was open to secular students, its roots were in traditional Augustinian monasticism, though with pastoral overtones. The epitome of the new professional master of whom Chenu speaks, the master unsure of his place in the Church and intent on organizing theology as a science with its own rules, this epitome we will not find among the Victorines, but rather in Peter Abelard (c. 1079–1142). *Sic et non*, "Yes and No," is the work in which Abelard provides the most explicit statement of his theological methodology.[69] It is composed of a preface and a series of 158 theological issues, for each of which Abelard presents a set of authoritative quotations that contradict each other—hence the title, *Yes and No*. These contradictions are left unresolved. Abelard conceived of *Sic et non* as a kind of exercise book for his students.[70] The idea was that, by means of the detailed rules of textual synthesis laid out in the preface,[71] they would learn how to build theology dialectically out of the quoted material. It is significant, of course, that the quotations, albeit unreconciled, are arranged according to specific theological topics and that these topics, in turn, are presented in a certain order.[72] Here we already see the outlines of the structure of Peter Abelard's theological system. It can roughly be summarized in the following schema:

Questions 1–4   The Nature of Faith
Questions 5–25   God and the Trinity
Questions 26–45   Divine Attributes
Questions 46–50   Angels

Abelard reshuffled his schema a number of times before producing what has come down to us as the final version of *Sic et non*, upon which the present discussion is based.[73] Unlike Hugh of St. Victor, he does not specify the rationale that holds his material together. Clearly, the structure of Abelard's theology is no longer tied to biblical history; it is more "logical" or "rational"—although Abelard's logic still leaves something to be desired. He begins with the nature of faith, whence he moves on to the principal object of faith, that is to say, God and the Trinity. There is no explicit treatment of creation—the "link" between God, the angels, and man, who are the subject matter of the next groups of questions. Since man falls, the Incarnation becomes necessary to save him. Hence the large set of questions on Christ, Mary, and the apostles. In the last third of *Sic et non*, we find a consideration of (some of) the sacraments and, finally, charity, together with its opposite, sin.

In his *Theologia*, which, like *Sic et non*, underwent several redactions, Abelard states the intended structure of his theological system much more directly. According to an Abelard expert, Constant J. Mews, "The version of the *Theologia* most familiar to Peter Abaelard's contemporaries"—including the author of the *Book of Sentences*—"was the *Theologia 'Scholarium.'"*[74] In the preface of this work, Abelard takes pains to justify the use of philosophy in theological matters. We must not forget that, at the time when he composed the *Theologia "Scholarium,"* his Trinitarian theology, with its emphasis on the comprehensibility of the Trinity by rational, philosophical means, had already been condemned once. The preface is followed by an overview of the work, the first book of which, as Abelard points out, "briefly contains a summary [*summam*] of the whole said treatise, namely, on faith, charity, and the sacraments."[75] These are "the three elements . . . in which the substance of human salvation [*hu-

manę salutis summa] consists."[76] While Abelard's own *Theologia* deliberately limits itself to the problem of the Trinity, this ternary division—no
doubt modeled on Augustine's treatise *Enchiridion, sive de fide, spe et
charitate*—was to become the classic structure of the more complete theological systems created by his followers.[77]

After this discussion of two of Peter Lombard's most influential predecessors, let us now, finally, examine the theological system of one of his
contemporaries. This will give us an idea of the immediate intellectual
landscape in which the creation of the *Book of Sentences* occurred, thus
enabling us to understand at least some of the respects in which the
sentence collections contemporaneous with the Lombard's work remained
open to improvement. Robert of Melun was conversant with all the major
philosophical and theological trends of his time. Born in England toward
the end of the eleventh century, he studied at Oxford before moving on
to Paris, where, around 1137, we find him teaching philosophy, or dia-
lectics, at Peter Abelard's school on Mount Sainte-Geneviève.[78] A few
years later, he left Mount Sainte-Geneviève for Melun, a town twenty-
eight miles southeast of Paris that was then quite important. There he
founded his own school of theology, again following in the footsteps of
Peter Abelard, who taught at Melun a few decades earlier. In the 1150s,
Robert seems to have moved again, this time to take up a chair at the
school of St. Victor. He was recalled to England around 1160, where he
was appointed to the bishopric of Hereford in 1163. Robert of Melun
died in 1167.

Given this intellectual background, it is not surprising that one of the
principal tasks Robert sets himself in his *Sentences* should be to reconcile
the theological traditions associated with the schools of Abelard and
Hugh of St. Victor. In his preface, which has been praised as unique in
the theological literature of the Middle Ages for the light it sheds on the
history and methodology of the sentence collections,[79] Robert asserts: "My
project will be complete, if after having gone briefly over the sacraments
of the Old and the New Testaments, I include a treatise on faith, hope,
and charity. In fact, in them the substance of human salvation [*summa
salutis humane*] is fully contained. For he who will have received the
sacraments, believed faithfully and persevered in charity, will surely partake of eternal salvation."[80] First, we should note that nothing is brief
about Robert of Melun's *Sentences*. It is a massive, multivolume work that
its author was never able to complete; the critical edition, which Ray-

mond Martin prepared in the 1930s and 1940s, breaks off before even having covered half the text. But let us comment on Robert's programmatic statement. Its first part alludes to the schema underlying Hugh of St. Victor's *De sacramentis*. As we know, in this work Hugh follows the order of the Old and New Testaments, distinguishing sacraments before and after the Incarnation. On the other hand, the reference to faith, hope, charity, and the sacraments—together with the phrase "the substance of human salvation"—reminds us distinctly of the *Theologia "Scholarium."*[81]

At the end of his preface, Robert draws attention to an important feature of his *Sentences*, namely, the fact that each book is divided into chapters with subject headings, as well as being preceded by a table of contents. Since he refers to the "custom" (*consuetudo*) of using such tools to facilitate the use of textbooks, titled chapter divisions and tables of contents must already have been quite widespread when he composed the *Sentences*.[82] Robert is not enamored of this custom, but he accepts the professional rules of his trade. Another feature that attests to what Marcia Colish has termed Robert's "thoroughgoing professionalism"[83] is his insistence on accurate quotation, lest the meaning of the authoritative sources be distorted.[84]

Let us now examine whether Robert's stated intentions about the structure of his work are in tune with its actual plan. The *Sentences* are divided into two books, respectively corresponding to the Old and the New Testaments. Book 1 comprises eleven parts, which are further subdivided into chapters. To these parts, three further sections are appended; their status is not entirely clear. Book 2 is in five parts, of which only the first two have been completed. The following schema sums up the arrangement of theological material in the *Sentences*:[85]

Preface

Table of Contents

Book I: The Sacraments of the Old Testament: From the Creation of the World to the Incarnation
Part I

Chapters 1–18	Scripture
Chapters 19–30	The Six Days of Creation

Part II

Chapters 1–9	God as Creator; Knowledge of the Trinity

Part III

Part IV

Part V

Part VI

Part VII

Part VIII

Part IX

Part X

Part XI

Second Part of the Principal Enumeration[86]

Second Part of the Principal Enumeration [*sic*]

Second Part of the Second Part of the Principal Enumeration

Book II: The Sacraments of the New Testament: From the Incarnation to the End of Time

Part I

Part II

Chapters 190–204	The State of Christ during the Three Days after His Death
Chapters 205–213	Christ's Descent into Hell; Hell and Purgatory
Part III (not executed)	The Sacraments
Part IV (not executed)	Faith, Hope, and Charity
Part V (not executed)	Last Things

Robert, it turns out, was not able to implement his program of reconciling the theological schemata of Hugh of St. Victor and Abelard. The *Sentences* break off before the categories of faith, hope, charity, and sacraments are treated. Even if this were not the case, though, it is not clear that Robert was planning to do much more than graft Abelardian theological categories onto an essentially Hugonian structure. There is, however, a simpler reason why Robert of Melun's *Sentences* could not become a successful and widely adopted textbook. It remained incomplete, the project a promise.

Masters other than Robert of Melun composed sentence collections around the time when Peter Lombard prepared his own *Book of Sentences*. We do not have the space to examine these works in the present context; furthermore, such an exercise would merely replicate existing research.[87] In the middle of the twelfth century, the Western tradition of Christianity was ready for a full-blown theological system—one that would render the faith as intelligible as humanly possible through comprehensive coverage of all its major themes in a methodical order and the application of dialectical procedures to several layers of authoritative texts. Peter Lombard was to create such a system.

PETER LOMBARD

Life and Works

According to a note jotted in the margin of a Florentine manuscript from the thirteenth century, Peter Lombard hailed *de Vico Lemononii, de Districtu*, "from the village of Lemononium, of the district [of Novara]."[1] Lumellogno, as the place is called today, is located just a few miles to the southwest of Novara in Lombardy (northern Italy). Peter Lombard's exact date of birth cannot be ascertained, but the details of his first appearance in datable historical records point to a time roughly between 1095 and 1100.

Almost nothing is known of Peter's family and early years. It seems certain, however, that he was poor, for as we shall see, he had to rely upon benefactors to help him make ends meet during his studies. In fact, several chroniclers relate that his mother made a living as a lowly washerwoman. Peter must have begun his education close to home, in the cathedral school of St. Mary's in Novara. He could then have pursued further studies either in Novara itself, or perhaps in Bologna, Parma, or Lucca. Lucca seems the most likely candidate, since it is there that Master Otto lectured, author of the *Summa sententiarum*, which has long been recognized as one of the principal contemporary sources of the Lombard's own *Book of Sentences*.[2] Moreover, it was the bishop of Lucca, Hubert, who recommended Peter to St. Bernard of Clairvaux when the Lombard felt drawn from his native land to France, the vibrant center of biblical and theological research in the twelfth century.

St. Bernard's Letter to the Abbey
of St. Victor

Sometime during the first months of 1136, Gilduin, abbot of St. Victor, received the following letter:

> To the reverend fathers and sirs, and dearest friends, to Gilduin, by God's grace venerable abbot of St. Victor in Paris, and to the entire holy convent, brother Bernard, called abbot of Clairvaux: greeting and all our prayers.
>
> We have to ask much, since much is asked of us, and we cannot spare our friends, since we are not spared by other friends. The Master Bishop of Lucca, our father and friend, recommended a venerable man to me, Peter Lombard, asking that, through our friends, I provide for him what is necessary for his sustenance, for the short time that he would stay in France to pursue his studies. I have done this while he stayed in Rheims. Now that he is sojourning in Paris I commend him to your love, asking that it may please you to provide him with food during the brief time that he has betaken himself here, up to the Nativity of the blessed Virgin Mary. Fare ye well.[3]

These few lines not only contain the first mention of Peter Lombard in a historical document; they also enable us to reconstruct at least the outlines of his journey to France. Peter was already a "venerable man" when Bishop Hubert asked St. Bernard to facilitate his stay in Rheims. He brought a small library with him, as Patricia Stirnemann has surmised recently.[4] But why did he choose Rheims to perfect his Italian education? The cathedral school there had established a reputation for itself in the eleventh century, and at the beginning of the twelfth its renown was further enhanced by the presence of several masters trained by Anselm of Laon.[5] Laon itself is only a short distance from Rheims. Peter no doubt used the opportunity to visit. In any case, the masters at Rheims and Laon were able to acquaint Peter with the state of the art in contemporary biblical scholarship, as it evolved around the Gloss. It is no surprise, then, that the Lombard's first work was an elaboration upon Anselm's Gloss on the Psalms. He may have begun this work during his stay in Rheims, though that is not certain.

Peter must have arrived in Rheims sometime after 1133, the first possible date for St. Bernard to have encountered Bishop Hubert in Italy—if we assume, with Joseph de Ghellinck and Ignatius Brady, that Hubert recommended Peter to Bernard on the occasion of a personal meeting.[6] Peter left Rheims for Paris in 1136, the year of St. Bernard's letter. The latter was evidently envisioning a fairly short stay for the venerable man from Italy, just "up to the Nativity of the blessed Virgin Mary." Undoubtedly Bernard recommended Peter Lombard to the Victorines because of their leading role in theological debates of the day. Hugh of St. Victor's *De sacramentis christianae fidei*, which we briefly discussed in the previous chapter, was completed in 1137, at a time when Paris was rapidly eclipsing other centers of learning, attracting the most celebrated masters of the time—including Peter Abelard.

St. Bernard's letter to Abbot Gilduin must not be overinterpreted. It does not imply that Peter Lombard actually stayed at St. Victor, although we may assume that the abbey became the center of his intellectual life. Of course, he will have attended Hugh of St. Victor's lectures, for Hugh's *De sacramentis* figures among the principal sources of the *Book of Sentences*, together with other works from Hugh's circle. There can also be little doubt that Peter Lombard must have sought out Peter Abelard, whose works he had come to know extremely well by the time he embarked on the *Sentences*.[7] During those years, we must imagine Peter in conversation with the thinkers who were most vigorously and courageously attempting to rearticulate the fundamental structures of the Christian faith. Yet the precise details of his first years in Paris remain shrouded in obscurity.

"Celebrem theologum vidimus Lumbardum"

Then, in 1144, we suddenly encounter Peter Lombard, "the famous theologian," which is what he is called in a poem by Walter Mapes:

Celebrem theologum vidimus Lumbardum,
Cum Yvone, Helyam Petrum, et Bernardum,

Quorum opobalsamum spirat os et nardum,
Et professi plurimi sunt Abaielardum.[8]

The famous theologian we have seen, the Lombard,
With Yvo [of Chartres], Petrus Helias, and Bernard,
Whose mouth[s] breathed balsam and nard,
And very many [of whom] professed [the teachings of] Abelard.

Peter must have become a master several years before this poem was composed. But where did he teach? All our evidence points to an affiliation with the cathedral school of Notre Dame. Brady's careful analysis of the charters witnessed by the canons of Notre Dame between 1133 and 1161 has revealed several documents that were signed by Peter Lombard.[9] His titles vary from *Petrus puer*, "Peter the child" (that is, cleric in minor orders), in 1145–1147 to *Petrus subdiaconus* in 1147–1152, *Magister Petrus subdiaconus, Parisiensis canonicus* (1150), *Petrus archidiaconus* in 1156–1157, and finally *Magister Petrus episcopus* (1159). However, the use of titles is not totally consistent in the charters; for example, Peter was certainly already a master before 1150. Analogously, he was appointed canon of Notre Dame earlier than 1150, most probably around 1145.

Peter Lombard's rising fame is attested to not only by his titles; he was now being called upon frequently as an expert in theological matters. Thus, during a visit to Paris in 1147, Pope Eugene III consulted him on the subject of fraternal correction. What to do about a fellow priest who denies a transgression to a superior, even if the superior knows for certain that the priest is guilty? Should the superior expose the priest's crime to others? No, Peter Lombard replied to the pope, for then "he would be disclosing his brother's crime like a traitor, not correcting it."[10] Indeed, the superior must stand by his priest even if he has admitted his transgression in private, but denies it in public.

In the same year, Pope Eugene held a consistory in Paris to discuss accusations against Gilbert de la Porrée, bishop of Poitiers, whose Trinitarian theology had been denounced by two of his own archdeacons. The consistory was adjourned, however, because the pope judged the difficulty of the case to require fuller deliberations at the Council of Rheims, scheduled for 1148. At that council, Peter joined St. Bernard, Suger of St. Denis, and many others in strongly censuring Gilbert's position.[11]

In late 1154, the Lombard accompanied the bishop of Paris, Theobald,

on a journey to Rome, where the bishop had to travel on diocesan busi-
ness. The sojourn in the Eternal City proved most useful to Peter, to
whom it afforded the opportunity to acquaint himself with the new translation of John Damascene's *De fide orthodoxa*, which Pope Eugene had
commissioned Burgundio of Pisa to prepare. Curiously, however, Peter
seems to have taken cognizance of this translation in a rather selective
manner. It has been noted that the *Book of Sentences*—on which Peter
was working at the time—quotes only those passages from Burgundio's
new Latin version that had already become available, slightly earlier, in
the partial translation of Cerbanus.[12] Did Peter, during a busy stay in
Rome, have to limit himself to checking material previously incorporated
into the *Sentences* against the newer, better translation? That would explain why quotations from John Damascene, which occur only in books
1 and 3 of the *Sentences*, seem to have been added rather hastily in parts
of book 3, where there even remain some of Cerbanus's translations.

Bishop of Paris

Bishop Theobald died in 1159. According to a credible chronicler, Robert
of Torigni, the person slated to succeed Theobald was no less than deacon
Philip, the king's own brother. But Philip declined, recognizing Peter
Lombard's superior qualifications. The chronicle calls Peter "a man of
great learning, and admirable above all the doctors of Paris." It continues:
"Master Peter Lombard obtained the episcopate of Paris, after Philip,
deacon of the same church and brother of the king of France, had been
passed over. It is said that he conceded his election to the same Peter."[13]

The Lombard's reputation as a teacher of theology must have been
redoubtable indeed for Philip, brother of the king, to renounce the pres-
tigious episcopal seat of Paris. King Louis VII ratified the election without hesitation. Peter Lombard was consecrated bishop about the time of
the feast of Saints Peter and Paul, toward the end of June 1159. Since
he died only one year later, on July 20, 1160, there is little to say about
his episcopate. He signed only three charters—the first one, interestingly,
a grant of tithes to the abbey of St. Victor. The accusation of simony that
Walter of St. Victor leveled against Bishop Peter some twenty years after
his death—along with venomous charges of heresy, diabolical arguments,
impious interpretation of the Fathers, and similar ones[14]—is without his-

torical foundation.[15] It shows, however, that Peter did have enemies and that his much-admired theological work was far from uncontroversial.[16] Original thinkers always have to walk a fine line between respect for the tradition and the courage to innovate. Indeed, in 1177 the Church rejected one of Peter Lombard's teachings, or what was believed to be such. About that we will hear more later in this book.

Peter Lombard was buried in the church of St. Marcellus, where his epitaph read:

> HERE LIETH MASTER PETER LOMBARD, BISHOP OF PARIS, WHO COMPOSED
> THE BOOK OF SENTENCES, GLOSSES ON THE PSALMS AND ON THE EPISTLES,
> [AND] THE DAY OF WHOSE DEATH IS AUGUST XIII.[17]

Sadly, Peter's grave was desecrated in 1793, and the church of St. Marcellus was destroyed in 1806. The boulevard Saint-Marcel still exists in Paris.

Peter Lombard, the Person

What kind of man was Peter Lombard? Was he humorous or serious? Kind, or did he have a short temper? What did he look like? These are, in fact, typically modern questions. They arise from an emphasis upon the uniqueness and specificity of the individual that was quite foreign to the Middle Ages. According to the well-known book by Colin Morris, the "discovery of the individual" took place only between 1050 and 1200.[18] Hence, for example, the puzzling lack of "historical accuracy" in medieval hagiographic accounts, which often attribute the same events and miracles to several different saintly figures. But, indulging for a moment our modern interest in personal details, and attempting to distinguish fact from fiction, what can we say about Peter Lombard, the man?

To begin, we know where he lived during his years as master at the cathedral school of Notre Dame. He owned a house close to the church of St. Christopher, which he bequeathed to the cathedral chapter, together with his other worldly possessions. The obituary of Notre Dame contains the following entry:

> On the same day, Master Peter, the bishop, died. We received thirty
> pounds in Parisian money for his soul, for payment of the *statio* on his
> anniversary day. For, that *statio* was paid from the house of Henry,
> the brother of Arnulfus Ruffus of Orliac, which at Henry's death came

into the hand[s] of the chapter; for Henry belonged to the family of the blessed Mary [that is to say, the cathedral]. That house is located close to St. Christopher. We also received an entire chapel, which contained a golden chalice, a dalmatic and tunic, two silver basins and two small silver vessels, to serve the water and wine, a breviary in two volumes, and a pallium [to be worn] before the altar. Moreover, we received all his glossed books, namely: the entire New Testament; in the Old Testament: the Psalter, the five books of Moses, the four major Prophets, the twelve minor [Prophets], the Canticles, Job, Esther, Tobias, Judith, the book of Wisdom, Ecclesiasticus; his Sentences, and the Decretals of Gratian.[19]

Brady interprets this document to imply that, after being elected to the bishopric, Peter Lombard rented to Henry of Orliac the house that he used to occupy as master. When Henry died, the house came into the hands of the cathedral chapter, which used the rental income to pay for an annual procession, or meal (*statio*), in memory of its revered former canon.

St. Christopher, which was demolished shortly after 1751, stood just outside the complex of churches around the old cathedral of Notre Dame (which under Peter Lombard's successor was replaced with the magnificent edifice that still exists today) on the Île de la Cité.[20] Peter therefore lived in convenient proximity to the cathedral to whose chapter he belonged and where he taught, in a neighborhood of clerics and professionals. Indeed, it is not unlikely that he held classes at his house as well, as masters of the time were wont to do.[21]

There are some contemporary reports of Peter Lombard's lectures that give us a glimpse of his style of teaching. From these reports, we can gather that his written doctrines did not always constitute his last word on a given topic. This is true especially in the case of some questions of Christology, which were the object of much contemporary controversy. Thus, a student of Peter's—possibly Peter Comestor—reports:

When asked whether [this statement] is to be conceded: "The divine essence is man or was made man," the Master first denied it and wrote it so, because it seemed to him that by these words the changeability [*versibilitas*] of a nature into [another] nature is indicated. Later, however, he corrected [his position] and conceded this [statement]: "The divine essence is man." The other one, however, he did not accept: "The divine essence was made man," because it explicitly indicates the changeability of a nature into [another] nature.[22]

Again with regard to a difficult Christological question, Peter makes a distinction between a position that he considers accurate theologically, but unsuitable to be expounded to the untrained layman, and a point of view fit for the non-expert: "When asked whether Christ, insofar as He is man, is something [*aliquid*], the Master . . . did not always deny this; in fact, he sometimes conceded it to external people. When he denied it, however, he spoke to safe ears, that is to say, to those whom he instructed."[23]

"Safe ears" (*tutis auribus*) should not be construed as meaning some esoteric circle of dissenters but, rather, as designating a group of people qualified to judge difficult theological matters. The expression was current at the time and remains so until the present day. Artur Landgraf has submitted the thesis that it was not uncommon for masters of the twelfth century to distinguish between opinions taught orally and more "official" statements committed to writing. He adverts to the existence of a principle according to which *quedam concedimus in legendo, que non concedimus in disserendo*, "we concede certain [positions] in lecturing that we do not concede in writing."[24]

On another subject broached in Peter's classes—the possibility of perfect charity turning imperfect—his student informs us: "I heard the Master hesitate on this."[25] In other words, Peter's classroom was not a place of dogmatic instruction, but a site for the open quest for the truth, a quest in which the master himself sometimes acknowledged his lack of certainty. "I did not hear the Master teach on this with certainty," the student remarks in the context of a question concerning the salvation of Jewish children before the institution of circumcision.[26] And we have another small piece of evidence which adds to the picture of a humble master who subordinates his own pride to the discovery of the truth of the faith. Around 1159, John of Cornwall heard the following words from Peter in one of his classes: "Shortly before he was elected bishop of Paris, he declared to me and everyone attending his lecture that this was not his assertion but only an opinion, which he accepted from the masters. He also added these words: 'Never, God willing, will there be an assertion of mine unless it be [in correspondence with] the Catholic faith.' "[27]

Finally, in our effort to gather some of the more personal details that have come down to us about Peter Lombard, we turn to an illuminated initial in one of the earliest manuscripts of the *Book of Sentences*, namely,

MS. *Troyes, Bibliothèque municipale 900*. This manuscript was completed in 1158 by a scribe named Michael of Ireland.[28] On its first folio, it carries an illuminated initial (see frontispiece) that shows Peter Lombard writing: *Omnes sitientes venite ad me*, "all you that thirst, come to me" (see Is 55:1 and Jn 7:37)—an allusion to the fact that the teaching of all masters ultimately goes back to the teaching of the Master.[29] Peter is wearing a blue coat with a hood on top of a white tunic and what appears to be an undergarment with blue stripes. On his head we see a black hat with an extension down the nape of the neck, which Stirnemann interprets as the headgear typical of either a master or a canon. This, then, is what Master Peter must have looked like as he taught his classes or walked down the streets of the Île de la Cité. Moreover, if it is true, as Stirnemann has suggested, that the illuminator who illustrated Troyes 900 worked for the abbey of St. Victor, he would most likely have encountered the famous theologian in Paris. Does his portrait therefore perhaps attempt to capture something of Master Peter's facial features?

Works

In speaking of the works of Peter Lombard, it is necessary to distinguish between notes that he prepared for his own use and writings meant for and circulated among a larger audience. In recent discussions, this distinction has sometimes become blurred, such that every gloss listed among the books which he bequeathed to the cathedral chapter is now regarded as a "work." The list in question, quoted above, does indeed allow us to infer that Peter left behind glosses that he had prepared on most of the books of Scripture: "the entire New Testament; in the Old Testament: the Psalter, the five books of Moses, the four major Prophets, the twelve minor [Prophets], the Canticles, Job, Esther, Tobias, Judith, the book of Wisdom, Ecclesiasticus." Father Ignatius Brady, the learned editor of the *Sentences* and undisputed authority on the life and works of Peter Lombard, has collected further evidence that can be adduced in favor of the existence of the glosses—all of it indirect, since these unpublished writings are no longer extant.[30] The works of Peter Lombard that were intended for the public are the *Book of Sentences*, his revision of Anselm of Laon's Gloss on the Psalter, an expanded version of the Gloss on the Letters of St. Paul, and sermons. With the exception of the

Book of Sentences, which will be treated in detail in the following chapters, I will now offer a brief description of each of these writings.

Gloss on the Psalter

The Gloss on the Psalter is Peter Lombard's earliest work, possibly already begun during his stay in Rheims.[31] One of his pupils, Herbert of Bosham, described it in the following terms:

> When he wrote this work, it never occurred to him, as I have learned from his own account, that he would read it [that is to say, lecture on it] in the public schools; it was composed solely for this [reason], to elucidate the obscure brevity of an older glossator, namely, Anselm of Laon. This is also why he was, in the event, less diligent (though sufficiently so at the time) in the selections of the expositors and in the interpretations of these same [expositors] which the same [Anselm] frequently offers. Very often, the words of the aforesaid glossator are interpreted, rather than [those] of the expositor. Make your own experience of what we are saying in reading [the work]. When, however, the said work was later, at the insistence of many and against expectation, read publicly by the Master, [and] when everything had not yet been fully cleaned up by the hoe of correction, he was promoted to be head of the Parisians and then, shortly thereafter, removed from human affairs.[32]

It is patent from this text that Herbert of Bosham already recognized certain shortcomings in the Gloss on the Psalter. Since the work was initially composed for Peter's private use in reflection and prayer, the author did not take great care in distinguishing the quotations of authorities, such as the Fathers, from Anselm of Laon's own glosses. Such scholarly accuracy was becoming an increasing concern at the time and was one of the reasons for the success that the *Book of Sentences* was to enjoy. Toward the end of his teaching career, Peter Lombard's students managed to talk the reluctant master into lecturing on the Psalms, on which occasion he began a revision of the work. That revision, however, was cut short by Peter's election to the bishopric and subsequent death. The Gloss on the Psalms has therefore come down to us as a relatively immature work.

Istius quod dicimus fac in legendo periculum, Herbert urges us: "find out for yourself in reading the work." And indeed, closer examination of the Psalms glosses reveals that, in composing them, Peter did not have recourse to original texts, relying exclusively upon the quotations assembled by Anselm and his pupil Gilbert de la Porrée. Moreover, the work has been judged to be theologically "jejune,"[33] remaining for the most part at the level of figurative interpretations of the Psalms without engaging in sustained and systematic reflection on theological doctrine. Nonetheless, and despite Herbert of Bosham's observations, the Lombard's contemporaries found his Gloss on the Psalms sufficiently impressive to range it among their standard works for biblical study. As such, it came to be known as the "Great Gloss," *Magna Glosatura*.

Marcia Colish, after carefully comparing the *Magna Glosatura* with other Psalms commentaries of the time, has offered a convincing explanation for the reputation it enjoyed. Most importantly, the Psalms Gloss proved superior to its rivals because of its holistic treatment of the Psalter. A detailed introduction, or *accessus*, provides an overview of the structure of the entire book, allowing Peter to situate each psalm within its broader context as he comments upon it. Similar *accessūs* introduce the individual psalms, which permits Peter to approach each verse from the perspective of the role it plays in its psalm as a whole. The *Glossa ordinaria*, by contrast, contented itself with commenting upon isolated words and phrases that presented special difficulties. Moreover, the *Magna Glosatura* stands out in that it draws attention to corruptions in the transmitted biblical text. Peter Lombard also moves in the direction of a more synthetic treatment of the authoritative quotations used to elucidate the text, not merely juxtaposing them, but comparing and weighing them. "In all of these respects," Colish sums up her analysis, "Peter's commentary on the Psalms lays a foundation for his commentary on the Pauline Epistles."[34]

Gloss on the Pauline Epistles

Peter's revision of the Gloss on the Pauline Epistles—his *Collectanea in epistolas S. Pauli*, materials "gathered together" on the letters of St. Paul, as the work is often referred to since the sixteenth century—underwent several redactions before reaching the final form that is available in print today.[35] Four manuscripts—two in the Vatican Library and two in the Bibliothèque Nationale in Paris—contain a "first edition" of the *Collectanea*, which the Lombard must have released for copying and circulation after the council of Rheims, in 1148, for the text contains explicit references to matters discussed at that council, in particular arguments relating to Gilbert de la Porrée's Trinitarian theology.[36] As Peter lectured on the Epistles of St. Paul, he continued to work with, and on, the *Collectanea*, both adding and removing material. This process stopped only when he was elected to the episcopate, thus ceasing to teach, sometime in 1159.

Although building upon techniques that Peter first practiced in composing the Gloss on the Psalms, the *Collectanea* is a very different work. Unlike the former, it draws upon a large array of sources in addition to those present in Anselm's and Gilbert's versions of the Gloss. In composing the *Collectanea*, the Lombard used quotations from works of Ambrose, Augustine, John Chrysostom, Ambrosiaster, Alcuin, Haymo, Remigius, and Lanfranc, as well as borrowing from contemporary authors, such as Hugh of St. Victor and Walter of Mortagne. Not all of these quotations, however, were derived from original sources. As was customary, Peter often availed himself of collections of excerpts; in the case of Augustine, in particular, he relied heavily upon a Carolingian compilation, Florus of Lyons's *Expositio epistolarum beati Pauli*.[37] To facilitate the consultation of his work, Peter carefully indicates the sources of his quotations in marginal rubrics, which also contain indications on the structure of the work and admonitions to the reader: "Question," "Response," "Reason," "Pay Attention," and so on. Further enhancing the value of the *Collectanea*, Peter rigorously applies the *accessus* method that he first learned and tested in the Psalms glosses. The resulting unity and coherence of the argument of the *Collectanea* did not fail to impress his contemporaries, for just like the Gloss on the Psalter, the Lombard's work on St. Paul's letters quickly became an exegetical classic.

Most importantly, however, Peter's Gloss on the Epistles of St. Paul offers much more than a commentary on the biblical text. In this work, we encounter the Lombard as it were torn between *sacra pagina* and systematic theology, that is to say, between the traditional mode of reflection on the faith, guided as that mode was by the narrative order of Scripture, and more recent attempts to articulate the elements of the faith in a logical system of doctrine. While Peter's Gloss does of course follow the order of the biblical narrative, his commentary frequently takes off from the text, especially in places where certain verses lend themselves to a more thematic approach. Thus, within the *Collectanea*, we find a number of relatively self-contained theological treatises—indeed, treatises so self-contained that some of them have recently been edited separately.[38] Many of these disquisitions, however, appear only in the first edition of the *Collectanea*. Peter Lombard eliminated some of them altogether from the text as it developed in later years, and he shortened others. As he started work on the *Book of Sentences*, he must have come to a clearer understanding of the differences between biblical commentary and the emerging structures of systematic theology. He realized, in other words, that an in-depth investigation of a theological theme (such as the procession of the persons of the Trinity or the Incarnation) occupies a specific place within a comprehensive system of doctrine—a system most logically expounded within a conceptual, not a narrative, order. The biblical commentary, Peter must have understood, is not the literary genre best suited to such logical and systematic exposition. The Christian "story" and the Christian "system" needed to be separated. Consequently, the Lombard decided to remove or abbreviate certain theological tractates found in the first version of the *Collectanea*. He did not, however, simply jettison the fruits of his reflection. Reworked, the material eliminated from the *Collectanea* made its way into the *Sentences*.

A good example of a theological treatise that appeared in the *Collectanea* before being reworked and mined for use in the *Sentences* is a treatise on the procession of the Son and the Holy Spirit, which is found in the four manuscripts of the first edition of the Gloss.[39] In the Gloss, the tractate originally functioned as commentary on Romans 11:36, "For of him, and by him, and in him, are all things: to him be glory for ever. Amen." Yet the presence of this elaborate dissertation was clearly disruptive to the flow of the biblical commentary. In the final redaction of the *Collectanea*, therefore, the treatise on the procession of the Son and the Spirit has disappeared.[40] But elements from it made their way into various parts of the first book of the *Sentences*.

The structure of the theological treatises contained within the text of the *Collectanea* affords us valuable insight into the process through which lectures on Scripture gradually took off from the biblical text, that is to say, mutated into lectures on systematic theology—in the case not only of Peter Lombard, but of the masters of the mid-twelfth century more generally.[41] A look at the treatise on the Incarnation from the first edition will be instructive in this respect.[42] Like all of the *Collectanea*, the treatise began as a revision of the *Glossa ordinaria*. The *Tractatus de incarnatione*, as Brady has entitled it, is triggered by Romans 1:3–5: "Concerning his Son, who was made to him of the seed of David, according to the flesh..." After a brief introductory paragraph, which provides a structured summary of the main points of the biblical text, the commentary starts as a long chain of quotations from various works of Augustine, Ambrose, Origen, and Cassiodorus. Peter Lombard only occasionally adds a few words of explanation. Even the questions raised are quotations. Throughout the treatise, however, the sources of the quotations are meticulously indicated in marginal rubrics. Particular attention is paid to accurate identification of authorship. One slightly humorous rubric reads: "Ambrose, in the Book of Questions on the Old and New Testament, which by ignorant people is attributed to Augustine."[43]

Then, four pages and fifteen quotations into the treatise, the Lombard raises a first question of his own: "Here is it asked, however, in what way Augustine is saying 'all' [totum] here, since he says elsewhere that the human and divine nature are not parts of that person [i.e., Christ]."[44] In other words, how can, according to Augustine, the person of Christ be all God and all man, if God and man are not "parts" of Christ? The functioning of this question is characteristic of the method of Scholastic inquiry, for it combines (1) investigation of a difficulty that originates in an apparent contradiction in an authoritative source with (2) focus on the meaning of a particular word, all in the service of (3) resolution of a theoretical problem. As one may expect, the solution consists in a distinction in the meaning of the word totum: "To which it is to be responded that totum [all, whole] is not understood here like something composed of parts." A confirmatio solutionis, "confirmation of the solution," from other Augustinian texts ensues, before a further difficulty is raised.

In the course of the treatise, Peter's questions become increasingly systematic rather than textual. In other words, the conceptual logic of the subject matter seems gradually to take precedence over the interpretation of the authoritative sources—although the two continue to work hand in hand. At one point, for example, the Lombard formulates the following problem: "Again, it is asked whether Christ must be said to be begotten twice [bis genitus], since he is said to be the son of God and of man."[45] This question is not occasioned by any textual difficulty, but Peter immediately adduces textual evidence to provide a solution. Frequently, solutions like this one are subjected to further inquiry, which then leads to extended controversial debate: *Opponitur solutioni*, "it is objected to this solution," is a phrase used in such a context, introducing arguments "con." These may then be followed by further arguments in favor of the solution (in a paragraph entitled *oppositio*), before the controversy comes to rest in a *determinatio*, or magisterial opinion, which reconciles the discordant voices by means of a distinction.[46] The *Collectanea* thus seems to reflect the rise of disputations in the schools, possibly in Peter Lombard's own classroom.[47] Disputations were a new method of instruction in which students were called upon to exchange authority-based arguments in favor and against certain positions, before the master would "determine," or resolve the opposition.

Sometimes, however, the texts of the tradition prove impossible to reconcile. Such cases call for a more personal theory—one not seamlessly derived from a consensus of authorities:

> Lo! it appears that the authorities [*auctores*] have held different positions on the question that has been laid out. That is why later generations reading those [positions] have maintained various and contrary teachings, taking their lead [*occasionem sumentes*] from the aforesaid [quotations].
>
> [*In the margin*: He solves it.] We, however, desiring to remove any hint of falsity and contradiction from the Sacred Pages, and adhering to the orthodox Fathers and Catholic doctors who are above any suspicion of a distorted understanding, say that . . .[48]

To sum up: in the *Collectanea*, scriptural passages are elucidated through authoritative texts from the tradition; tensions in these texts crystallize theological difficulties; and these difficulties, in turn, are resolved by means of distinctions. The result is more clearly defined theological doctrine. In some cases, when differences in interpreting Scripture (and hence, the faith) remain irreconcilable, teachings are presented as more personal opinions.

The treatise on the Incarnation demonstrates, in the space of two dozen pages, how scriptural interpretation turned into theological doctrine in the twelfth century. What distinguishes the *Book of Sentences* from the *Collectanea*, as we shall see, is not the fundamental structure of this method, but abstraction from the narrative order of the scriptural texts that originally gave rise to its application.

Sermons

Besides his work as master of theology, Peter Lombard's duties included preaching in the cathedral to which he belonged. Thirty-five of his sermons have been discovered so far, a thirty-sixth being of dubious authorship.[49] Most closely studied in an old dissertation by Félix Protois, Peter's homiletic work has generally been judged as falling short of the brilliance of his more theoretical productions. Nonetheless, the Lombard's sermons compare positively with those of many of his contemporaries, who tended to cultivate a style of fire and brimstone. Peter was competent and calm as a preacher, preferring affectionate exhortation and charitable compassion to violent diatribes.[50] Although his sermons are not without moments of great eloquence, Master Peter's goal was "to instruct rather than to move" his audience.[51] Since they were composed in Latin, the sermons must have been intended for an educated audience, such as his colleagues and students at the cathedral school. Indeed, less sophisticated congregations would hardly have been able to follow Peter's often subtle distinctions—usually threefold, as Protois has observed. At least two of the homilies, numbers 14 and 31 in Brady's list, were given at St. Victor.

According to contemporary canon law, it was incumbent upon deacons to preach upon the New Testament, while minor clerics were to limit themselves to the Old.[52] We may assume, therefore, that those of the Lombard's sermons which deal with the Old Testament were written and delivered before he became deacon and those on the New Testament after he attained the diaconate. Protois has pointed to differences in maturity that might provide another criterion to date Peter Lombard's homiletic work. Moreover, some of the sermons exhibit clear parallels with either the commentary on the Psalms, the *Collectanea*, or the *Book of Sentences*, indicating that Peter was able to draw upon these works as he composed certain homilies. The contents of sermon number 20 allow us to assign it to the period of the episcopate. The sermons were collected and published after Bishop Peter's death; several manuscripts of such collected sermons have come down to us, though the number of homilies they contain varies from seventeen to thirty-one.

More research in this field clearly is an important desideratum, allowing us as it would to round out our understanding of the Lombard's spirituality and ideas. In fact, the sermons sometimes touch upon matters that are not discussed anywhere else in his writings.

The "Magna Glosatura"

Finally, a word on the way in which Peter's Glosses on the Psalms and the Pauline Epistles eventually came to be part of the "official" Gloss on the Bible. Apart from shedding light upon the intellectual effect of Peter Lombard, this discussion will give us an opportunity to appreciate the coherence of different aspects of medieval culture. For the life of the mind and material culture are intertwined, constituting each other in an indissoluble link—not only in the twelfth century.

We already know that toward the middle of the twelfth century, Anselm of Laon and his circle placed a new tool of biblical interpretation in the hands of contemporary scholars: the *Glossa ordinaria*. Gilbert de la Porrée was responsible for an expanded version of the Gloss on the Psalms and the Pauline Epistles, which twelfth-century scholars regarded as the central books in the Old and New Testaments, respectively for their moral guidance and doctrinal richness. Gilbert's Gloss in many respects paved the way for Peter Lombard's work, for he transformed the short marginal and interlinear glosses of the *Glossa ordinaria* into a continuous text. Gilbert's revision came to be referred to as the *Media Glosatura*. It circulated side by side with the standard Gloss, rather than superseding it. By contrast, Peter Lombard's *Magna Glosatura*—that is, his Gloss on the Psalms and on the letters of St. Paul—ended up replacing the respective portions in the *Glossa ordinaria*, so that "by the end of the third quarter of the twelfth century a full set of glossed books of the Bible comprised the Psalter and Pauline Epistles with the Gloss of Peter Lombard, and all the other books of the Bible with the Gloss compiled in the schools of Laon."[53]

Paleographer Christopher de Hamel has discovered a fascinating development in the page layout of the three stages of the Gloss just described.[54] Initially, in the first copies of the *Glossa ordinaria*, the scribes divided each page into three roughly equal columns. The middle column was reserved for the biblical text, around which the glosses were arranged on lines ruled separately from, and more tightly than, those on which the scriptural verses were written. Since the biblical text was invariably copied first, the columns reserved for the gloss sometimes proved insufficient, and sometimes overly generous. The result was a rather uneven, unbalanced appearance of the page. Soon, however, the scribes learned how to create a more attractive and economical page layout. They began to adjust the respective widths of the three columns as a function of the proportion of scriptural text and commentary that had to be fitted onto a single page. Then further techniques were invented with the same goal of balancing the spaces occupied by Scripture and gloss, including techniques such as glosses written across the whole width of the page. The result of these scribal experiments was a much closer relationship between Scripture and gloss, which now visually appeared as a unified whole, rather than as a central text with some marginal remarks haphazardly added to it (see fig. 1). De Hamel comments: "The *sacra pagina*, both theologically and in practice, became a single entity comprising Gloss as well as biblical text."[55]

The arrangement of Gilbert's *Media Glosatura* went a step further. As already noted, Gilbert's Gloss came in the form of a continuous text, unlike the *Glossa ordinaria*, which was made up of marginal and interlinear notes on particular words and verses. In its first manuscripts, the *Media Glosatura* was presented as an independent piece of writing, without the full text of Scripture accompanying it. (Gilbert's Gloss incorporated lemmata, short quotations of the beginnings of verses and of other keywords, to indicate what part of Scripture was being referred to.) But the need was felt for a full biblical text side by side with Gilbert's work, to facilitate its consultation and comprehension. When scribes responded to that need, they created manuscripts in which they wrote out the *Media*

FIG. 1. Page layout of the *Glossa ordinaria* in the mid-twelfth century. Drawing from de Hamel, *Glossed Books of the Bible*, 17. Reproduced by kind permission of Boydell & Brewer Ltd., publishers.

Glosatura first and subsequently added, as best they could, the scriptural text in its inner margins. "The arrangement of the text and gloss is now effectively reversed from the layout of the early twelfth century," de Hamel remarks.[56] In terms of the well-balanced and efficient allocation of space, the results of the new layout tended to be disappointing (see fig. 2).

Just like the *Media Glosatura*, Peter Lombard's revision of the Glosses on the Psalms and the Pauline Epistles was initially copied without the full biblical text accompanying it. But when this was added, the scribes applied extraordinary care to the page layout. Their crucial innovation consisted in the idea of using a single set of rules for the texts of both Scripture and Gloss, which gave the page an impression of great homogeneity and proportion. To distinguish the words of Scripture clearly from those of its commentator, the biblical verses were written on alternate lines and in a larger script—in fact, a new display script which exhibited many features of what was to become Gothic. Initially, both Bible and Gloss ran across the entire width of each column, but later scribes refined the layout further by placing blocks of scriptural text along the left edges of the columns, so as not to interrupt the continuity of the Gloss (see fig. 3). From the 1160s onward, the alternate-line method initially devised to balance Scripture and Gloss in the *Magna Glosatura* was applied, with some modifications, to the Glosses on all of the books of the Bible.

De Hamel toys with the idea that "it was Peter Lombard himself who originally worked out the ingenious system of writing the text beside the

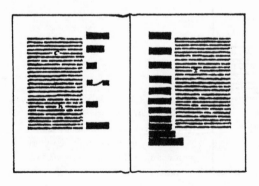

FIG. 2. Layout of the *Media Glosatura*. Drawing from de Hamel, *Glossed Books of the Bible*, 20. Reproduced by kind permission of Boydell & Brewer Ltd., publishers.

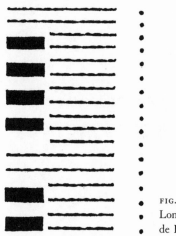

FIG. 3. Alternate-line method used in Peter Lombard's *Magna Glosatura*. Drawing from de Hamel, *Glossed Books of the Bible*, 23. Reproduced by kind permission of Boydell & Brewer Ltd., publishers.

gloss on alternate lines"—an idea which he ultimately dismisses.[57] But that is not the important point here. Rather, what the evolution of the page layout of the Gloss shows us, very palpably, is a shift of emphasis in the relationship between the Word of God and its human interpreters, and that in the space of just a few crucial decades. Whereas in the arrangement of Anselm's *Glossa ordinaria*, the human commentators play nothing but, literally, a marginal role, after Peter Lombard's revisions the status of the glosses is greatly enhanced. They now form an integral unity with the biblical text, with which they closely intermesh on the page. In some books of the Bible—the Psalms and the Pauline Epistles—Scripture now occupies the margins, in order to make room for the lengthy treatises of the theologian. Only the size of its script makes it stand out. The page is set for the birth of systematic theology.

THE *BOOK OF SENTENCES*

Structure, Method, and Theological Vision

In the 1150s, after many years of teaching, Peter Lombard became dissatisfied with the limitations that the literary genre of the gloss imposed upon theological reflection. He turned to the composition of a sentence collection, a form of writing that he knew from his contemporaries; from his studies at Lucca, for example, he was familiar with Master Otto's *Summa sententiarum*, a work of Victorine inspiration. Nonetheless, the step from the gloss to the sentence collection remained a daunting one. To be sure, Peter had conducted systematic theological investigations in the many treatises that his Gloss on the Pauline Epistles contained. Yet there is a crucial difference between treatises on individual theological topics, such as the Incarnation or marriage, and a system of theology in which every important topic not only receives treatment, but occupies a logical place within a general schema. Faced with this task, the Lombard had to choose between two possibilities: the Victorine attempt to organize the theological material along the lines of salvation history, most clearly seen in Hugh's *De sacramentis*, and the Abelardian experiments with conceptual structures.

Date of Composition

Like Peter Lombard's glosses, in particular the Gloss on the Letters of St. Paul, the *Book of Sentences* was not a static work, but underwent a process of revision. Two main stages can be distinguished. A first version of the *Sentences* was completed after Peter's journey to Rome in 1154, during which he incorporated passages from Burgundio's new translation of John Damascene into his text. He then "read," or taught, the *Sentences* in the academic year 1156–1157, releasing a first edition for publication. But he continued to work on the book, as we know from remarks in manuscripts of his students, who frequently distinguish two *editiones* or *lectiones*. The students noticed that when Peter taught his second course on the *Sentences*, in 1157–1158 (the academic year before he returned to the Psalms, which was to be his last), he added numerous notes and *glossae volatiles*, "flying glosses," in the margins.[1] The second edition appeared in 1158, when Michael of Ireland completed copying the text that has come down to us in MS. *Troyes, Bibliothèque municipale 900*.[2] It is estimated that there are between six hundred and nine hundred extant manuscripts of the *Book of Sentences* today, an incredible number for a medieval piece of writing. Even works that were fairly influential in their own day are sometimes preserved in only a single copy.

Sources

Paramount among the sources that Peter Lombard used in compiling the *Sentences* was, not surprisingly, material from his own glosses, in which he had developed his theological positions throughout his earlier career.[3] Apart from the influence of his glosses, we can also discern that of the Gloss, around which so much theological reflection crystallized in the first half of the twelfth century. Peter employed the *Glossa ordinaria* as a mine for authoritative quotations from the Fathers and early medieval theologians, but also as an authority in its own right, when the *Glossa* left sources unidentified or offered comments due to Anselm and his school. In such cases, Peter referred to it simply as *auctoritas* or, sometimes, *expositor*. Among the original works Peter read, those of Augustine stand out, unrivaled, as his principal source of *originalia*. He had firsthand knowledge of the treatise *On Christian Teaching*, the book *Of Eighty-Three*

Questions, the *Retractations*, and the *Enchiridion*, but apparently not of the *On the Trinity*. Combined, the Lombard's firsthand and derivative quotations from Augustine number almost 1,100.[4] In view of this fact, it would not be wrong to say that the *Book of Sentences* belongs squarely in the Augustinian tradition. It is perhaps the last great work of theology in the Western tradition of which this statement can be affirmed so unambiguously.

Hilary of Poitiers was an important inspiration for Peter's Trinitarian theology, as was John of Damascus, whose *De fide orthodoxa* moreover helped Peter formulate some of his Christological insights. The Lombard drew on canonical material assembled by both Ivo of Chartres and Gratian, heavily so in his discussion of the sacraments. He appears to have had access to a treatise from Visigothic Spain, Julian of Toledo's *Prognosticon futuri saeculi*,[5] a major source of his eschatology. Finally, he was well acquainted with the works of the principal theologians of his day, which again served him as sources both of older quotations and of contemporary teachings. In this context, we must mention, on the one hand, Hugh of St. Victor's *De sacramentis christianae fidei* and the Victorine *Summa sententiarum*,[6] and, on the other hand, two works by Peter Abelard, the *Theologia "Scholarium"* and *Sic et non*. Yet Hugh of St. Victor and Peter Abelard are not the only contemporary masters whose views are documented in the *Book of Sentences*. Indeed, Joseph de Ghellinck has remarked that one of the great strengths of the *Sentences* is to have gathered together, into one complex mosaic, all the influential theological opinions of its time.[7] But the contemporaries are never identified by name; rather, Peter employs expressions such as "some people say," *quidam dicunt*, or "here it is asked," *hic quaeritur*.

To us, it must seem strange, and very unscholarly, that so many of Peter's quotations were not garnered from original works, but simply repeated second- or thirdhand from some other source. *Ce "plagiaire,"* Father de Ghellinck jokingly called Peter Lombard.[8] But let us be careful not to project the conventions and methods of contemporary scholarship onto another age, which had totally different conceptions of literary propriety and little regard for the "originality" that we so prize.[9] More remarkable than Peter Lombard's reliance upon derivative quotations is the large number of authoritative works that he did, in fact, read in the original. Marcia Colish cites Peter's "own independent reading of his sources" as one of the reasons for the superior quality of the *Book of*

Sentences.[10] Evidently, the comprehension of a quotation is greatly enhanced when that quotation is replaced in its original context, where the intent and reasoning of the author can much more easily be discerned than in a couple of excerpted sentences. Thus, his reading of original texts gave Peter Lombard a decisive edge in grasping nuances in the meaning of traditional teachings and, if necessary, in overcoming discrepancies among them.

The Structure of the *Book of Sentences*

We have already seen a number of times that with regard to the key question of systematic theology—the arrangement of more specific topics within the overall account of the Christian faith—thinkers in the middle of the twelfth century were faced with a stark choice. They could follow the example of Hugh of St. Victor and his school, which attempted to elaborate a comprehensive system of theology without renouncing the narrative order of the Bible. This approach certainly required a degree of abstraction from the "stories" of the Old and New Testaments; after all, the *De sacramentis* or the *Summa sententiarum* were not glosses. Yet the fundamental guiding thread holding the topics of reflection together was not their logical relationship, but rather their chronological succession in salvation history. Thus, the Victorine approach was a "traditional" one, emphasizing the primacy of the Word of God in theological instruction. One could view it against the background of the religious history of the abbey of St. Victor itself. St. Victor was a community of canons who had adopted a more monastic, traditionally Augustinian way of life in reaction to the increasing secularization that they lamented in the cathedral chapters. Originally, the intention of the canons regular at St. Victor and elsewhere had been to reform the cathedral chapters. When that hope was disappointed, the canons regular severed their ties with the dioceses to which they belonged, forming a new religious order.[11]

On the other side of our twelfth-century religious spectrum, we have the figure of Peter Abelard: a restless seeker, brilliant, no doubt, and faithful in his intentions, but with a track record of scandal and condemnation. Abelard experimented with much more innovative methods of theological systematization, methods leaving behind the scriptural order of salvation history. Abelard and his followers divided the theological enterprise into faith, charity/ethics, and sacraments—or dogmatic theology, moral theology, and a separate theology of the sacraments. Note the clear division between the theoretical and practical realms of inquiry; we are no longer in a monastic setting, where reflection is indissociably embedded in a life of worship and prayer.

In between the two poles defined by the Victorines and the Abelardians, we find Master Peter Lombard. Without making a silly attempt to reduce the life of the spirit to social and historical circumstances, I would nonetheless like to note that Peter's personal situation and the institutional setting of his teaching put him at something like an equal distance from Hugh of St. Victor and Abelard.[12] Peter, though sympathetic to the Victorines, never joined their ranks; instead, he became one of the "secularized" canons of the diocese of Paris. He led a life outside any religious order, in his own house, with a relatively loose attachment to the cathedral of Notre Dame. Yet his was an extremely stable existence, incomparable with the peregrinations of Peter Abelard, who never seemed to be sure of his place in life and in the Church.

Enough biographical speculation, and back to the facts. How did Peter Lombard structure the *Book of Sentences*? He took his clue from a reading of the first book of Augustine's work *On Christian Teaching*, which we have already had occasion to discuss briefly in chapter 1. This is how the first book of the *Sentences* commences:

> **All doctrine is of things or of signs.** While we were again and again pondering the contents of the Old and New Law in a diligent examination, the prevenient grace of God hinted to us that the treatment of the sacred page principally turns upon things and signs. For just as the eminent doctor Augustine says in the book, *On Christian Doctrine*, . . .[13]

Three points are worth noting before we have a closer look at Peter's use of the Augustinian signs-things distinction: first, the allusion to the Lombard's long teaching career, a career devoted to what we would call "biblical studies." The author of the *Sentences*, consequently, regards the project upon which he is about to embark as a study of the "sacred page," *sacra pagina*—which shows how deeply rooted systematic theology is for him in the text of Scripture, despite the fact that the *Sentences* contain many more references to theological authorities than to the sacred text.

The *Sentences* are clearly a work of reflection on the tradition of scriptural learning, and of reflection on Scripture only through the lens of that tradition. Systematic theology is born at a certain distance from the original "story" of Scripture. Finally, it is more than a rhetorical cliché that Peter Lombard alludes to divine grace as having provided him with the key inspiration which allowed him to find a structure for his "treatment of the sacred page."

The paragraph just quoted continues with a text from *On Christian Teaching* in which Augustine explains the fundamental difference between things (*res*) and signs (*signa*): things do not signify anything, whereas signs do. All signs, however, are things—simply in the broader sense of being something—but not all things are signs (that is to say, things signifying). Peter Lombard employs this Augustinian distinction, which he has understood quite correctly, for a purpose that remains rather marginal in *On Christian Teaching*, namely, to define the sacraments and, moreover, distinguish between sacraments of the Old and New Testaments.[14] For some signs, Peter explains, merely signify grace without justifying, and these are the sacraments of the Old Law. (Circumcision is the standard example of such a vetero-testamentary sacrament.) Other signs, however, do not only signify grace but confer it: these are the "evangelical sacraments." The sacraments are the subject matter of book 4 of the *Sentences*.

Peter now turns to an analysis of "things," again closely following Augustine's lead while adapting his ideas to a new purpose—the structuring of a comprehensive theological system. He introduces a further distinction, this time between things that are to be used (*uti*), things that are to be enjoyed (*frui*), and things that are objects of both use and enjoyment. Only the triune God, who is capable of giving us beatifying happiness, is the proper object of enjoyment; every other thing is to be used as a mere means in the quest for beatitude. Human beings and the angels form an exception, Peter notes, for they are both to be used as a means on the journey to God and to be enjoyed, though only "in God." Another case that deserves special consideration is that of the virtues, such as charity, joy, peace, and patience. The difficulty surrounding the status of the virtues shows itself in an apparent disagreement between Augustine and Ambrose, which Peter however finds easy to resolve. He makes quite an eloquent statement:

We however, desirous of putting out of the way those [points] concerning which there seems to be an incompatibility of authorities, say
that the virtues are to be pursued and loved for their own sake, and
yet for the sake of beatitude alone. They are to be loved for their own
sake, because they delight those that possess them in a sincere and
saintly manner, and bring about spiritual joy in them. Nonetheless,
one must not stop here but proceed further. The process of love does
not remain fixed here, nor is the end-point of love here, but this [whole
dynamism] is referred to that highest good to which alone one should
cleave absolutely, since it is to be loved for its own sake alone and
there is nothing to be sought beyond it: for it is the highest end.[15]

An objection affords Peter the opportunity to render his solution more
precise. The virtues are not themselves objects of enjoyment, he concedes,
but are that through which we enjoy: *per virtutes fruimur, non eis*.[16] This
means that the virtues do not occupy the same intermediary position as
men and angels, but rather are special among the things to be used.

An epilogue sums up the whole rather detailed discussion, of which
we have only seen a rapid summary:

Epilogue. "This is the sum of all that has been said in our treatment
of things":[17] There is a difference between things to be enjoyed, things
to be used, and things to be enjoyed and used; among those that are
to be used, some are those through which we enjoy, such as the virtues
and powers of the soul, which are natural goods. Of all this, we have
to treat before treating of signs; and first [we will treat] of the things
to be enjoyed, namely, of the holy and indivisible Trinity.[18]

This, then, is Peter Lombard's outline of the structure of the *Book of
Sentences*. A discussion of the Trinity (things to be enjoyed) will precede
a treatment of creation (things to be used), which will lead to a third
part of the work devoted to man and angels (things that are objects of
both enjoyment and use). This will be followed by a theology of the
virtues (things through which we enjoy), before the work comes to an
end in a part on the sacraments (signs). Does this outline correspond to
the actual execution of the work? Roughly, yes; but not quite.

In book 1, we do indeed get a very detailed treatment of the triune
God. The book is entitled "On the Mystery of the Trinity." Book 2 carries
the title "On the Creation of Things, and the Formation of Spiritual and
Corporeal Entities, and Many Other Matters Pertaining to These." These
"many other matters" include the creation of man, his prelapsarian state,

the Fall, sin, and related issues. Book 3 then turns to "the Incarnation of the Word." How does it fit into the schema just outlined? This, alas, Peter does not explain, as his short prologue to this book situates it within the whole of the *Sentences* without, frustratingly, any mention or even allusion to the thing/sign, enjoyment/use distinctions. But it is not too difficult to supply the missing argument. In becoming flesh, God deigned to be not only the ultimate end of human existence, but the road to that end as well; in other words, God, the ultimate object of enjoyment, allowed himself to be used for human salvation. That is, indeed, how Augustine presents the Incarnation in a fascinating passage from book 1 of *On Christian Teaching*: "So although it [wisdom] is actually our homeland [*patria*], it has also made itself the road [*viam*] to our homeland. And although wisdom is everywhere present to the inner eye that is healthy and pure, it deigned to appear even to the carnal eyes of those whose inner eye was weak and impure."[19] Book 3, interestingly, also addresses the virtues—that is, those things to be used through which we enjoy. The virtues find their place in book 3 because Peter approaches them from the point of view of the human Christ; put differently, Peter analyzes the virtues in their most perfect and exemplary state. Finally, book 4 is dedicated to the signs of grace, or the sacraments. A short opening sentence explicitly reminds his readers of Peter's initial plan: "Having treated of those matters which pertain to the doctrine of things that are to be enjoyed, that are to be used, and that are to be used and enjoyed, we approach the doctrine of signs."[20]

Method and Vision of
the Theological Project

Given the beginning of book 4, it would be preposterous to suggest that Peter Lombard somehow forgot about his initial plan for the work in the process of composing it. Nevertheless, it is undeniable that, with the exception of that short sentence, he makes no effort whatsoever to show his readers how his work unfolds, logically, in function of the Augustinian distinctions.[21] Indeed, as already indicated, at the beginning of book 3 he offers what seems to be an alternative rationale for the structure of the *Book of Sentences*:

The contents of this volume are briefly stated in a summary.—Thus, the order of reason [*ordo rationis*] demands that we who, in the first book, have said something about the inexplicable mystery of the most high Trinity, through the irrefragable witness of the Saints, and then, in the second book, have thoroughly penetrated into the order of the creation of things and the fall of man, following the model of certain authorities; consequently in the third and fourth book[s] examine his redemption, accomplished through the grace of the Mediator of God and men, as well as the sacraments of human redemption by which the bruises of man are bound up and the wounds of sinners are healed: just as the Samaritan comes to the wounded, the physician to the sick, [and] grace to the wretched.[22]

While Peter's Augustinian and "rational" accounts of the division of the *Sentences* are not incompatible with each other, they do represent different emphases. The Augustinian plan presented at the beginning of the work replaces the narrative order of Scripture with an arrangement that can claim the authority of one of the greatest "Saints," or Church Fathers. The summary that introduces book 3, on the other hand, sounds as though the Lombard has opted for the Abelardian way of structuring theology, namely, in accordance with an order exclusively based upon rational considerations.

Perhaps Peter Lombard's lack of methodological rigor is simply indicative of the fact that reflection on method was not his forte. He excelled in grasping the subtlest shades of meaning in the theological positions of the tradition and of his contemporaries, in synthesizing and arranging material, but he was not able to lift the procedures that he intuitively employed in his work of theological systematization onto the level of methodological clarity—the kind of clarity one finds in the preface to Peter Abelard's *Sic et non*. There is method in the *Book of Sentences*, one could say, yet little methodology, or systematic reflection upon method. Indeed, where such systematic reflection occurs, it is not quite coherent, as in the two accounts of the structure of the *Sentences*.

This explanation is possible, but it is not the only possible one. Rather, one could argue that Peter quite deliberately avoided the emphasis on methodology that was so typical of some of his contemporaries—people such as Abelard, but also Gilbert de la Porrée. These thinkers approached theology with the heavy artillery of logic and semantics, which they had developed in commentaries upon Boethius. This background furnished them with the tools to articulate theology as a science, "science" in the sense of knowledge constituted by means of a method that is itself the subject of critical reflection and control. In the twelfth century, the transition from *sacra pagina* to theological science stalled, in part due to the influence of Peter Lombard, in part due to the inadequacy of the conceptual tools available at the time. If, as Marie-Dominique Chenu has argued, in the thirteenth century theology finally adopted the scientific paradigm, this development occurred precisely as a result of the availability of enhanced conceptual tools (through the discovery of the Aristotelian tradition) and their subsequent application to theology.[23]

Peter Lombard wanted to keep theology closer to its roots in Scripture and in reasoning from authority, without however taking the side of "traditionalists" like Hugh of St. Victor. In his summary of the *Sentences* at the beginning of book 3, we have noticed his reference to the "irrefragable witness of the Saints," as well as his stated desire to follow "the model of certain authorities." This is a programmatic statement, not a mere *captatio benevolentiae* to please his readers. The preface contains very similar remarks on a volume compiled "from witnesses to truth that are founded in eternity," a volume entirely made up of "the teachings of the Fathers," in which the author's voice makes itself heard but rarely.[24] By contrast, the *Sentences* abound in derogatory remarks on those the Lombard calls *garrulos ratiocinatores, elatiores quam capaciores*, "garrulous reasoners, more lofty than capable,"[25] *de ingenio suo praesumentes*, "those making presumptions concerning their abilities,"[26] *de suo sensu gloriantes*, "those boasting of their understanding,"[27] and *illi scrutatores*, "those scrutinizers."[28] In book 3, discussing a question on the Resurrection, he declares: "These and other subtleties [*argutiae*] have their place in creaturely matters, but the sacrament of faith is free from philosophical arguments [*a philosophicis argumentis est liberum*]."[29]

While not rejecting the use of philosophy lock, stock, and barrel, Peter prefers an attitude of humility when it comes to the great mysteries of faith. More than once in the *Book of Sentences* we find him admitting his inability to resolve a question: "this question is insoluble, surpassing human understanding," he remarks on one such occasion, in the context of Trinitarian theology.[30] Just a few pages later, he concedes, "This question, as well, is inexplicable, since it surpasses the weaknesses of man."[31]

Let me suggest that it is precisely the positive character of Peter Lombard's theology that ensured its continued success over the centuries. Had

Peter forced the theological material "into any one, preemptive, philosophical mold,"[32] subsequent generations would have found it difficult to use his collection of authorities as the basis for their own reflections. The fact that the coherence of the *Book of Sentences* is real, but not rigid, afforded it the malleability necessary to make it a classic.

If, therefore, the structure of the *Book of Sentences* is exceptionally clear, such clarity is not the hallmark of a system logically generated from the rigorous application of explicitly formulated and examined principles. Rather, it is largely an extrinsic clarity, one added to the system when it was already complete. I am referring to the consultation aids with which Peter deliberately and meticulously equipped his work. These consultation aids are, on the one hand, a detailed table of contents and, on the other hand, rubrics guiding the user of the book through its argument and identifying the principal authorities quoted.

The table of contents appeared such an important feature to Peter himself that he even drew attention to its existence at the end of his preface: "In order that what is sought may turn up more easily, we have preceded [the work] with the titles by which the chapters of the individual books are distinguished."[33] The table of contents makes it possible to find Peter's treatment of a particular theological question quickly, without thumbing through the entire volume. That made it particularly suitable as a textbook. The chapter headings from the table of contents correspond, though not always literally, to the rubrics placed at the beginning of the first paragraph of each chapter. At that point, the reader will frequently find a short reflection defining the logical place of the topic under consideration within the larger whole: "After the witnesses of the Old Testament . . . , let us now turn to the authorities of the New Testament";[34] "let us now return to the question mentioned earlier";[35] "now, after we have scrutinized the coeternity of the three persons . . . , it remains at this point to say something about their equality";[36] and so on. At major junctures, we find brief overviews explaining the structure of the subsequent discussions: "**What is to be considered on [the subject of] the angels.** On the angelic nature, these [points] are therefore to be considered first: . . . ; then, . . . ; moreover, . . ."[37]

These brief overviews and sentences marking logical transitions were to give rise to the division of the *Sentences* into "distinctions," which was not due to Peter Lombard himself. Originally, the work was divided only into four books, with 210 chapters in the first, 269 in the second, 164 in the third, and 290 in the fourth book. Alexander of Hales, who was the first master to use the *Sentences*, rather than Scripture, as the basis of his theological lectures, grouped the chapters further into topical units, employing the indications that the Lombard himself had furnished. This move occurred at Paris, sometime between 1223 and 1227. Once Alexander had introduced these units, or distinctions, the chapters were renumbered accordingly, now being counted within each distinction.[38] That is how the *Book of Sentences* has been cited ever since—for example, *Book of Sentences*, book 1, distinction 5, chapter 3.[39]

Let us now turn to the rubrics. These are words often written in red characters (the Latin *ruber* means "red"), either within the columns of text or in the margins, which fulfill several functions:[40]

1. They provide the titles of chapters, thus making it possible easily to retrieve titles from the table of contents and to orient oneself within the work; for example, **All doctrine is of things or of signs** (book 1, dist. 1, chap. 1, no. 1) or **On the mystery of Trinity and unity** (book 1, dist. 2, chap. 1, no. 1).

2. They mark subdivisions within the chapters, thus helping the reader to follow the structure of the argument; for instance, **Here is it asked whether God enjoys or uses us** (book 1, dist. 1, chap. 3, no. 6) or **Epilogue** (ibid., chap. 3, no. 11).

3. They identify the sources of quotations; for example, **Augustine in book VI of the De Trinitate*** (book 3, dist. 36, chap. 2, no. 3) or **Augustine, to Jerome*** (ibid., no. 5). The care Peter Lombard takes in identifying the sources of his quotations—wherever possible, by name, book, and chapter—provides the basis for a genuinely critical discussion of the meaning of the texts cited, as opposed to a use of authorities as mere tokens to illustrate predefined stereotyped positions. In many cases, dots at the beginning and end of quotations, together with red lines running down the left-hand side of the column, indicate the precise lengths of quotations, thus fulfilling the function of modern-day quotation marks.

4. They advert to important or difficult issues to which the reader should pay particular attention; for instance, **Be careful*** (book 1, dist. 3, chap. 3, no. 1) or **Pay attention here*** (book 3, dist. 15, chap. 3, no. 2). Such rubrics are relatively rare, however.

Reconciliation of Authorities

There is one aspect of Peter Lombard's method in the *Book of Sentences* that we have only touched upon briefly so far, although it is crucial to Peter's theological project, as well as—more generally—to the progress of theological reflection in the Middle Ages: the reconciliation of authorities. For the function of the *Book of Sentences* is not only to collect the *sententiae*—the sentences—of the Fathers and other authoritative theologians and to arrange them in a systematic order; it is "to put out of the way those [points] concerning which there seems to be an incompatibility of authorities," as Peter put it in a passage quoted earlier in this chapter. In the task of synthesizing authorities, the *Book of Sentences* did not have to reinvent the wheel, being able to draw upon a long Christian tradition that ultimately remounts to Jesus himself: "I am not come to destroy, but to fulfill" (Mt 5:17). The main steps in the development of this tradition were, of course, outlined in our first chapter. In Peter Lombard's own day, Abelard codified procedures of synthesis in his *Sic et non*, which Peter knew and used. These procedures ranged from the recognition of terminological differences between Latin and Greek Fathers and the need to work upon the basis of sound texts, through the distinction between an author's own opinion and a report of the teachings of others, to the suggestions that sometimes an author's expression might be idiosyncratic or that what he says could be meant to apply only to particular times and circumstances. If there is no other way to surmount differences, Abelard further recommends, the weightier, more trustworthy authority should prevail.[41]

Let us now examine the structure of a typical chapter in the *Book of Sentences*, so that we may form an idea of the literary form that characterizes this great work, while also coming to understand some of the strategies of argumentation that Peter Lombard employs in it. Note that in the following paragraphs, I will comment on the contents of the text only insofar as understanding its structure requires it. Our example is book 1, distinction 5, chapter 1.[42]

"**Here it is asked**," the rubric at the beginning announces, "**whether the Father has begotten the divine essence or it [the divine essence] the Son, [and] whether the essence has begotten the essence or it [the essence] has neither begotten nor is begotten**." Not too difficult a question, it appears, since all Catholic authors agree at least on the first crucial point: the divine essence is not begotten by the Father. Several reasons can be adduced to support this answer: "**The first reason why it is so***"; "**a second one***"; "**a third and more powerful reason**"—each of these rubrics, two of them marginal, opens a paragraph that contains references to or quotations from Augustine, which are accompanied by Peter's own elucidations. But then, in spite of the consensus, a problem arises: "**This seems to be opposed**" by some Augustinian texts, where Augustine speaks as though the Father had begotten the divine essence. In the (pseudo-) Augustinian *De fide ad Petrum*, for instance, the bishop of Hippo writes that "as God begot the Word, he begot what He Himself is."[43] Now what "He Himself is" is obviously His essence. Is the divine essence actively involved in the process of generation? No, Peter replies, "those words are to be understood in this manner, [as though they were] saying: 'The Father has begotten from Himself what He Himself is,' that is to say, the Son, who is what the Father is." This interpretation brings Augustine back into line with himself, as it were, as well as defusing a theologically dubious use of his authority. For let us not forget that what may appear to us as anodyne details from the theology of a time long past represented issues of burning interest in Peter Lombard's own day. No doubt the quotation from *De fide ad Petrum* was invoked by some contemporary theologian to defend a position according to which the Father begot the divine essence, or the divine essence begot itself. If mainstream Christians no longer hold such a position today, it is precisely because debates in previous centuries have shown it to be incompatible with a coherently articulated statement of their faith.

"**He pursues other parts of the question**"—note the third person, which the learned Franciscans who prepared the first edition of the *Sentences* (1882) took as an indication of the fact that the rubrics could not be attributed to the Lombard himself, an opinion in which they were seconded by de Ghellinck. It has been shown, however, that other contemporary masters used the same kind of third-person rubrics.[44] In this paragraph, Peter adds two conclusions to the previous discussion. First, the divine essence cannot have begotten the Son, for "if the Son were the divine essence, then the Son would be the thing from which He was begotten; and then the same thing would have begotten itself." This argument is a little strange, unless I have misunderstood it. It seems to be based upon the assumption that the previously disproven position is in fact correct, namely, that the Father has begotten the divine essence.

Since the Father has undisputedly also begotten the Son, the Son would be the divine essence. Secondly, the divine essence cannot have begotten the divine essence, because then "the same thing has begotten itself, which absolutely cannot be."

Again, there are counterarguments to be addressed: "**Points that seem to be opposed to what was said above**." The points amount to three quotations from Augustine, passages in which the saint seems to be insinuating that the divine essence has, in fact, begotten itself. The Lombard quotes each text, then explains, as clearly and objectively as possible, the interpretation that it has been given. These explanations usually begin with a standard phrase, such as *et hic videtur dicere*, "and here he seems to be saying," or *ecce aperte dicit his verbis*, "lo and behold! he expressly says in these words."

Peter, of course, does not agree, so that there now follows a "**Determination of those points that seem to be opposed***." When Augustine says that in God, essence is from essence or substance from substance, he does not mean that the divine essence or substance has begotten itself. Rather, his words must be taken to mean that "the Son, who is wisdom, which is substance, is from the Father, who is the same wisdom and substance." Again, "so as to speak more clearly, we say that the Son is wisdom from the Father [who is] wisdom, and we say that the Son is substance begotten by the Father and from the Father [who is] substance." Two quotations from Augustine are adduced to confirm this reading. Peter's strategy, then, consists in an attempt to arrive at an interpretation of Augustine in which the bishop of Hippo's various texts are as consonant with each other as possible. Consistency of an author with himself remains an important hermeneutic principle even today. One does not have to read deconstructionist theorists, however, to realize that it is not an unproblematic one. Augustine is an excellent example of an author whose thought remained in evolution throughout his career. But let us not stray too far from our path.

In the *Book of Sentences*, the interplay of pro and con, of *sic et non*, continues. Peter Lombard is not content with a superficial examination of the questions he raises. Since there is a further argument in the essence-begot-essence debate that either could be brought up in the present context or that was, in fact, put forward by a contemporary master, the Lombard gives it a hearing. "**What seems contrary to the aforesaid exposition**," the next rubric reads. In this paragraph, our attention is turned to texts from another Church Father, Hilary. Hilary's *De Trinitate* seems to contain passages in which the divine essence or nature is said both to have begotten and to be begotten. The gist of the argument is summed up in a rubric right in the middle of the text: "**That the nature of God, remaining in its own form, took on the form of nature and of bodily weakness.**" If God did not become other than Himself in the Incarnation, that is, if He remained in the form of His nature, then nature must have begotten nature.

"**How the words of Hilary just mentioned are to be understood.**" Before offering his own reading of the controverted texts, Peter quotes Hilary in enunciating an important principle of interpretation—one not to be found in Abelard—*non sermoni res, sed rei est sermo subiectus*, "the thing is not subordinated to speech, but speech is subordinated to the thing." In other words, in interpreting the words of Hilary, and of the Fathers more generally, let us not slavishly adhere to the letter of their texts, but instead read these texts in light of the inherent logic of the subjects being investigated. In the present case, this maxim translates into the following, perfectly orthodox paraphrase of Hilary's sentences: the Son "has nothing, insofar as He is God, than what He has received in being born, and precisely in being born does He have the self-subsisting nature of the Father in Him." Hilary's own words in another passage from *De Trinitate* actually confirm this interpretation: "**He confirms his exposition through the words of the same [Hilary].**"

Having examined various imperfect and misleading formulations of the role of the divine essence in the inner-Trinitarian process of generation, Peter now moves into the final part of his chapter, which is devoted to the account he judges to be orthodox. The rubric announces, "**That one reads: The Father has begotten the Son from his substance, and the Son is of the substance of the Father.**" The meaning of "that one reads" becomes clearer in the next sentence: "It is also said, and one frequently reads in Sacred Scripture, that the Father has begotten the Son from his substance." Several quotations from Augustine, accompanied by the Lombard's own brief paraphrases and explanations, support this position. The chapter seems to come to a serene conclusion in the last paragraph: "**Providing a summary of what has been said above, he discloses in what sense it should be understood.**" Yet before Peter Lombard closes the debate, he once again admits the strength of the arguments according to which the divine essence is an active element in the process of generation:

These words just quoted [from Augustine] seem to intimate that the divine substance has begotten the Son, and that the Son is begotten from the substance of the Father, and that from God there is a co-eternal nature, and that the Father has begotten what He Himself is. But what He Himself is, is the divine substance; and thus one can deem that the divine essence has begotten.—These words move us strongly; I would rather hear from others than to propound [myself] in what way they are to be understood. Nevertheless, so that I may speak without rash judgment and temerity, the quotations can be understood in the following sense: "The coeternal nature is from God," that is, the Son, who is coeternal with the Father, is from the Father, such that [the Son] is the same nature as [the Father] is, or of the same nature.

Two quotations from Augustine wrap up the chapter. In it, Peter Lombard has examined all of the major points of a controversial contemporary debate: the role of the divine essence in the process of generation. Has the Father begotten the divine essence? Or has the divine essence begotten the Son? More generally, is the essence of God in any way, actively or passively, involved in the process of generation? Peter answers these questions in the negative, although he is acutely aware of the possibility of interpreting certain Fathers, especially Augustine, otherwise than he does. Peter's conclusion, then, is exhaustively argued but nonetheless humble and provisional.[45]

We now have a better understanding of the literary form, structure, and method of the *Book of Sentences*—the rhythm, as it were, of this great text. Let us turn to the theological substance of the work.

THE *SENTENCES*, BOOK I

On the Mystery of the Trinity

The work of the historian of ideas occurs in a space that is characterized by a fundamental tension—one could call it the tension of immanence and transcendence. But in fact, it is simply the tension of human existence. On the one hand, the historian of ideas utilizes the methods of historical research, which means that he or she examines the way in which the intellectual life is rooted in the conditions of the past. There is no piece of philosophical or theological writing that does not, upon close inspection, turn out to be completely composed of its "sources," so much so, in fact, that the originality of the author appears reduced to the stitching together of the borrowed material in a certain order. While this patchwork quality lies at the very surface of the literary genre of the sentence collection, it can be verified, as well, in works in which the formative genius of the author has left a much clearer imprint. There is no sentence in, say, *Being and Time* that is not reminiscent of Augustine, Kant, Hegel, Kierkegaard, Husserl, or some other great predecessor of Heidegger's.

On the other hand, however, the historian of ideas is dealing with productions of the human mind that intend a certain transcendence of their sources. Put differently, whatever the degree of their awareness of their debt to the past, philosophers and theologians intend to speak the truth about the subjects addressed in their writings, although not necessarily the truth in the sense of verity transcending all possible times and conditions. Nonetheless, authors intend to make statements that possess relevance for an audience that, from the point of view of the writer, is necessarily future. This intention cannot adequately be captured by the methods of historical deconstruction (a term I employ in its literal meaning here). What is required, rather, is a method that focuses on the synthetic unity of the works under consideration, that is to say, their attempt to articulate truth adequately and coherently.

This is the method that I plan to apply in the following five chapters. We have seen that the *Book of Sentences* is not a *creatio ex nihilo* by any stretch of the imagination. It belongs to a long tradition of Christian reflection and arose from lively exchange with the intellectual currents of its time. Other scholars have shown how each of the four books of the *Sentences* fits into the theological landscape of the mid-twelfth century, which idea Peter Lombard borrowed from whom, and in opposition to which contemporary master certain pages of the *Sentences* were composed.[1] There is no need to replicate this research. In what follows, we will therefore concentrate on the theological substance of the *Book of Sentences*, only occasionally introducing historical observations where they are needed. Let us find out what kind of account of the Christian faith the *Book of Sentences* renders.

The Structure of Book 1

An overview of the contents of the first book of the *Sentences* will help us orient ourselves in Peter Lombard's argument. The book opens with the use/enjoyment distinction, with which we have already acquainted ourselves (dist. 1). There follows a section comprising several chapters in which the Lombard examines the evidence for the existence of three persons in the one Godhead—evidence that he finds both in the Old and New Testaments, as well as in certain analogies of the Trinity in creation (dist. 2 and 3). Distinctions 4 through 7 turn to questions concerning the inner-Trinitarian generation of the Son. It is not entirely clear why these discussions appear at this point; they might have found a better place later in the book.[2] In distinction 8, Peter examines properties that belong not to any of the divine persons, but to God's essence as such, properties like immutability and simplicity. Distinction 9 returns to the relationship between the Father and the Son. Distinction 10 then begins the Lombard's exceptionally long and rich pneumatology, which extends through thirty-eight chapters up to, and including, distinction 18. After this treatment of the Holy Spirit, at the very center of book 1, we are offered reflections upon the properties of the three persons in their relationship to each other: their equality, mutual inherence, and so forth (dist. 19–21). In the next chapters, our attention is drawn to the "different names that we use in speaking about God," as Peter formulates it in the table of contents.[3] The divine names fall into six categories, which are the subject of detailed examination in no fewer than sixty chapters (dist. 22–34). In the relationship between God and the human being, two properties of the divine essence are of particular importance: God's knowledge and God's will. Peter's discussion of God's knowledge includes questions concerning foreknowledge, providence, and predestination, as well as a series of chapters on immanence and transcendence (dist. 35–41). The section pertaining to the divine will addresses a number of issues, ranging from the problem of whether God could have done better or other than He has, to the question of the relationship between God's will and evil (dist. 42–48).

The Trinity: Scriptural and
Philosophical Evidence

Peter's attempts to approach the mystery of the Trinity intellectually are prefaced by an extended reflection upon the limitations of the human mind when it is faced with the "light of the ineffable and inaccessible Godhead."[4] We could dismiss these words as a mere cliché, a protestation of humility that was expected of any theologian writing in the middle of the twelfth century. But such a dismissal would be a mistake. Peter's humility sets the tone for his entire treatment of the Trinitarian mysteries. His theology is permeated by a sense of awe that keeps his intellectual endeavors tied to the intuitive piety of the believer. Theology, for Peter, is more than mental gymnastics.

To the modern reader, it might seem surprising that the *Book of Sentences* finds allusions to the Trinity in the Old Testament. However, for the Christian, the God who spoke through the prophets of the Old Testament is the same God the story of whose Son the apostles relate in the

Gospels; moreover, patristic and medieval authors universally believed that the Old Testament foreshadowed its fulfillment in the New. Peter Lombard therefore discovers evidence of the divine unity and Trinity in the pages of the Old Testament. On the subject of God's unity, he quotes Deuteronomy 6:4, among other passages: "Hear, O Israel, the Lord our God is one Lord." That Genesis speaks of the Creator in the plural, on the other hand, is taken as a hint at the plurality of divine persons: "The Lord simultaneously discloses the plurality of persons and the unity of nature in Genesis, when He says: 'Let us make man to our image and likeness' [Gn 1:26]. For in saying, *let us*, and, *our*, he discloses the plurality of persons; but in saying, *image*, [he discloses] the unity of essence."[5] What is more, for Peter Lombard, the Old Testament even alludes to the Son and the Holy Spirit. Does Psalm 2:7 not read, "The Lord hath said to me: Thou art my son, this day have I begotten thee"? And what about, "The spirit of God moved over the waters" (Gn 1:2)?

After several pages devoted to the Old Testament, the *Sentences* address the New Testament evidence for the divine triunity much more briefly. Since passages such as "Going therefore, teach ye all nations; baptizing them in the name of the Father, and of the Son, and of the Holy Ghost" (Mt 28:19) or "I and the Father are one" (Jn 10:30) abound, both in the Gospels and in the apostolic letters, Peter feels that he can refrain from extended discussion: "Almost every single syllable of the New Testament," he writes, "points consistently at the ineffable truth of the unity and trinity."[6]

The biblical evidence having been examined, we move to the question of whether, and how, the Trinity can be known through "Catholic reasons and suitable likenesses."[7] The Lombard clearly views the approach to the Trinity through "reasons" as secondary by comparison with the analysis of Scripture; the only use that he is able to discern in it is to satisfy the inquisitiveness of—we already know this phrase—the "garrulous reasoners, more lofty than capable."[8] However, he finds justification for the rational approach in Scripture itself, which asserts that the human being has access to God not only through faith, but through reason as well: "For the invisible things of him, from the creation of the world, are clearly seen, being understood by the things that are made; his eternal power also, and divinity" (Rom 1:20).

Logically, it is necessary to ask "**how the Creator could be known through created beings**"[9] before addressing the possibility of knowing, more specifically, that God is one essence in three persons. There are four "reasons" or "ways," *rationes* or *modi*, by means of which God's existence can be established. First, creation contains certain kinds of beings that cannot have been brought about by any creature, notably, heaven and earth. Secondly, we have to realize that "what is changeable can have its being only from that which *is*, simply and immutably."[10] Thirdly, "whatever belongs to the group of substances is either a body or a spirit, and something that is a spirit is better than something that is a body, but far better still is that which has made spirit and body."[11] Fourthly and finally, there are sensible forms, such as bodies, and intelligible forms: everything spiritual. Spirit is more formlike (*magis speciosa*) than body, but both have received their being as forms from "a first and unchangeable form."[12]

What I have just summarized are not four philosophically sophisticated proofs of God's existence, as Marcia Colish has claimed. In her laudable desire to give the author of the *Book of Sentences* his due, she sometimes overshoots the mark, and her commentary on the so-called proofs is a case in point. While her account of the first reason is inaccurate—Peter does not say "that all created beings must have causes since they are incapable of causing themselves"[13]—she overinterprets the remaining three. To be sure, Peter was familiar with the philosophical debates of his time, with the positions of the likes of Abelard and Gilbert de la Porrée, but, as I have argued, he made a deliberate decision to limit the role of philosophy in what he still regarded as *sacra pagina*. The *Book of Sentences* contains nothing in the way of proofs of God's existence that could rival the philosophical acumen of some later authors. That is how Peter Lombard wanted it to be. He mentions the four *rationes vel modi* as though in passing, without dwelling on them or according them any special importance.

Now, let us move on to the possibility of discerning traces of the Trinity in the created world. Everything that is, Peter suggests, possesses a certain ontological unity, a shape or form, and displays some order in its relationship to the world (bodies have weight and belong in some place, while souls have definite directions in their desires). "And in this manner, a vestige of the Trinity shines forth in creatures,"[14] namely, insofar as the Creator is the principle of their being, bestows upon them the beauty that is consequent upon their form, and gives them the various directions they follow in their existence. The idea here is that, while God's creative action is one and indivisible, creaturely unity points to the Father, beauty to the Son, and order or direction to the Spirit. Of course, this is not a conclusive argument, as the Lombard himself acknowledges, distancing himself implicitly from the Abelardian claim according to which the Trinity was already discovered by the ancient philosophers: "It is not and was not possible to have sufficient knowledge of the Trinity through the contemplation of creatures, without the revelation of teaching or inner inspiration."[15]

Creation in general may contain a vague trace of the Trinity; the human being, however, is made in the image and likeness of God. It is only later, in book 2, that Peter will explicitly discuss Genesis 1:26, but the scriptural text was certainly on his mind when he composed the two chapters which examine "**how an image of the Trinity is in the soul.**"[16] As with so much of the material in the first book of the *Sentences*, the Lombard is taking his inspiration from Augustine in responding to this question. In fact, the human soul is constituted of three principal powers—memory, intelligence, and love or will—whose relationship mirrors the triunity of its Creator. First, memory, intelligence, and will, as three distinct faculties, inhere in a mind that remains indissolubly one, just as the distinctness of the three persons of the Trinity does not impinge upon the unity of the divine essence. Furthermore, the comprehension of each and all of the faculties in any of the others images the circumincession of the divine persons, "for I remember having memory and intelligence and will; and I understand that I understand and will and remember; and I will that I will and remember and understand."[17] It is not possible that any of the three faculties should operate in isolation from the other two. These two important similarities notwithstanding, we must not forget—Peter reminds us—that the human mind is a mere image of the Trinity. An image is not identical with its original, because of the dissimilarities that obtain between them. In the case of the Trinity and its human image, the most striking dissimilarities are two in number. First, the human being is not his memory, intelligence, and will. We "have" these faculties, just as we have arms and legs. In God, by contrast, there is nothing but complete unity and simplicity. God has no parts. The divine essence does not, therefore, "have" a Father, Son, and Holy Spirit. As Peter Lombard warns in a rubric about the three persons: "**Careful: They are not of one God, but rather one God!***"[18] Secondly, the human being who has memory, intelligence, and will is one person, whereas God is three persons.

There is, however, another way of analyzing the image of the Trinity in the human soul. This new way possesses the advantage of allowing us a faint glimpse of the inner-Trinitarian processions, rather than producing a merely static image of the Godhead. For, if we say that the human soul is composed of mind, knowledge, and love (*mens, notitia, amor*), we can liken the mind to the Father, knowledge to the Son, and love to the Holy Spirit. The mind "begets" knowledge of itself, and in knowing itself, loves itself, just as the Father begets the Son, or Wisdom, and Love between them—the Spirit—ensues.

The Divine Essence

Before turning to a closer examination of the three persons of the Trinity and their relationships, let us jump ahead a few pages to distinction 8, which is devoted to the divine essence. After a precise metaphysical definition of God's being, this distinction proceeds to a systematic derivation of the most fundamental properties that follow directly from the ontological constitution of the divine essence. Distinction 8 underscores that Peter Lombard was certainly not inept philosophically, even if he adopted a cautious attitude with regard to philosophy's role within theology. Indeed, Peter's priorities are obvious from the way he begins this discussion—with a biblical quotation, "God said to Moses: I AM WHO AM. He said: Thus shalt thou say to the children of Israel: HE WHO IS, hath sent me to you" (Ex 3:14). But if God has revealed Himself as He who is (*qui est*), then surely God is essence: "For just as *sapientia*, or 'wisdom,' is said from that which *sapere* ['to be prudent or wise'] consists in," Peter writes, quoting Augustine, "and just as *scientia*, 'knowledge,' is said from that which *scire* ['to know'] consists in, so *essentia*, 'essence,' is said from that which *esse* ['to be'] consists in."[19] Indeed, the Lombard explicitly maintains that, in God, essence and being are the same thing: "God alone is properly said to be essence [*essentia*] or being [*esse*]. That is why Hilary says, in book VII of his *De Trinitate*: 'Being [*esse*] does not belong to God accidentally, but is subsistent truth.' "[20] This statement sounds proto-Thomistic, as a perceptive commentator has noted.[21] The distance between Peter Lombard and Aquinas, however, is considerable, despite the striking similarity at the surface of their doctrines. Peter arrives at his identification of being and essence in God through the reconciliation of authorities, as well as through etymological analysis: *essentia* derives from *esse*, hence ultimately denoting nothing but that which "to be" consists in. Aquinas, on the other hand, presents extended metaphysical analyses to underpin his identification of essence and existence in God. This remark is not meant to detract in any way from the Lombard's intellectual achievement; it is simply not the same kind of achievement as Aquinas's.

A number of consequences follow from the statement according to which God is fundamentally "to be." First and most importantly, God, as pure *esse*-nce, is not subject to time. There are two seemingly contrary ways of putting this insight. Either one can say that God "was" not and "will" not be, but simply "is." For what "was," no longer is, whereas what "will be," is not yet. But this insight can also be framed positively, an approach that Peter much prefers: God, we thus say, always was, is, and will be.

Secondly, not subject to time, God is immutable. By the same token, He, and He alone, possesses true immortality. Even the immortal souls of angels are vulnerable to death, namely, spiritual death in sin.

Furthermore, in contradistinction to the ontological composition that is characteristic of creatures, God is simple. The composite nature of creatures is obvious in the case of physical entities, yet even souls are far from a state of total unity: "for it is one thing to be skillful, another to be without skill, another to be sharp; memory is one thing, cupidity another, yet another is fear and another joy, and sadness another"—all attributes a soul may possess or emotions it may undergo at different points of its existence.[22] The simplicity of God's essence does not, of course, imply any kind of ontological dearth. Rather, it means that attributes which, in the creaturely realm, are distinct from the substance in which they inhere, coincide with God's essence. Thus, God is substantial wisdom, strength, and so forth because "the simplicity and purity of His essence is such that there is nothing in it that is not *it*, but rather possessing [an attribute] and being possessed are the same." The rubric is even more lapidary: "**That there is nothing in God that is not God.**"[23] In virtue of God's perfect simplicity, it is preferable, Peter argues, to speak of His essence rather than His substance. A substance subsists for something that is in a subject, namely, accidents. God, however, has no accidents.

Later, in distinctions 35 through 37, Peter Lombard will approach the question of divine foreknowledge and predestination, as well as the problem of immanence and transcendence, on the basis of the same metaphysical principles. It is appropriate to summarize the main points of that discussion here.[24]

Although God's wisdom, foreknowledge, (pre-)arrangement, predestination, and providence are commonly distinguished—Peter Lombard begins—this distinction is valid only from a creaturely point of view, namely, insofar as God's complete unity fans out, as it were, into a multiplicity of different effects:

> One should know that, although the knowledge or wisdom of God is one and simple, it is nonetheless assigned several and diverse names, on account of the various states of things and the diverse effects. For it is not only called knowledge, but also foreknowledge or foresight, arrangement [*dispositio*], predestination, and providence.—Now foreknowledge or foresight is of future things only, although of all, good and bad; arrangement, however, concerns things to be done [*faciendis*]; predestination is about the salvation of men, as well as the goods through which they are freed here [on earth] and with which they will be crowned in the future.[25]

Since God is pure *esse*-nce, and hence simple, His knowledge of all things past, present, and future is *one* knowledge. Moreover, whereas creatures have to move outside of themselves, as it were, in order to know what is other than themselves, God knows all in Himself. Past, present, and future all merge in the eternal present of His inner life.[26] Is God's knowledge of creation identical with His knowledge of Himself, then? Peter Lombard gestures, one could say, at this theory, but he does not spell it out: "God does not know those temporal things in such a manner as to be ignorant of Himself; rather, He alone knows Himself perfectly. By comparison with His knowledge, all knowledge of the creature is imperfect."[27]

Distinction 36 now takes up several questions that arise from the theory just developed. First, if everything created is present in God's knowledge, and if God's knowledge is identical with His essence (in virtue of His simplicity), then is all of creation not contained in God's essence? No, is Peter's answer. His argument, however, is not very strong. He quotes a passage from Augustine in which the bishop of Hippo argues for the presence of the elect in God's knowledge, but not in His nature. Peter explains the passage, with the caveat that it could be interpreted differently. There is much room for development here by future commentators, to whom the Lombard bequeaths an important theological question *sans* answer.

The second major problem that distinction 36 addresses concerns God's knowledge of evil. If God knows all, He must know evil as well; it must even be *in* Him in some sense. Indeed, in Scripture we read that "from him, and by him, and in him, are all things" (Rom 11:36).[28] Also, clearly God must be aware of our sins. On the other hand, evil is neither "from" God (*ex ipso*), nor "by" God (*per ipsum*), so perhaps it is also not "in" God (*in ipsum*). Peter does not find this reflection quite satisfactory yet, adding a further distinction. Surely there must be a difference between God's knowledge of good and His knowledge of evil. The difference, Peter decides, consists in the fact that God views good things with approval and pleasure, but the latter are obviously absent in the case of His knowledge of evil. But His approval and pleasure are necessary for us to say that anything is in God: "It is on account of such knowledge that anything is said to be in God; namely, that He knows it in such a way that He also approves of it and that it pleases Him, that is, that He knows it insofar as He is its Author."[29] Distinction 36 ends with an extended analysis of the scriptural phrase "from him, and by him, and in him are all things." The upshot is important: not everything that is from God (*ex ipso*) is also of God (*de ipso*). Otherwise, all of creation would be *of* God's substance. That would be pantheism. Again, Peter Lombard's insight is crucial, but his arguments leave much room for further development.

Let us take a glance at distinction 37, before we return to the earlier parts of book 1. If all things are in God—not substantially, and evil excepted—then is God also in all things? We are dealing with the fascinating question of divine immanence and transcendence. Peter distinguishes three cases, which he describes in the following text:

> **That God is in all things by essence, power, and presence, and in the saints through grace, and in the man Christ through union*.** One should know that God, always existing immutably in Himself, is presentially, potentially, and essentially [*praesentialiter, potentialiter, essentialiter*] in every nature or essence, [but] without definition of Him; in every place without circumscription; and in every time without mutability. Moreover, He is in the saintly spirits and souls in a more excellent manner, namely, inhabiting them through grace. And He is in the most excellent fashion in the man Christ, in whom "dwelleth

all the fullness of the Godhead corporeally" [Col 2:9], as the Apostle
says. For in him, God dwelled not through the grace of adoption, but
through the grace of union.[30]

This eloquent and beautiful passage, resonant with the paradoxes of negative theology, leaves not the slightest doubt about the fact that God is
intimately present to all of creation. He is present to the very essence of
all things through His power—this is how one might tentatively interpret
praesentialiter, potentialiter, essentialiter. Peter himself, alas, has frustratingly little to offer to elucidate this phrase, which he adapted from Gregory the Great's commentary on the Song of Songs. Instead, he declares
that "the sublimity and immensity of this consideration" totally surpasses
the capacities of human reason.[31] It is true, even with the benefit of
knowing the tradition subsequent to the Lombard, that the paradox of
God's transcendent immanence remains one the most difficult questions
of philosophical theology.

Even more intimately than to all of creation, God is present in the
lives and souls of the saints, whom He inhabits through grace. And
finally, God is not only present in Christ or inhabits His soul, but is
united to His human nature.[32]

Interestingly, when an opportunity arises to clarify what might be
meant, more exactly, by God's essential presence to creation, Peter regards
the explanation with great suspicion. Without rejecting it out of hand,
he insists that those who attempt to reduce the mystery of God to the
capacities of human reason—it is Abelard and his circle whom Peter
must have in mind—are gravely mistaken. The passage in question is
worth quoting, since it sheds further light upon the Lombard's reluctance
to open wide the door to philosophical reasoning in theology; he wants
the door to be no more than slightly ajar:

> **The opinion of some people who presume to demonstrate how God
> is everywhere through essence, power, and presence.** Some people,
> however, presuming to measure the immeasurable by their own ca-
> pacity, have taught that this will have to be understood in the following
> way: God is said to be everywhere through His essence, not because
> the essence of God is properly in every place and in every creature,
> but because every nature and everything that is naturally, in whatever
> place it may be, has its being through Him [*per eum habet esse*]—as
> does every place in which it is.... But although these [statements],
> which they assert in order to explain the meaning of the aforesaid, are

true, nonetheless one has to believe that in those words, by which it is said that God is everywhere through His essence, more is contained than a living human being is able to grasp.[33]

The same people whom Peter thus rebukes also raise subtle objections concerning God's omnipresence, for example, the question of whether God is not defiled by the filth of creation. "This is so frivolous," Peter exclaims, "as to be unworthy of an answer."[34] The point of the *Book of Sentences* is not to satisfy every human curiosity, but to clarify a solid and profound faith, to which questions about the defilement of God appear impious, and blasphemous even. Yet Master Peter had students who may not have been content with such an old-fashioned attitude. Therefore, he offers an analogy to explain why God's intimate presence to creation in no wise implies that He comes into contact with its filth: are the rays of the sun, which fill the entire earth, befouled by the dirt upon which they shine?

The Trinity: Father and Son

Peter Lombard's discussion of the generation of the Son is governed by the same principles that we have already discovered to be seminal in his analysis of the divine essence: God is pure *esse*-nce, pure being, which implies that He is exempt from the flux of time and is ontologically simple. In distinction 6, Peter's insight into God's transcendence of time helps him resolve the problem of whether the Father has begotten the Son voluntarily or necessarily, indeed, whether there is anything such as "willing" and "not willing" in God. The idea according to which the generation of the Son occurs of necessity is dismissed first, with the simple statement that "there is no necessity in God."[35] This assertion finds no further justification; perhaps the Lombard regarded it as obvious because there is no entity existing above God that could constrain Him in any way. Such a course of reasoning would, of course, still leave open the question as to whether God's internal constitution might be such that certain actions necessarily flow from it.

Peter's treatment of the role of the will in the generation of the Son is less sketchy. The key here is his realization that "for God, to know or to will is nothing else than to be [*nec est aliud Deo scire vel velle quam esse*]."³⁶ There is, then, no will in God that could precede or be a mere accident of His wisdom, or indeed of any of His other attributes. God the Father "begot the Son without willing before begetting."³⁷ Since the notion of willing seems to be indissolubly tied up with the idea of temporal precedence—how could I say that I "willed" to do X unless there was a will preceding my doing of X?—it is legitimate to assert that the generation of the Son occurred entirely outside the domain of willing or nonwilling. As in other contexts, however, Peter prefers a more positive, less "apophatic," way of couching his teaching: "For if the Father is said to have begotten the Son [being] wise and good, why not also willing?"³⁸ What is crucial is to understand that for God, willing is not different from being.

Sometimes in the *Book of Sentences*, Peter Lombard indicates that he is taking up a question reluctantly, not because of its inherent value but only in order not to pass over a point featuring prominently in contemporary debates. The following issue, raised in connection with the role of the divine will in the generation of the Son, is of this nature:

> **Here it is asked whether the Father had the power, or willed, to beget the Son.** At this point, some people are wont to ask whether the Father had the power, or willed, to beget the Son. For if, they say, He had the power and willed to beget the Son, then He was able to do and did will something that the Son was not able to do and did not will, since the Son neither was able nor willed to beget the Son.³⁹

The theological problem here is the conclusion that the Father possesses a capacity and will that the Son does not possess, which contradicts the fact that they are one God, sharing one essence. Peter is quite dismissive of this problem, ironically referring to its *versutia*, or "cleverness."⁴⁰ According to him, it is born of a fundamental disregard of the difference between divine and merely human power and willing. Again, the Father "did not will or have power before He begot; just as He *was* not before He begot, since He has been from eternity and has begotten from eternity."⁴¹ To say, "begetting the Son is something that is subject to the Father's power and will, but not the Son's," is misleading, since the Father's power and willing *are* His begetting of the Son. Moreover, according to Augustine, begetting is nothing that lies outside the powers of the Son; it is just something that did not behoove Him (*not oportuit*). What exactly does this mean? "It is not clear to us how to explain in what way this [statement] is true," Master Peter admits, "and hence it would be better to pass it over in silence, if the insistence of questioners did not compel me to say something about this."[42] The Son, he continues, is not at all incapable of begetting; it was simply not appropriate for Him to do so. In the following chapter, he elaborates further: since the Father and the Son share the same nature, they share the same power as well. It is in virtue of the same essential power, then, that the Father has the power to be Father, and the Son has the power to be Son.

Let us stop for a moment to reflect upon Peter Lombard's ambiguous attitude toward the theological debates of his time, or at least toward certain aspects of these debates. He seems to be genuinely appalled by the direction the study of theology is taking in certain quarters: cleverness, conceit, and curiosity are taking the place of humility in the face of the mystery of God. But Master Peter is teaching at Notre Dame in Paris, a city quickly developing into the center of the Scholastic movement. His students are not willing to accept declarations of humility in lieu of well-reasoned doctrine, and so Peter accedes to their demands. What a paradox! The book that was to become the cornerstone of Scholastic theology has an author who was not a little suspicious of professional, rational, philosophical theology and who shows signs of having despised the new type of Christian intellectual that produced it.

Now let us examine the role of time in the generation of the Son. The three persons of the Trinity are said to be coeternal, but then, how are we to understand the relationship between the Father and the Son? For a father has to be prior to his son. Peter's answer is prefaced, as we are now accustomed to expect, by two paragraphs of reflection upon the ineffability of the generation of the Son. He then offers a formula that captures the central characteristic of the father-son relationship—that of begetting and being begotten—while also doing justice to the fact that God transcends time: the Son "is always begotten" (*semper gignitur*) or "has always been begotten" (*semper genitus est*). Which of these two phrases is more adequate is a discussion that occupies the Lombard for several pages, because Gregory the Great prefers *semper genitus* or *natus est* (which emphasizes the "perfect" state of the Son), whereas Origen defends the formula *semper gignitur* or *nascitur* (which emphasizes the eternal splendor of the Wisdom of God). Peter has a slight preference for *semper natus*, "has always been born," which—when correctly understood—combines reference to the perfect state of the Son's generation, in which there is nothing missing or outstanding, with an indication of the fact that the birth of the Son from the Father has no beginning or end in time.

The Holy Spirit

Peter Lombard's presentation of his pneumatology is logical and well structured. Its starting point is the time-honored Christian belief according to which the Holy Spirit is the bond of love between the Father and the Son: "The Holy Spirit is the love, charity, or affection [*amor sive caritas sive dilectio*] of the Father and the Son. Hence Augustine says in book XV of the *De Trinitate*: 'The Holy Spirit is not of the Father alone, nor of the Son alone, but belongs to both. On that account, it indicates to us the common charity through which the Father and the Son mutually love [*diligunt*] each other.' "

Peter seems to regard *amor*, *caritas*, and *dilectio* as synonymous, using them interchangeably throughout his discussion of the Holy Spirit. Both *caritas* and *dilectio*, but not *amor*, served as Latin translations of the Greek term ἀγάπη as it appears, for example, in 1 John 4:8 and 16 ("God is charity"), the scriptural text Peter cites immediately after the passage just quoted. Peter knew both the Vulgate's translation, *Deus est caritas*, and— through Augustine—the Vetus Itala's *Deus est dilectio*. The fact that, unlike *caritas* and *dilectio*, *amor* could have some "low," sensual connotations does not seem to bother him. Further describing the Holy Spirit, Peter speaks of it as the unity of peace kept between the Father and the Son (see Eph 4:3), their ineffable community.[44] In virtue of this community, "love" and "charity" are particularly apt as designations of the Holy Spirit, although, of course, God as a whole is substantial charity. Indeed, the Trinity can be described as a community of love: "one [person] loving him who is from the first, and one loving him from whom he is, and love itself."[45] Following Augustine, the Lombard is not enthusiastic about the term "friendship" in the context of Trinitarian theology.

The Christian Churches of the West and East are divided by the vexed question of the *Filioque*: does the Holy Spirit proceed from the Father and the Son, as the Latin Church professes, or from the Father alone, as the Greeks hold? Peter relates, and then refutes, several arguments adduced in favor of the Eastern position. He does not believe, however,

that the difference between the Western and Eastern terminologies be-
speaks an insuperable theological disagreement: "**That the Greeks agree
with us on the level of meaning, even if they are different in the words
[they use]**" is the rubric with which he opens chapter 2 of distinction
11. Numerous Eastern Church Fathers, he claims, have clearly expressed
their belief in the procession of the Spirit from the Father and the Son,
among them Athanasius, Didymus, Cyril, and John Chrysostom.

It is important to uphold the distinction between the processions of
the Son and of the Holy Spirit, that is, the fact that the Son is born from
the Father, whereas the Holy Spirit is given or, better, a gift. If we started
confusing the attributes of the three persons, the Spirit would be said to
be "born," just like the Son—and that would make him a son as well,
namely, of the Father and the Son. That would be most absurd, Peter
maintains. Yet for us in this life, it is not possible to understand what,
fundamentally, the distinction between the generation of the Son and the
procession of the Spirit expresses, beyond the mere verbal difference.
Once again, the author of the *Book of Sentences* avows his ignorance.[46]

Despite the irreducible difference between the birth of the Son and
the donation of the Spirit, the processions of the two persons exhibit
important parallels. The Spirit's procession is twofold, eternal and temporal: eternal insofar as the Spirit proceeds from the Father and the Son
as the bond of their mutual love, and temporal insofar as the Spirit is
sent by the Father and the Son into this world.[47] Peter Lombard proposes
to reserve the term "gift" (*donum*) for the Holy Ghost qua proceeding
eternally, while it should be described as "given" or "gifted" (*datum vel
donatum*) in relation to its temporal mission.[48] It makes sense, in fact, to
speak of the eternal gift of the Holy Spirit as being given to man. The
temporal donation of the Spirit occurs in two forms: visibly and invisibly.
The Spirit's visible mission is testified to in Matthew 3:16, where the
Spirit of God is said to have descended upon Jesus as a dove. The events
of Pentecost as related in Acts 2:2–4 provide another example of the
Spirit's visible mission. The invisible mission, by contrast, means the in-
fusion of the Spirit into the hearts of humans.[49] We will turn to the
Lombard's interesting thoughts on this matter in a moment, after a brief
consideration of the parallel procession of the Son:

> **That the Son is said to be sent in two ways.** To which [namely, the pre-
> ceding question] we say that the Son is said to be sent in two ways, in

addition to that eternal generation [*genitura*] which is ineffable, [and] according to which He can also be said to be sent, as it seems to some people; though according to this [generation] He is better and more truly said to be born. In addition to the latter, then, He is said to be sent in two ways, namely, either when He appeared visibly in the world, having assumed flesh, or when He "conveyeth" Himself "into holy souls" [Wis 7:27] in such a way as to be perceived and known by them.[50]

Now to the temporal, invisible donation of the Holy Spirit. Peter Lombard's teaching on this point was already controversial in his own day and was subsequently to become the object of considerable debate among the commentators on the *Book of Sentences*. The Catholic tradition ultimately rejected it, although it was never formally condemned. According to Peter Lombard, the human love of God and neighbor is nothing but the unmediated presence of the Holy Spirit in the soul. Let us read the opening paragraphs of the famous distinction 17:

> **On the mission of the Holy Spirit by which it is sent invisibly.** We now come to determine the mission of the Holy Spirit by which it is invisibly sent into the hearts of the faithful. For, the Holy Spirit itself, who is God and the third person in the Trinity—as has been shown above—proceeds temporally from the Father and the Son, as well as from itself, that is, it is sent or given to the faithful. But what this mission or donation is, or how it occurs, is to be considered.
>
> **Something is said first which is necessary for this exposition, namely, that the Holy Spirit is the charity by which we love God and neighbor.** In order for this [point] to be able to be taught more intelligibly and to be perceived more fully, something needs to be said first which is very necessary for this [discussion]. It has already been said above and demonstrated through sacred authorities that the Holy Spirit is the love [*amor*] of the Father and the Son with which they love [*amant*] each other, as well as us. To these [words] it should be added that this same Holy Spirit is the love or charity [*amor sive caritas*] with which we love [*diligimus*] God and neighbor. When this charity is in us in such a manner that it makes us love God and neighbor, then the Holy Spirit is said to be sent or given to us; and he who loves that very love with which he loves his neighbor, loves God in that [neighbor], since God is love itself, that is [to say], the Holy Spirit.[51]

First, let us note that this passage, and the many pages that follow it, are unambiguous in the doctrine they present. "In speaking of the Holy

Spirit as the love bonding believers to each other, and to God," Peter Lombard does not mean, as Marcia Colish would have it, "strictly, the effects of the Holy Spirit, which assist man in developing the virtue of charity and other virtues."[52] On the contrary, the Lombard explicitly writes:

> Charity—that is, the Holy Spirit—brings about the other acts and motions of the virtues by the mediation of those virtues whose acts they are; such as the act of faith, which is to believe, by mediating faith, and the act of hope, which is to hope, by mediating hope: for it [charity] brings about the aforesaid acts through faith and hope. The act of loving, however, which is to love, it [charity] brings about through itself alone, without the medium of any virtue [*diligendi vero actum per se tantum, sine alicuius virtutis medio operatur, id est diligere*].[53]

In other words, the Holy Spirit does not create the virtue of charity in the soul, so that we may love God and neighbor through that virtue; indeed, there is no such thing as the "virtue" of charity.[54] There is only the Holy Spirit, who is the charity that makes us love. One commentator, Johann Schupp, has gone so far as to claim that, for Peter Lombard, it is not we who love, but God Himself who loves in us.[55] The entire subsequent tradition has not misunderstood Peter Lombard—which is Colish's unlikely claim.

The Lombard was well aware of the kind of counterarguments that his teaching on charity was likely to provoke; indeed, a lively controversy about it seems to have started during his own lifetime. A century later, Thomas Aquinas would still echo some of the principal counterarguments in his commentary on the *Sentences*. Aquinas explicitly repudiates the Lombardian conception of charity: "The Master wants charity not to be some habit created in the soul," he writes with some indignation, "but simply an act that arises from free will moved by the Holy Spirit, whom he calls charity." *Sed hoc non potest stare*, he protests, "but this cannot stand."[56] God united Himself with human nature only once, in Christ. It is not acceptable, therefore, to maintain that the will of those who have received the gift of the Spirit is united with the Spirit. The saints act charitably not because their will is conjoined with the Spirit, but because God has infused them with a form, a habit, that functions as the proximate cause of their charitable acts. This habit is precisely what the virtue of charity consists in. We have seen in the second excerpt quoted above that Peter Lombard anticipated the "mediating virtue" argument, which forms the backbone of Aquinas's critique. Why, then, did he hold fast to his conviction that charity, fraternal love, *is* the Holy Ghost?

It is important to realize that the Lombard's teaching on charity could claim a long tradition for itself. This tradition took its main inspiration from two scriptural passages, 1 John 4:7–8 ("God is charity") and Romans 5:5 ("And hope confoundeth not: because the charity of God is poured forth in our hearts, by the Holy Ghost, who is given to us"). Augustine suggested the identification of the charity in our soul with the Holy Spirit in book 15 of *De Trinitate*, and this idea was repeated more or less · unchanged by Carolingian authors such as Alcuin, Paschasius Radbertus, Rabanus Maurus, and Sedulius Scottus. In the twelfth century, William of St. Thierry—St. Bernard's close friend—subscribed to it, whereas dialecticians such as Abelard and Gilbert de la Porrée insisted on the clearer distinction between the divine and human spheres that the *habitus* theory implies.[57] In its own time, then, Peter Lombard's theory was the more traditional one. That may have been one reason why Peter preferred it over the Abelardian-Gilbertian account, with its emphasis upon the autonomy of the created soul in its own, finite sphere of action.

It is undeniable that the Lombard's position, according to which it is God Himself, the Holy Spirit, who acts in "our" love of God and neighbor, raises philosophical questions. The quotation marks around the word "our" indicate what these are: if God acts immediately in us when we love, in what sense do charitable acts belong to us? Is the autonomy of human nature and action not violated? There is little doubt that Thomas Aquinas's critique of Peter Lombard makes sense once we accept the presupposition that the spheres of divine and human action need to be clearly separated, because the created world possesses an autonomy of action that flows from its own natural forms. Spiritually, however, the idea that the love of God and neighbor is the very presence of the Holy Spirit in our midst is of a powerful beauty. Being aware of possible criticisms, Peter Lombard opted for the less "scientific," more spiritual account of charity. It is interesting to note, too, that Protestant theology received the Lombard's teaching on charity much more positively than Peter Lombard's immediate medieval successors. In his *Handbook of the History of Dogma*, Adolf von Harnack described the identification of charity with the Holy Spirit as "remarkable," seeing in it "the seeds of a more evangelical attitude" because of its refusal to reduce grace to divine assistance for human merit.[58] Harnack reports that the Lombard's position found approval in the writings of Johannes Pupper von Goch (c. 1400–1475), whose works foreshadowed important themes of the Reformers; Johann von Staupitz (c. 1468–1524), Luther's predecessor as professor of theology at Wittenberg, defended it as well. And even Luther himself regarded the Lombard's position not without sympathy.[59]

The Divine Names

Considering the human language about God, its kinds and limits, is an important part of the theological enterprise, which attempts to articulate the faith in a precise and coherent manner. Of course, "speaking about the ineffable Unity and Trinity"[60] involves a fundamental paradox. Nevertheless, even in acknowledging our ultimate inability to capture the divine mysteries in adequate terms, we need at least to avoid the crassest confusions. Thus, Peter Lombard distinguishes six different kinds of names that we employ in speaking about God:[61]

1. A first group of divine names refers to the divine essence. Examples of this category would be "wisdom," "power," "greatness," "truth," and suchlike. "Person," as well, is an essential name of the Godhead, although it functions somewhat differently than the other designations in this first group. In fact, whereas the other substantial names apply both to the essence and to the individual persons in the singular, "person" cannot be predicated of the divine essence except in the plural: the Father is a person, the Son is a person, the Holy Spirit is a person, and the three together, constituting the divine essence, are three persons. The essence, however, is not "a person."[62] The *Book of Sentences* does not attribute much importance to the terminological difference between the Latin and Greek traditions of referring to the Father, Son, and Holy Spirit. While the West prefers the term "persons," the East speaks of three "substances" or "hypostases." Are not both the Latin and the Greek languages wanting in the face of their ineffable subject matter?[63]

   The numbers one, two, and three are predicated of the divine essence as well: God is "one," but also "three persons"; the Father and the Son are "two persons"; and so forth. Yet the meaning of these numbers is entirely negative, Peter rules, in that they ex-

clude numerical or quantitative multiplicity (namely, in the case
of "one") while also negating the idea that God might be solitary
and single (in the case of "two" and "three"). In short, applied to
God, the numbers lose their quantitative sense.[64]

2. A second category of divine names is used with reference to the
individual persons. The theologian knows these names as "properties," "notions," or "relations."[65] Most fundamentally, the Father
is characterized by the property of "begetting" (*genuit*), the Son is
"born" (*natus est*), and the Holy Ghost "proceeds" (*procedit*).[66]
These properties are predicated relatively to each other, because to
beget means to beget someone who will be born; analogously, to
be born means to have been begotten; and to proceed implies proceeding from somewhere, namely, from the begetter and the one
born. Moreover, the properties are not accidental, without however being attributable to the divine substance. For, although the
divine substance is not born and does not proceed, birth and procession are not accidental to God, since the eternal and immutable
relationships among the individual persons constitute them as persons. Indeed, the persons are nothing but these properties. The
Father does not have a substance different from the Son's that
happens to have begotten the latter, for there is only one divine
essence. Rather, the Father *is* the begetting of the Son, and the
Son *is* the having-been-begotten by the Father.[67] This Trinitarian
dogma possesses enormous metaphysical potential, which the *Book
of Sentences* leaves unexplored. The identity of property and person means that the tension between substance and relation, or inside and outside, is a merely creaturely attribute, not affecting the
Godhead at all. In the human realm, a person is who he or she is
over against other creatures, relating to them in an accidental
manner. No human being could ever be totally "outside" of him-
or herself, reconciling the embrace of the other with complete inner rest. Put more simply, we experience ourselves as torn between our own interests and the demands of the world around
us. This is precisely what must be totally different in the three
persons of the Godhead. The Father does not hold back anything
from His relationship with the Son, because He *is* that relationship—without being in danger of losing His own identity.

The difficult question arises of how the properties, which are
so fundamental to the distinction of the persons, can leave unaf-
fected the divine essence in which they inhere. The Father begets
the Son, indeed *is* His begetting of the Son; the Father and the

Son are of the same essence; yet the essence neither begets nor is begotten. How is that to be explained? At this point, Peter once again retreats to a profession of ignorance: "In no wise is it allowed to us to 'search the majesty' [Prv 25:27], to impose a law upon the power, to set bounds to the infinite."[68]

3. Certain names are predicated of God in relation to creation, and even to time, such as "Creator," "Lord," and "Refuge." Similarly, the Holy Spirit is said to have been "gifted" (*donatum*) to humans. Peter notes that, although these designations are relative in their meaning—Creator, for example, is said relative to "creature"—they must not be taken to indicate any relation in God, only in creation. He examines the case of time. God is the Lord of all things that have come to be in time, but He is not, on that account, subject, or in any way relative, to time: for He is the Lord of time.[69]

There are three further classes to be distinguished among the names of God. Peter only mentions them in passing, without offering any detailed examination:

4. "Trinity" is not predicated of the three persons severally, but only collectively. It is not a substantial name of God.[70]

5. Some names applying to God carry a temporal sense, although they are not predicated of Him relatively, as are the names in category 3. Examples are "incarnate" (*incarnatus*) and "having become human" (*humanatus*).[71] What Peter seems to have in mind here is the fact that the relationship between Creator and creation is of a different nature than the relationship between the second person of the Trinity and Christ. Christ, who was sent to creation, nonetheless remained fully God in His incarnation. Christ is not "other" than God in the sense in which creation is other than the Creator.

6. Finally, names such as "splendor" or "mirror" are predicated of God in a merely metaphorical sense. Their epistemological value in helping us come to a better understanding of God is therefore minimal.[72]

THE *SENTENCES*, BOOK II

On the Creation of Things, and the
Formation of Spiritual and Corporeal
Entities, and Many Other Matters
Pertaining to These

We are moving from an examination of the divine nature itself, and of the inner-Trinitarian mysteries, to a consideration of God's effects in creation. In book 2 of the *Sentences*, we are therefore treading on less sacred ground than that covered in book 1; there is more room here for human insight, and our language can become somewhat less hesitant, less stammering. The words "ineffable" (*ineffabilis*), "ineffably" (*ineffabiliter*), and "ineffability" (*ineffabilitas*) occur forty-five times in the *Book of Sentences*. But thirty-one of these occurrences are in the text of book 1, whose subject matter—we may safely conclude—Peter Lombard found far more "ineffable" than that of the remaining three books.[1] At the beginning of book 2, he writes: "We have diligently gone through what is considered to pertain to the knowledge—albeit 'in part' [1 Cor 13:9]—of the mystery of the divine unity and Trinity, to the extent to which we were able [to do so]. Now let us move on to the consideration of creatures."[2]

The structure of book 2 is straightforward. Distinction 1 opens the book with reflections on the concept of creation and its reasons. Distinctions 2 through 11 are devoted to the first element of creation: the angels. Then, distinctions 12 to 15 offer a hexaemeron, that is to say, Peter Lombard's thoughts on the six days of creation as recounted in Genesis. Distinctions 16 to 18 focus more specifically on the creation of mankind, distinction 18 being devoted exclusively to the creation of woman. Next, the condition of the human being before the Fall is addressed in distinctions 19 and 20. The Fall forms the subject matter of distinctions 21 through 29, and this section is logically followed by an extended treatment of original sin (dist. 30–33). Finally, Peter discusses actual sin—sin resulting from an individual act of free will—in distinctions 34 through 44.

The Concept of Creation
and Its Reasons

In the first chapters of distinction 1, Peter Lombard demarcates the Christian concept of creation from Platonic and Aristotelian notions. Against Plato—and the school of Chartres, which attempted to appropriate the *Timaeus* for a Christian account of creation—Peter emphasizes that the principle of creation is one, as well as explaining the difference between creating and making:

> **On what grounds "creator" is properly said, and what creating and making are.** The creator, in fact, is someone who makes something from nothing [*qui de nihilo aliqua facit*], and creating, properly [speaking], is to make something from nothing. Making [*facere*], by contrast, [is] not at all to bring about something from nothing, but rather from matter. This is why man or angel is said to make something, but not to create, and is called "maker" or "artificer," but not "creator."[3]

Thus, the Christian God is a Creator-God, and not a kind of Platonic demiurge, who fashions things out of preexisting matter and form: "Plato supposed that there were three initial elements, namely, God, an exemplar, and matter; and [, moreover,] that the latter were uncreated, without beginning, and that God was a kind of artificer, not the creator."[4] The Aristotelian theory according to which "the world always is and has been" is contrasted with the Christian belief, that "God created the world at the beginning of time."[5] Peter does not know, or seem to care a great deal about, the philosophies underlying Plato's and Aristotle's positions, philosophies that could not conceive of creation *ex nihilo* because of the ancient Greek view of time as circular and eternal. Thomas Aquinas and his contemporaries would later, after the rediscovery of Aristotle's *Physics* and *Metaphysics*, have to wrestle more seriously with the problem of the eternity of the world. What counts for Peter Lombard is simply the prima facie incompatibility of Platonic and Aristotelian notions with the Christian idea of God as Creator.

God created not at all out of necessity, but rather to communicate His own goodness, so that others could share in it. That also explains why God made rational creatures, that is, angels and human beings; for participation in Him requires an intellectual nature that is capable of understanding and love. The purpose, then, of intellectual creatures is "to praise God, serve Him, and enjoy Him."[6] Here, "serving" must not be construed as an activity for God's benefit, but rather for our own. God needs nothing, so that serving Him profits us, not God.

If human beings were made to serve and enjoy God, the world in turn was made to serve humanity. The human being thus occupies a position in between God and nonrational nature: *positus est ergo homo in medio*, as Peter puts it.[7] The angels, he adds, who are superior to us in this life, will be our equals in the life to come; indeed, one could say that the angels were made for our use, for it is "for our sake" that they are "sent into their ministry."[8] For Peter Lombard, human existence has its center in God, but the world centers on man. The tripartite structure of the created world as a whole, which is composed of pure spirits, incarnate spirits, and irrational nature, mirrors the Trinity of Him who brought it into being.[9]

But was it necessary to unite the human being so closely with the corporeal world, to bring it right into him? Peter offers three possible answers to this question as to why the human soul was united with a material body. First, he declares, "God wanted it, and His will is a cause not to be questioned."[10] He does not stop there, however, immediately adding a second explanation. He views the union of body and soul as a faint image and prefiguration of the "blessed union that exists between God and the spirit, [and] in which He is loved 'with [our] whole heart' [Mt 22:37] and seen 'face to face' [1 Cor 13:12]."[11] In other words, the union of the human soul with the flesh—a union so close that the spirit clings to it with all its force—prefigures what the union between created and uncreated spirit will be like. Thirdly and finally, Peter speculates that the human soul was united to the body to increase its rewards in the hereafter.

Angelology

Angelology is the wallflower of contemporary theology, a seemingly mythical residue in our enlightened discourse about God. In the early 1970s, Rob van der Hart wrote, " 'Angelology'—the theology of spirits— is a subject untouched and almost forgotten."[12] Father van der Hart went on to report a controversy triggered by the then famous—or infamous, depending on one's perspective—Dutch Catechism, which referred to angels only in the vaguest and most noncommittal of terms, causing the displeasure of some Dutch Catholics and, of course, of Rome. In the follow-up debate between Dutch and Roman delegations of theologians, the Dutch explained biblical references to angels as part of the social and historical framework of Revelation; if God wanted to speak to His people, and be heard by them, He had to employ a language they understood. Angels, the Dutch argued, are part of the cultural language used to convey God's message, rather than an integral part of that message itself.

It is not up to us, in this book, to pronounce ourselves on the theological status of angels. Yet we must measure the distance between our own time and Peter Lombard's twelfth century, attempting to understand why angels used to be more for theologians than an embarrassing curiosity. The Lombard devotes ten distinctions, or fifty-seven chapters, to angelology—about one fifth of book 2 of the *Sentences*. It forms an important part of his thought.

An ἄγγελος (*angelos*), in Greek, is a messenger. The angels of the Christian Scripture are messengers that mediate between the transcendence of God and the world here below, rendering present mediately the sacred within the secular and profane. Through these messengers, who sometimes appear as kings, sometimes as priests, as prophets, or indeed as natural forces such as fire and wind,[13] the Lord reaches into this world in order to make His voice heard. Since ancient Greek times, however, the gods have increasingly withdrawn from the world of Western man. The explanation of nature in terms of nature—in terms of elements, causes, laws, and finally quantifiable forces, and not in terms of supernature—has provided us with a powerful tool to master our natural environment. Consequently, nature is no longer permeated by a sense of the sacred, but has become a mere resource for economic and technological progress. And if we still believe in God, we make sure to separate

Him neatly from His creation, just as we distinguish rigorously between faith and reason. However, as Father van der Hart suggests:

> Perhaps we are mistaken, perhaps our world is full of angels without our knowing it, perhaps—to quote Hebrews 13:2—we are "entertaining angels unawares." It is indeed one of the common features of practically all the biblical angel stories that the people in them only later realize that they have been conversing with angels. First of all they think ordinary men have visited them. And then they are compelled, as it were, to admit that something more is involved; suddenly they realize that their own small world, their own sphere, has to be understood as resting within the wider sphere of the divine.[14]

Peter Lombard certainly understood his world in this premodern way. It was a world in which the germinal state of natural science left much unexplained and mysterious that we now understand without having to have recourse to the supernatural. Yet it was also a world that was more open to mystery, in recognition of its own inability to explain the All.[15]

At the beginning of distinction 2, the Lombard lays out the structure of his treatise on the angels in the following words:

> **What is to be considered on [the subject of] the angels.** On the angelic nature, these [points] are therefore to be considered first: when it was created, and where, and how it was made when it was first brought into existence; then, how it was affected by the turning away [from God] of certain [angels] and by the conversion [to God] of others; moreover, something has to be said about its excellence, its orders, and the difference of its gifts, and about its tasks and names, and many other things.[16]

Together with unformed matter, the angels represent the first stage of creation. They and the four elements were created at the same time. That is how Peter Lombard—following Augustine—interprets Genesis 1:1, "In the beginning God created heaven, and earth." "Heaven" stands for spiritual creatures, while "earth" signifies matter. The angels, therefore, did not exist before the beginning of time, but rather are contemporaneous with the inception of the world.

The angels were created in the empyrean, that is, the highest heaven, which is situated above the firmament (created on the second day) and not to be confounded with it. Again, the creation of the empyrean and of the angels was simultaneous: "at the moment that it was made, it was filled with the angels."[17] And just as matter was initially unformed (Peter uses the Greek word *chaos* to characterize it), so the angels, as well, lacked any form beyond the most fundamental aspects of their nature. What Peter means is that the angels were "formed," properly speaking, only by their love of, and turning toward, the Creator—or, indeed, by their turning away from Him. This movement of *conversio* or *aversio*, however, did not occur simultaneously with the creation of angelic nature. Peter speaks of "some short delay, albeit extremely brief"[18] between the coming into being of the angels and their decisions for or against God.

As for the natural properties that the angels possessed from the very beginning of time, the Lombard distinguishes four: a simple, indivisible, and immaterial essence; personhood; intelligence, memory, and will—all three in virtue of reason; and finally, free will. Although the angels are all pure spirits, and hence immortal, God endowed them with different degrees of dignity, degrees measured by the tenuity or subtlety of their essence, the perspicacity of their wisdom, and the power of their free will. How exactly these distinctions in dignity are to be understood, however, lies beyond the grasp of human reason: "Only He who made everything 'in measure, and number, and weight' [Wis 11:21] was able to comprehend and ponder these intelligible distinctions of the invisible natures."[19]

All the angels were created good. This goodness accrued to them in virtue of their nature, and not as a result of any moral perfection or merit. It would be perverse, Peter emphasizes, to assume that God created bad angels: "the most excellent Creator could not be the author of evil."[20] By the same token, the angels in the state of nature, during that extremely brief moment between their coming into existence and their conversion or aversion, were neither blessed nor wretched, but rather remained in a state of innocence.

We now come to the "formation" of the angels, that is to say, their transition from innocence to moral responsibility. Significantly, it is only in this transition that grace enters into the world. Peter Lombard explains:

On the conversion [to God] and confirmation of those remaining steadfast, and the turning away [from God] and fall of those falling. After this, our consideration prompts us to inquire in what manner they were affected when they were divided by aversion and conversion. For after creation, some soon turned toward their Creator, while others turned away. Turning toward God was to cling to Him in charity; turning away, [by contrast, meant] to have hatred and be envious: for the mother of envy is pride [*superbia*], by which they wanted to make themselves equal to God. In the converted, God's Wisdom, by which they were illuminated, began to shine as though in a mirror; but those who turned away were blinded. The former were converted and illuminated by God through the aid of grace [*gratia apposita*]; the latter, however, were blinded not because they were sent anything bad, but because grace forsook them—[and] they were forsaken by grace not in such a way that grace which had previously been given was taken away, but because it was never given to them so that they might be converted. This, then, is the conversion and aversion by which those who were good by nature, were divided, so that some might, through justice, be good over and above that goodness, and others might be bad through transgression while that [natural goodness] was destroyed. Conversion created just [angels], and aversion unjust ones. Both the one and the other belonged to the will, and the will in both cases was free.[21]

A theologically charged passage! We are at the intersection of some of the most fundamental concepts of the Christian faith, and perhaps of religion as such: nature and grace, transgression and punishment, good and evil. The Creator endowed all angels with a good nature, which included free will. Soon after their creation, the angels take a decision: some turn back to their Creator in a movement of love, with which they respond to the divine goodness (and to the intrinsic bent of their own nature created in goodness). Others, by contrast, turn away in mad hatred, envy, and pride, unable to reconcile themselves with their finitude— with the fact that they are not God. *Superbia*, pride, the desire to be "above" (*super*) that which one really is, lies at the root of all sin. The humble and loving angels are rewarded with a share in God's Wisdom, whereas the proud and hateful ones are struck with blindness, which we may interpret as a metaphor for their utterly distorted view of the order of creation. The good nature of the former is further perfected, whereas the latter forfeit even their innate goodness. Now, for God's reward and punishment to be just, the angels' decisions have to be attributable to their free will: if the conversion of the good angels were solely due to the gift of grace while the aversion of the bad angels was directly caused by a refusal of that grace, God would be rewarding and punishing creation for His own actions. On the other hand, would it not contradict the very finitude of creation, which the good angels recognize, if it were possible for a creature to bring about its own perfection—especially a perfection "over and above" (*supra*) natural goodness? Can God be made to raise nature beyond its created limits by meritorious acts of justice arising from within that nature?

Evidently, it is necessary to mediate between the conflicting claims of an autonomous nature and the gratuity of grace. Peter Lombard finds this mediation in the concept of *gratia cooperans*, "cooperating grace," that is, grace that assists and strengthens the free will in its conversion, without however bringing that conversion about by turning nature around as though against its will (which would be the effect of *gratia operans*, grace capable of justifying even the sinner).[22] The proud angels do not receive this cooperating grace because their natural goodness would have enabled them to remain in their innocent state, which they freely abandoned in their quest for autonomous (and hence unnatural) supernatural perfection. By contrast, the angels freely deciding to content themselves with their place in the order of creation are gratuitously lifted beyond it.

Angels from all levels of the angelic hierarchy have persisted in goodness, just as all kinds of different angels have fallen. In distinction 6, we learn that, as a consequence, the realm of fallen angels is hierarchically structured, with Lucifer at the very top. Lucifer is not only the most powerful of the demons; before his fall, he was the greatest of all the angels. Since Lucifer's rebellion, he has been banned from the empyrean and cast into the "dark air," together with the other evil spirits. Some demons, however, are in hell, where they torture the souls of the wicked.

Peter Lombard now proceeds to a consideration of the properties of the angels after their conversion (or, as the matter may be, aversion), before examining more closely the different orders of angels. Let us note some of his most important points. The Lombard teaches that the decision of the angels to turn toward, or away from, God is irreversible. That is not because their free will has been suppressed, but rather because the free will of the good angels is too firmly rooted in holiness to be perturbed, whereas the free will of the demons has become obdurate. Peter acknowledges the power of magic, emphasizing that all the power and knowledge of the devil derives from God, who uses him to bring the bad to fall as well as to admonish and test those who are just. No demon is capable of creating in the technical sense, though some have been known to make frogs and serpents! However, the biblical story of the magicians' inability to make *cinifes*—sciniphs, as the Douay-Rheims version calls these insects (see Ex 8:16–19)—proves again that the power of the demons depends upon God, and is limited by Him, as well as by the good angels. The Lombard is certain that the angels are capable of appearing in bodily form, but hesitates as to the precise nature of these apparitions: do they use extrinsic physical shapes (perhaps specially created by God) to clothe their own spiritual bodies, or are they capable of transforming their spiritual bodies at will when they appear in the world here below? He leaves the question open, just as he limits his remarks on what spiritual bodies might be to a brief report of Augustine. Speaking of himself in the third person, he writes: "Note, reader, that he does not solve the stated question."[23] He seems uncomfortable with such speculations and ends up not even deciding whether angels are corporeal (having rarefied spiritual bodies) or incorporeal.[24] One thing is beyond doubt, however: God Himself never appears to human beings in His own form.

In distinction 9, Peter comes to the discussion of the different orders of angels. There are nine orders, or three groups each comprising three kinds of angels—an arrangement mirroring the Trinity, as Peter remarks. Each of the orders is associated with a particular office, or gift, although the Lombard takes pains to emphasize that these gifts should not be understood as exclusive of each other. The seraphs are the most elevated of the pure spirits, burning more than any of the others with love for God. They are followed by the cherubs, whose particular gift is wisdom. The thrones are associated with God's judgments, including their communication to mankind. This brings us to the second triad in the celestial hierarchy, which is made up of the dominations, principalities, and powers. Peter says little about the dominations, except that they "surpass the principalities and powers."[25] In any case, they constitute the link between the first and the second triad. The principalities are spirits of action, possessing as they do the particular gift of leading the other angels in the task of implementing the "divine mysteries."[26] The powers are assigned the task of keeping in check the demons, whose ability to tempt human beings never escapes the powers' control. In the final triad, the virtues are particularly responsible for the execution of miracles, whereas the archangels and angels are the carriers of more or less important messages.

Other Christian thinkers—above all, Pseudo-Dionysius the Areopagite in his *Celestial Hierarchies*—have developed more speculative accounts of the angelic orders. Still, even Peter Lombard's succinct treatment transmits some of the most important insights of this aspect of angelology. First, it is clear that the orders of angels form a descending hierarchy, from the spirits whose offices associate them most closely with God in the first triad, down to the angels of the third triad, who are charged with the execution of tasks that place them in close communion with the natural world and the world of humans. The celestial hierarchy thus comprises several layers of mediation through which God's grace is channeled to the physical universe. Put differently, the angels mediate between grace and nature, buffering, as it were, the effects of God's action in creation. Secondly, and this point is related to the first, the celestial hierarchy provides a structure for divine grace, such that there are angels for all the major aspects of the relationship between the sacred and the human: judgment, divine governance, temptation and evil, signs and miracles, and so forth.

In a later chapter of distinction 9 (chap. 4), the *Book of Sentences* addresses the question as to whether the angelic orders have existed from the very beginning of time. In line with what we have learned earlier about the formation of the angels, the answer is negative. Since the celestial hierarchy is an order of grace, it cannot have come into being before the conversion and aversion of the angels. This does not exclude, however, that there obtained a certain natural order of precedence among the spirits even before the granting or removal of grace.

Finally, Peter Lombard teaches the existence of guardian angels. Indeed, every human being is accompanied not only by a good but also by an evil spirit. Peter considers it conceivable that one and the same angel is charged with assisting or tempting (depending on whether it is a good or a bad angel) several humans. Otherwise, we might run into problems with an excessive number of angels. Again, let us make an effort to understand this idea in its medieval context. We are used to attributing the impetus for good and evil actions entirely to our own initiative, to our internal psychological and moral makeup. This is why the modern cure and punishment of behavioral abnormalities aims at the "inside" of people: psychoanalysis belongs as much in this category as do long prison sentences that pursue the goal of inner reform through psychological torment. Contrast psychoanalysis with exorcism, and long-term incarceration with physical torture: exorcism views evil as an outside force that has temporarily befallen the human soul, while torture punishes the body through which the offender has harmed the community or challenged its authorities. Horrific as they are, both practices accord the human soul, the "inside," a certain immunity. Of course, Peter Lombard and other medieval thinkers did not deny free will and the responsibility of human beings for their actions. Yet evil did not, ultimately, originate in the human sphere. In a sense, it remained "outside." Modernity, by contrast, has internalized it. The result is undeniable progress—who would want to return to the medieval penal system, for example?—but internalization has its own price.[27]

The Hexaemeron

Since Augustine, the Western Christian tradition has taken into consideration allegorical interpretations of the six days of creation. Such interpretations, which deny any temporal dimension to the act of creation, instead maintaining that God created all at once (*simul*), continued to be the object of lively debate in the mid-twelfth century.[28] These debates find their echo in distinction 12, where the *Sentences* take up this subject:

> **That the saintly authors seem to have handed down as it were conflicting [accounts] on this [subject], some saying that everything was made at once in matter and form, others [claiming that creation occurred] in intervals of time.** In fact, some of the saintly Fathers, who have investigated the words and mysteries of God most excellently, seem to have written as it were conflicting [accounts] on this.—Some have taught that everything was created at once in matter and form; which is what Augustine seems to have supposed.—Others, however, have rather proven and asserted this [theory], that raw and unformed matter was created first, in a state of commixture and confusion of the four elements; but after that, in the intervals of the six days the genera of corporeal things were formed according to their proper species. Which is the teaching that Gregory, Jerome, Bede, and many others recommend and prefer, [and] with which the Book of Genesis, from which the original knowledge of this subject has flown to us, also seems to agree more.[29]

Peter Lombard's own preferences are quite clear from this passage: he leans to the more literal interpretation, which he deems to be doing greater justice to the scriptural texts. He does, however, place the six days within a broader theoretical framework that allows him to accommodate certain refinements, such as the possibility of development in the natural world after God's initial creative act. According to the Lombard, creation occurred in four steps: first, God laid out the order of creation in His Word; then, simultaneously and out of nothing, He created the angels and the unformed matter of the four elements; during the six days God, in a third step, "distinguished and reduced to their proper forms everything that he had made *simul* materially";[30] finally, from "hidden" or "primordial" seeds that God placed within material creation, new natural forms are continually able to arise.[31]

Distinctions 13 through 15 offer a detailed account of the six days. Each day contributes to the final structure of creation by introducing distinctions into the unformed, chaotic matter God originaly made. On the first day, God divided light from darkness; on the second, He divided heaven from earth; on the third, land from sea, so that plant life could appear; on the fourth, He created the heavenly bodies that enable us to distinguish years, seasons, and days and to count hours (it is only at this stage that the sun came into existence, for the sun is different from the light of the first day); on the fifth day, God made the animals living in water; and, finally, on the sixth day, He created those living on land. Peter Lombard's treatment of these matters is straightforward and, admittedly, not very speculative. At one point, he introduces the promising concept of duality (*binarius*) as the "principle of alterity and sign of division,"[32] a concept that could have served him to penetrate the logic of the six days of creation more thoroughly. But he does not pursue the idea, being more interested in providing a down-to-earth account of the scriptural evidence.

Toward the end of distinction 15, the Lombard returns to the question of creation *simul*, repeating that the Catholic tradition seems split on the interpretation of the six days. He affords ample space to a detailed summary of the position of those authors who, like Augustine, have maintained that "all was made at the very beginning of time," and who have argued, further, that Moses had to clothe the account of creation in the graphic language of time for the benefit of "the coarse and carnal populace."[33] Yet, once again, he begs to differ, for "the letter of Genesis seems to lend more support" to the teachings of those taking the six days literally, in addition to the fact that "the Church approves" these teachings more.[34] The issue of the six days throws Peter Lombard's method into high relief: he deliberately chooses to be more of a positive theologian than a speculative one. On the other hand, he is reluctant to foreclose discussion. His detailed and fair summary of creation *simul* ensures that readers of the *Sentences* are furnished with the essential terms of the debate.

The Creation of Man and Woman

We already know why and with what end in view God created humanity: God created the human being out of goodness, so that men might enjoy Him. But what was the metaphysical constitution of the first human beings? To this question, we now turn.

With the entire Christian tradition, Peter Lombard follows Genesis 1: 26 in holding that God made man to His "image and likeness." The question "What is man?" therefore has no immanent answer, but immediately refers the human being to his divine exemplar. We are what we are because of God, and in relation to Him. Human nature ultimately possesses no autonomous intelligibility. In what, then, do the image and likeness of God consist? Peter Lombard is open to a number of different theories, among which he does not decide:

> **In what the image and likeness are considered [to consist].** The human being, then, is made to the image and likeness of God [*ad imaginem Dei et similitudinem*] according to the mind, with regard to which he surpasses the irrational [creatures]; but [he is made] to [God's] image according to memory, intelligence, and love; [and] to [His] likeness according to the innocence and justice that are naturally in the rational mind.—Or the image is considered [to consist] in the understanding of truth, the likeness in the love of virtue; or the image [is considered to consist] in everything else, the likeness in the essence, since it is immortal and indivisible.—Which is why Augustine [says] in his book *De quantitate animae*: "The soul is made like God, since God has made it immortal and indissoluble." The image, then, pertains to the form, the likeness to the nature. The human being consequently is made, according to his soul, to the image and likeness not of the Father or the Son or the Holy Spirit, but of the entire Trinity.[35]

According to the first theory that the Lombard mentions in this passage, the image of God in the human being would consist in the way in which the triune metaphysical structure of the human mind mirrors the divine Trinity, whereas the likeness would be connected with the moral goodness that the created mind possesses in virtue of its nature. The second theory shifts the understanding of the image of God in man in a more epistemological direction, associating it with the human ability to comprehend truth. The third and final theory approaches the image-likeness distinction in a rather different manner, viewing the likeness as consisting in the indivisible and immortal essence or nature of the human mind, while the image is associated with "everything else"—presumably all the other attributes previously mentioned. Incidentally, Peter Lombard seems to be using the word *form* here in a sense similar to the one we encountered earlier in this chapter in connection with the "formation" of the angels.

The human being is said to be made "to" (*ad*) the image and likeness of God in order to distinguish the way in which man mirrors God from the way the Son does. Due to His equality with the Father, He is simply God's "image" (see Col 1:15).[36]

The human soul, we learn in distinction 17, was created by God "from nothing," and it was immediately placed in the human body. On this question, the Lombard distances himself from Augustine's position according to which the human soul was initially created without body.[37] Moreover, God created Adam as an adult, an action that, to be sure, did not follow the normal course of nature, but which was nonetheless not "unnatural": "such things," Peter explains, "happen against nature only for us, to whom the course of nature has come to be known otherwise; for God, however, nature is what He does."[38] Moreover, the natural causes of things include the possibility of such divine intervention.

Just like the angels, Adam was first created in a purely natural state, without enjoying any special grace. Only subsequently to his creation did God, through an act of grace, assign him to paradise—which is a real place, not just an allegory of the future state of the Church. Incredibly pleasant, fecund, and replete with fruit-bearing trees, paradise is probably to be found somewhere in the East, Peter speculates. In the Vulgate, Genesis 2:8 reads, "And the Lord God had planted a paradise of pleasure from the beginning: wherein he placed man whom he had formed," but the Septuagint has *ad orientem* ("toward the Orient") in lieu of *a principio* ("from the beginning"). Thus, paradise might be located somewhere in the Eastern parts, separated by vast masses of water and land from the known world; moreover, it is elevated, touching the circle of the moon.

We come to the creation of woman, which Peter discusses in distinction 18. Explaining why Eve was created from Adam's side—not from his head or feet—he argues that this mode of creation symbolizes the fellowship of love, as well as the equality, that was meant to govern the relationship of the sexes: "Since woman was not destined to be either the ruler or the servant of man, but his companion, she was to be brought forth neither from his head nor from his feet, but from his side."[39] Just a few distinctions after this passage, however, Peter suddenly speaks of a master-servant relationship between man and woman to illustrate the domination of the higher aspects of reason over the lower ones.[40] This reversal is no doubt inspired by Genesis 3:16, a biblical verse that presents woman's subjection to man as a punishment for sin. As far as Eve's soul is concerned, it was not made from Adam's soul, as some heretics would have it—such as the traducianists, who also held that all the other human souls stem from Adam's—but from nothing.

Peter Lombard now addresses the question of man's (and woman's) state before the Fall. The human body, we learn, was a material body, not the spiritual kind of body that will come to be in the hereafter. As such, it required food for its sustenance. The prelapsarian body was, however, not yet mortal—but neither was it immortal. Rather, it was characterized by a strange state in between mortality and immortality, which Peter attempts to capture as the possibility of both dying and not dying: "in that first state, it had the *posse mori* and the *posse non mori*—the being-able-to-die and the being-able-not-to-die."[41] In other words, the human body, as yet untainted by sin, was not yet "formed," in the sense we have encountered previously; it existed in a state of metaphysical neutrality. Had man eaten from the tree of life, and not from the tree of knowledge of good and evil (see Gn 2:9), he would have been able to transform this being-able-not-to-die (*posse non mori*) into a not-being-able-to-die (*non posse mori*), which would have constituted immortality, properly speaking. But that, of course, did not happen.

Procreation did not actually occur while Adam and Eve were in paradise, but if it had, it would have involved sexual intercourse without lust, and childbirth without pain. It is easy to see why the labors of birth are viewed as the result of sin; after all, pain, along with disease, is a sign of human mortality. But, following Augustine, Peter Lombard regards lust, too, as a "lethal sickness."[42] He offers no detailed explanation for this judgment, but the context and comparison with other passages makes it clear that it is rooted in the fact that lust indicates a loss of control of reason over the senses, and hence a reversal of the natural order of the human person. Further speculating on the hypothetical nature of procreation before the Fall, Peter significantly limits the role of miraculous, supernatural elements. Thus, he maintains that human beings would not have been born as adults, nor have reached full physical and mental maturity immediately after birth, but that they would have grown up "according to the same law that we even now observe as governing human birth."[43] We have noticed that, throughout his treatment of the highly speculative question of human nature before the Fall, Peter Lombard keeps his theories as straightforward as possible: no soul without body, no body without food, no preternatural immortality, no birth of fully developed children. In this attitude, we see another sign of the Lombard's humility with regard to the mysteries of faith. Indeed, in the first paragraph of distinction 19, he distances himself from the "curiosity" with which these questions are sometimes treated—an undisciplined and self-confident eagerness to know that gives free rein to the imagination.[44]

The Fall

We have already learned why certain angels—above all, Lucifer—decided to abandon God. In distinction 5, Peter Lombard wrote that "turning away [was] to have hatred and be envious: for the mother of envy is pride [*superbia*], by which they wanted to make themselves equal to God." Aspiring to be above (*super*) the state naturally assigned to them, the evil angels envied God His perfection, with the paradoxical result that their illicit desire to be like God turned them away from Him in resentment and hatred. The same envy that brought about the aversion of the angels from God is the reason why the devil tempted mankind in paradise:

On the envy of the devil through which he undertook to tempt the human being. Seeing, then, that the human being, through the humility of obedience, is able to ascend to where he himself had fallen from due to pride, the devil envied him; and he who was initially, through pride, the "devil"—that is to say, the one fallen downwards—through the zeal of envy was made "Satan," that is to say, the enemy.[45]

Unable to stand the sight of the human beings who, through humility and obedience, have a chance to be raised above their nature, to God, the devil attempts to pull them down with him. Peter Lombard's etymology of the Hebrew term *Satan* is quite correct, but *diabolos*, in Greek, literally means "slanderer," being derived from *diaballein*, "to throw or carry across," "to attack, accuse."

The devil schemed to tempt humankind by approaching the woman because he knew of her greater weakness, due to her less developed rationality. He had to disguise himself, lest he be recognized immediately, but on the other hand, his disguise could not be so perfect as to deprive (wo)man of any chance of detecting his deceit—which would have rendered the Fall inevitable and, hence, unjust. That is why God allowed the devil to tempt Eve only in the form of a serpent, although he would rather have taken on the more deceptive form of a dove.[46] Eve did not fear the serpent because she assumed that God had given it the ability to speak.

The *Book of Sentences* interprets the devil's words in Genesis 3:5 ("For God doth know that in what day soever you shall eat thereof, your eyes shall be opened: and you shall be as Gods, knowing good and evil") as containing a threefold temptation: gluttony in the promise of food, vainglory in the promise of likeness to God, and intellectual greed in the promise of knowledge. The fact that the human being gave in to the temptation of another—in other words, the fact that Eve's sin was not without occasion—makes the human transgression remediable: "For he who had someone inciting [him] to [do] evil, not unjustly [also] had someone restoring [him] to [become] good."[47] The fall of Lucifer and the other demons, by contrast, cannot be undone, for the angels' *aversio* was a totally autonomous decision, prompted by no one.

Adam's temptation was not quite of the same nature as Eve's: "for he did not believe what the devil suggested to be true."[48] Why, then, did he allow himself to be seduced by Eve? "Adam, however, did not believe this, and pondered God's punishment and mercy while, humoring his wife, he yielded to her attempts to persuade him, since he did not wish to make her sad and leave her estranged from him, for fear lest she perish. He had come to the opinion that this [transgression] would be a venial, not a mortal crime."[49] From our contemporary perspective, the Lombard's description of Adam's motives for sinning must appear slightly amusing: while Eve was animated by passion and proud presumption,[50] Adam merely misjudged the seriousness of the sin he was about to commit—to commit because he did not wish to sadden his weak companion and expose her to the dangers of life without his protection. In accordance with this manner of viewing the situation, Peter Lombard decides, though not without hesitation, that Eve's transgression was more serious than Adam's.

As we have already seen, the devil's temptation of Eve and Adam in paradise did not occur outside the realm of divine providence: God ensured fair play, as it were, in preventing the devil from appearing in the guise of a dove. That gives rise to the question as to why, knowing man would fall, God permitted the temptation at all. Peter offers a number of possible explanations, the first being that it is more glorious not to yield to temptation than not to be capable of being tempted. In other words, God wanted to give the human being a chance of greater glory. But He did foresee that we would fall, did He not? This question finds a possible answer in the Augustinian statement that God preferred His creatures to be what they decided to be, rather than creating them incapable of choice. Ultimately, however, we must realize, Peter emphasizes, that we cannot penetrate the mystery of the divine will.

The Lombard leaves no doubt about the fact that he considers the story of Adam, Eve, and the serpent to represent an actual event in the history of humankind. Yet he adds a second, more allegorical interpretation, according to which Adam, Eve, and the serpent illustrate the three parts of the soul, which play a role in the psychogenesis of temptation:

> **That the woman, man, and serpent are in us, and in what manner*.**
> For just as at that time the serpent incited the woman to evil and she consented, and she then gave it to her husband, and thus the sin was consummated; so now in us, too, there is the sensual motion of the soul in place of the serpent, [there is] the inferior part of reason in place of the woman, [and there is] the superior part of reason in place of the husband.[51]

Peter is suggesting that sin typically originates in the sensual part of the soul, which then attempts to implicate reason in its illicit desires: first by inciting the lower part of reason, knowledge (*scientia*), to take delight in the idea of the transgression, and then by seeking the assent of the higher aspect of reason, namely, wisdom (*sapientia*), which controls the will. On the basis of this schema, the Lombard is able to distinguish between venial and mortal sins. The former are sins that remain at the level of ineffectual desires of the sensual soul; the latter are transgressions committed with the full assent of the will. Sinful tendencies that rise to the level of consciousness remain venial if they are immediately repelled by wisdom, but if the consciousness revels in them, the sin is mortal, even if the contemplated act is never brought to execution.[52]

Distinctions 24 through 29 are devoted to the grace that the human being enjoyed before the Fall. Twice in this chapter already, we have witnessed Peter Lombard grappling with issues at the intersection of nature and grace, namely, in connection with the themes of the formation of the angels and the meaning of the celestial hierarchy. The present treatment, however, is by far the most detailed in the *Sentences*. What is at stake in the discussion of the relationship between nature and grace is the extent to which the human being is able to give positive meaning to his or her own life, the role of God in creation, and, ultimately, the autonomy or heteronomy of the created world. Can human nature fulfill itself, or is it utterly helpless without God? These are not easy questions. They have perplexed Christian thinkers since patristic times, and the different ways in which they have been answered in the course of history have created sharp divisions, most notably the division between the Catholic and the Protestant traditions. Due to the complexity of the issues at hand, differences tend to express themselves in minute distinctions. In the last analysis, however, we are dealing with fundamental stances on the relationship between nature and supernature.

Peter Lombard's treatment begins: "It should be known that—just as we have said about the angels—the human being has, in creation, been given assistance through grace and, together with it, the power through which he could remain steadfast, that is to say, not turn away from what he had received; but he was not able to make progress to the extent that he would, by the grace of creation without any other [kind of grace], be capable of earning salvation."[53] Just like the angels, the human being was initially created in a natural state, without any special kind of grace, except the grace of creation itself. This *gratia creationis* signifies nothing but the ability to "remain steadfast" (*stare*) in the state of innocence; it is not justifying, thus bringing salvation. More precisely, the natural endowment of the *gratia creationis* consists in the free will: "For there exists in the rational soul a natural will, by which [the soul] naturally wills the good, albeit tenuously and feebly unless grace assists it; which, when it arrives, assists it and raises it up so that it may effectively will the good."[54]

The effect of the Fall was that "the natural goods in man were destroyed, and the gratuitous ones were taken away."[55] The reference to "gratuitous goods" (*gratuita*) makes us stop for a moment, for Peter just declared that before the Fall, the human being was endowed only with a *gratia creationis*. Or does Peter assume that at some stage between the creation of man and the Fall, grace was added to the first human beings' natural innocence? Some commentators believe this to be the case.[56] Their interpretation is confirmed by several texts, including one at the beginning of distinction 29 which states unambiguously that the human beings before the Fall required both operating and cooperating grace, without which they could not have willed the good effectively.[57] As Artur Landgraf has noted, it is not clear why, before the Fall, Adam and Eve would have needed any *gratia operans*, which in the context of the angels was defined as the power to justify sinners.[58] What is missing in Peter Lombard's treatment—as well as in that of his contemporaries—is a sufficiently clear definition of the "good" that the first humans could or could not reach without grace. If this good is understood as the supernatural perfection that human nature is promised in the hereafter, then it is logical to assume that this supernatural good cannot be attained without supernatural assistance. Sometimes, Peter Lombard hints that this is precisely what he is struggling to say: "This, however, we hold steadfastly and unhesitatingly, that without prevenient and assisting grace the free will does not suffice to obtain justification and salvation."[59] This prevenient grace, we further learn, consists in faith and charity. On the other hand, there is no compelling reason as to why human nature should be unable to accomplish all manner of finite goods even without any special grace: "Nevertheless, we do not deny that, before and beyond that grace, goods are done by man through the free will, as [Pseudo-]Augustine teaches in his *Answers against the Pelagians*, where he says that human beings through free will cultivate fields, build houses, and do many other good things without cooperating grace."[60]

But we must return to the effects of the Fall upon human free will.

The *Sentences* distinguish four states in the history of the human *liberum arbitrium*:[61]

1. Before the Fall, the free will possessed the *gratia creationis*, through which it was able to will the good without impediment, not being subject to any inclination to evil. Moreover, at some stage after creation, the human being received the grace necessary to strengthen the free will, so that it might pursue the ultimate good effectively.

2. Eve and Adam's sin both destroyed the grace of creation and led to the removal of the supernatural gift of grace. The consequences of sin therefore left humanity in a situation in which it tended to evil instead of good, being unable not to sin. This does not mean, however, that the free will became subject to some necessity to sin. Indeed, "before sin and after, the will is equally [*aeque*] free from necessity."[62] What Peter presumably means is that even the will of sinners is free from external constraint; that as an inner movement of the soul, the will "can never be forced."[63]

3. Christ's saving work restored the grace liberating human freedom from sin, although this freedom is not an absolute one. Even after the redemption, humans still retain a tendency to do evil, such that it is impossible for fallen man to avoid sinning altogether. What is possible for humans *post reparationem*, newly strengthened by grace, is to live without committing mortal sin.

4. Finally, in the hereafter, man will enjoy complete freedom from misery, that is to say, he will neither be overcome nor indeed be oppressed by any sinful tendencies. In a word, he will enjoy the *non posse peccare*, the not-being-able-to-sin.

Original Sin

After humbly apologizing for any defects in his discussion of the Fall, Peter Lombard moves on to the topic of original sin. Most significantly in this context, Peter insists on the reality—even physical reality—of original sin, despite the inherent difficulty of the idea of guilt without personal responsibility. Some contemporaries, such as Abelard, dismissed the idea of original sin for that very reason.[64] In our own age of individualism, it must appear even more counterintuitive that someone should be held responsible for the transgressions of another human being who lived many generations ago. Collective responsibility tends to be embraced most reluctantly. It is not easily defined. In what sense, for example, does a German born twenty years after the war bear guilt for the Holocaust?

Characteristically, Peter Lombard readily admits to the difficulty of the subject matter upon which he is about to embark: about original sin, he writes, "the saintly doctors have spoken somewhat obscurely, and the Scholastic doctors have held various [positions]."[65] According to the *Sentences*, however, original sin possesses a reality that precedes the acts of individual sinners, affecting each and every human being from the moment of conception. Thus, Adam's sin continues to mark all of humanity not only in an allegorical way, insofar as all sinners can be said to be following Adam's example. No, Adam's sin is in all of us. We literally carry it in our flesh. It is an inherited guilt that consists in concupiscence—not in an individual act of concupiscence (for that would be actual sin, not original sin), but rather in the kind of concupiscence that constitutes the underlying condition of sin, the "tinder of sin" (*fomes peccati*), as Peter puts it.[66]

Concupiscence is the "law of the flesh," the *lex carnis*, with which the human being is afflicted owing to his very constitution as an incarnate spirit: "Sin itself is said to dwell in the flesh."[67] The sensuality of the flesh is a breeding ground for illicit desires, which constantly threaten to corrupt the soul—an explanation that is in consonance with Peter's earlier discussion of the psychogenesis of sin. The paradigm of concupiscence is sexual intercourse, which since the Fall is pervaded by lust. Now each time a man and a woman come together in the sexual act, they transmit to the offspring they beget the taint of their own lust: "The very flesh, which is conceived in vicious concupiscence, is polluted and corrupted. From contact with it, the soul, which is poured into it, takes on the stain by which it is polluted and made guilty, that is to say, [it takes on] the vice of concupiscence, which is original sin."[68] Even the "goods of marriage" cannot do more than "excuse" the guilt of concupiscence, which is inherent in the sexual act.

We still want to know how exactly the transmission of original sin occurs. Peter's theory is surprisingly physical. Some "followers after words" (see Prv 19:7), he reports, have raised objections against the idea according to which original sin is transmitted in the flesh; for how could all of humanity carry atoms from Adam's body? Surely the number of human beings subsequent to Adam and Eve exceeds the quantity of atoms that made up Adam's flesh? The Lombard's response almost sounds like modern genetic theory. He speaks as though original sin were some kind of defect in our DNA structure:

> **Response in which it is disclosed how [all human beings] were in Adam according to a seminal reason [*secumdum rationem seminalem*], and in what manner they descended from him, namely, by the law of propagation.** One can respond to these people that everything which exists naturally in human bodies is said to have been materially and causally, not formally, in the first human being. It descended from the first parent by the law of propagation, and was increased and multiplied in itself [*in se*], without any exterior substance passing into it; and it will resurrect in the future. It has nourishment from food, but the food is not transformed into the human substance, which descended from Adam through propagation.
>
> **How it descended through propagation.** For Adam transmitted a modest amount from his own substance to the bodies of his sons when he begot them, that is to say, some small amount from the mass of his substance divided itself and thence the body of the son was formed, and, through self-multiplication [*suique multiplicatione*] without the addition of anything extrinsic, it was made to grow.[69]

Actual Sin

Original sin provides the soil, as it were, on which actual sin can grow. Yet whereas original sin is a condition of the flesh, actual sin is an interior motion of the will, which often translates into an exterior act.[70] Peter Lombard emphasizes the fact, however, that sin is first and foremost an interior act, for it is in a perverse will that evil acts have their root, just as a bad tree produces bad fruit.[71] We can recognize the quality of the will from the end that it pursues. A righteous will acts in view of only one goal: to come closer to the kingdom of God through love of God and neighbor. Reflecting the "consensus view" of the time,[72] the Lombard's ethics has strong intentionalist tendencies.

Distinction 40 discusses at length Augustine's thesis according to

which certain acts are always and intrinsically wrong, quite independently of the intention with which they are executed. Who would claim,
for example, that we are allowed to steal from the rich in order to realize
our good intention to give to the poor? Or that we could commit adultery
if the act were done with a praiseworthy goal in mind? In spite of these
objections, Peter is reluctant to give ground. He ends up suggesting,
though in an indirect mode ("some people say"), that intrinsically evil
acts cannot be performed with a good intention. This position would
leave his basic claim intact: *Praecipue tamen in voluntate peccatum consistit*,
"nonetheless sin consists chiefly in the will."[73]

To illustrate the effects of sin, the *Book of Sentences* refers to the
biblical parable of the man traveling from Jerusalem to Jericho who fell
into the hands of robbers and was stripped and almost killed (see Lk 10:
30). The devil is just like those robbers, Peter argues: he strips the sinner
who falls prey to him of all grace, in addition to inflicting serious wounds
to his nature as a rational being. As a consequence of this weakening of
man's healthy nature and the removal of grace, more sins will inevitably
follow from the first one, acting as punishment for it. This vicious dynamism of sin engendering ever more sin will remove the sinner further
and further from His maker:

> **How the human being distances himself from God, namely, through
> the dissimilarity that sin produces.** [The human being] distances him-
> self from [God] through sin—not in terms of local distance, since
> [God] is everywhere in His entirety and is present to all.... Through
> sin, therefore, somebody comes to be far removed from God, [though]
> not in terms of place: he comes to be far removed in that he abandons
> His likeness; and the further he is removed, the more dissimilar does
> he become.... There is nothing that makes the human being more
> unlike God than sin.[74]

This passage reveals another dimension of Peter's conception of the image
and likeness of God. The likeness, in fact, appears to possess a moral dimension, such that sin diminishes it, whereas righteousness will increase it.

The *Sentences* propose a threefold classification of sin. Augustine distinguishes sins out of cupidity and out of fear. Jerome, on the other hand,
believes that all sins fall into one of three categories—sins of thought,
speech, and act—to which one could add a fourth category, namely, sins
of habit. Finally, it is possible to categorize sins according to their object:

God, self, and neighbor. It is not necessary to choose among these approaches, for they focus on different aspects of sin: its source, medium,
and object.

A consideration of the seven principal vices, the sin against the Holy
Spirit, and the divine origins of the human power to sin completes book
2 of the *Sentences*. In this book, Peter Lombard presents his ideas with
his usual sense of humility, recognizing the limits of the human mind in
coming to grasp why man was created as an incarnate spirit, how precisely the details of angelic nature are to be understood, or why God
allowed the devil to tempt humanity, knowing as He did that we would
fall. This humility produces three consequences. First, the Lombard
shuns excessively speculative explanations, attempting to keep his account
of matters such as human nature in its prelapsarian state as straightforward as possible. Secondly, Peter leans strongly to the literal reading of
scriptural texts, as we have seen in the examples of the Genesis account
of creation and of the Fall. Such literal readings in fact minimize the
need for speculation. Thirdly and finally, the *Book of Sentences* is reluctant
to foreclose discussion, often preferring a multiplicity of voices to assertion of the truth of one particular human point of view. Thus, there is
no one theory in the *Sentences* on such a question as the image and
likeness of God in man. Even in cases where Peter Lombard has a clearly
stated preference (as with the interpretation of the hexaemeron), he is
loath to dismiss alternative accounts altogether. The *Book of Sentences*,
then, often remains precisely this: a book, a collection of "sentences," that
is, of authoritative opinions. One could say that, in the mid-twelfth century, the Christian tradition was not yet ready for a more definitive synthesis, for which it lacked certain conceptual tools and intellectual practices.[75] Or one could maintain that it was, rather, an acute sense of
humility in the face of God and the All that prevented thinkers like
Peter Lombard from developing more rigorous syntheses. The two explanations taken together might work best.

THE *SENTENCES*, BOOK III

On the Incarnation of the Word

On May 28, 1170, Pope Alexander III addressed a letter to William of Champagne, the archbishop of Sens and papal legate in France. He wrote:

> When you were once in Our presence, We enjoined you verbally [*viva voce*] that you explicitly urge and effectively summon your suffragans who are associated with you at Paris to renounce the vicious doctrine of Peter, erstwhile bishop of Paris, in which it is said that Christ, insofar as He is man, is not something [*non est aliquid*]. It is thus that We command you as a brother through Apostolic writing [*per Apostolica scripta*] that ... you convoke your suffragans at Paris and, together with them and others, take pains to renounce completely the aforementioned doctrine, as well as ensuring that the schoolmasters who study theology there teach Christ to be perfect man, consisting of body and soul, just as He is perfect God.[1]

As though these words were not clear enough, seven years later Pope Alexander pronounced a formal anathema against Peter Lombard's "vicious doctrine" (*prava doctrina*) on the hypostatic union, in a letter to the same Bishop William, who had at that stage been transferred to Rheims: "Since Christ, perfect God, is [also] perfect man, it is astonishing with what temerity someone would dare say that Christ was not something insofar as He is man. Lest great misuse should arise and error be introduced in the Church of God, We command that, by Our authority, you forbid in peril of anathema that anyone dare say henceforth that Christ is not something insofar as He is man; for just as [He is] true God, so He is true man, subsisting on the basis of a rational soul and human flesh."[2]

In the long run, the condemnation of Peter Lombard's Christology, that "vicious doctrine," did not detract from the esteem in which the Lombard's theology was held. Its greatest ecclesiastical triumph came in 1215, after over a half century of heated and often acrimonious debate— we remember some of Walter of St. Victor's accusations, including his charges against Bishop Peter's personal integrity. The Fourth Council of the Lateran solemnly recognized the orthodoxy of Peter Lombard's Trinitarian theology, which had been just as embattled as his Christology: "We however, with the approbation of the sacred Council, believe and confess with Peter Lombard that there is one highest entity, incomprehensible and ineffable, which is truly Father, and Son, and Holy Spirit: [etc.]."[3]

The purpose of this chapter is not a historical study of the controversies that surrounded the *Book of Sentences* before it became the standard textbook of theology in the Christian West—fascinating as such an investigation would be.[4] But we will have to examine the strange doctrine that seems to have marred the Christology of the *Sentences*, a doctrine according to which *Christus secundum quod est homo, non est aliquid*, "Christ, insofar as He is man, is not something." Christ the man—simply "nothing"? Did God not truly become man, then? And why would Peter Lombard have entertained such an idea, which appears to undermine the most deeply held belief of the Christian faith? Did he in fact subscribe to this "Christological nihilianism," as the position has come to be called?[5] In order to answer these questions, we will have to place the famous distinction 10 of book 3 in its proper context.

The Structure of Book 3

Despite Otto Baltzer's surprising claim that "in the Lombard, Christology seems to dissolve into almost disconnected particular questions," the order of questions being "purely extrinsic" and "in some cases ... accidental,"[6] the structure of Peter Lombard's Christology appears quite coherent and logical.[7] Distinctions 1 through 14 are devoted to the being of Christ, that is to say, to fundamental questions concerning the constitution of Christ as God-man. These distinctions include discussions of the reasons why it was the second person of the Trinity that became flesh; of the immaculate conception; of the precise mode of the relationship between the divine and human natures of Christ (the hypostatic union); of the problem of Christological nihilianism; and of certain attributes of Christ, such as His wisdom and power. Thereafter, distinctions 15 through 22 turn to the passion of Christ and His saving work, distinctions 18 and 19 treating, in particular, the precise manner in which He liberated humanity from the devil and from sin. In distinctions 23 to 36, Peter Lombard analyzes the virtues, both theological (dist. 23–32) and cardinal (dist. 33), which analysis is followed by his treatment of the seven gifts of the Holy Spirit (dist. 34–35). Peter considers the latter to be virtues as well, and in distinction 36 argues that all the virtues are rooted in charity. Distinctions 37 through 40 conclude book 3 with a discussion of the Ten Commandments, which further specify the contents of charity in men's relation to God and to each other.

Several contemporary authors have followed Baltzer in his judgment concerning the flawed structure of book 3 of the *Sentences*. It is especially the inclusion of the virtues in Christology that has met with the disapproval of historians of theology. Thus, the German *Handbuch der Dogmen- und Theologiegeschichte* alleges that the *Sentences'* treatises on the virtues and the commandments are "less well worked out and placed" in the whole than other parts of book 3.[8] The *Handbuch* continues: "It is the relationship of the virtues, gifts, and commandments only to salvation and grace, but not to creation and nature, that seems to be taken into consideration here."[9] Marcia Colish agrees: "From a schematic point of view, ethics is the major subject on which his gift for lucid organization deserts [Peter]. He does not take up all the points relevant to this topic in one place. . . . his principal analysis of virtue, both the theological virtues, the cardinal virtues, and the gifts of the Holy Spirit, occurs in Book 3, in connection with the moral aptitudes of the human Christ."[10]

It is a fact that Peter's discussion of the virtues opens, in distinction 23, with the question of whether Christ possessed faith and hope, just as He possessed charity. The Lombard thus approaches the problem of virtue from an unabashedly Christological point of view. But there is no inconsistency here. The Lombardian conception of virtue is different from our own, insofar as he prefers to show us virtue in its perfect state, that is to say, in its realization in Christ. One could say that Peter Lombard approaches virtue "from above," from a quasi-divine angle, and not from the point of view of its instantiation in ordinary human nature. Does this option—shared by many of Peter's contemporaries, especially in the Victorine school—entail a privileging of grace over nature, as well as a lack of consideration of nature in its pure state? It most likely does. The twelfth century still exhibited some of the typically Neoplatonic, idealistic traits that the Christian Middle Ages inherited from the Church Fathers. We have discovered an example of such idealism earlier in this book, namely, in Peter Lombard's close association of sin with the flesh and the senses. The rediscovery of Aristotelianism in the thirteenth century would force a rethinking of many of these assumptions, which tended to regard man's physical nature with suspicion, strongly emphasizing the need for spiritual purification, and even mortification. Such views are certainly out of tune with the bent of modern anthropology; but that does not render them incoherent or absurd. My claim, then, is that the placement of the virtues in book 3 of the *Sentences* represents a logical consequence of Peter Lombard's understanding of human nature in its fallen state, and of his conviction that the human being needs to emulate the exemplary perfection of Christ.

The Incarnation and the Trinity

At the beginning of his discussion of the Incarnation, Peter reminds his readers of his earlier statements on the two missions of Christ, in distinction 15 of book 1: "In fact, the mission of the Son is the Incarnation itself: for he was sent so as to appear visibly to the world in the form of man. About which enough has been said above."[11] Through this sentence, Peter adverts to the connection between Trinitarian theology and Christology, which belong closely together, despite the different places that they occupy (and must occupy) in the theological system of the *Sentences*. But why was it the Son who assumed flesh, rather than the Father or the Holy Spirit? This is the first question book 3 addresses. We learn of three possible answers.

First, it is appropriate that God, who created the world in His wisdom, should also restore it through His wisdom. Put differently, the creation that came from God through the Word fittingly returns to Him through the Word as well. Furthermore, it was appropriate for the second person of the Trinity to be sent into the world because it is *ab alio*, "from another," whereas the Father is *a nullo*, "from no one." It makes sense that the Son, who is begotten of the Father, is sent into the world by the Father, who Himself could not have been sent by anyone else. Finally, it was suitable for the Son of God to become the son of man as well; had another person of the Trinity become incarnate—the Father, say—the same person would play the role of Father in the Trinity and of son in the human realm.

It is noteworthy that Peter does not present the three reasons for the Incarnation of the Word as compelling necessities, but instead frames them in terms of "suitability" or "fittingness" (*ordine congruo* and *congruentius* are the expressions he uses). Indeed, he points out that, just as the Word was made man, so the Father or the Holy Spirit could have become incarnate; in fact, the Father and the Holy Spirit could still become incarnate now. Thus, Peter does not wish to suggest that the scope of God's possible action is limited to what actually occurred in history.

The final point raised in the first distinction concerns one of the central principles of Trinitarian theology: the indivisibility of the divine essence and, hence, of God's action. Since the second person has become man, must we not assume that the Father and the Holy Spirit have become incarnate together with the Son? The answer Peter Lombard supplies is merely verbal; we are dealing with a truth of the Christian faith that does not appear to be susceptible of further elucidation: "We say that the Son does nothing without the Father and the Holy Spirit, but [that] the action of these three [persons] is one, indivisible, and nondissimilar; and yet the Son, not the Father or the Holy Spirit, has taken on the flesh. . . . The Trinity, then, brought to pass the assumption of flesh, but through the Word, not through the Father or the Holy Spirit."[12] "This is my faith too," Peter Lombard adds, quoting Augustine, "since it is the Catholic faith."

The Incarnation and the Flesh

The primary purpose of distinction 2 is to emphasize the fact that, in assuming the flesh, the Word took on all of human nature, with all its properties and accidents, and not this or that particular aspect of humanity to the exclusion of others. This was necessary, Peter explains, for a soteriological reason: since the whole of human nature was corrupted by sin, the whole had to be assumed in Christ to be healed and sanctified. Due to the subtlety and simplicity of the divine essence, as well as its incomparable superiority to the human body, made as that is from "the mud of the earth,"[13] the Word became united with the flesh through the mediation of the soul. The need for mediation between the essence of God and the flesh should not, however, mislead us into believing that the Word took on the human soul first, and the body only subsequently. Similarly, the fetus that was conceived in the Virgin's womb never existed in a merely human state; rather, it was conceived as the Word incarnate. Again, the *Book of Sentences* insists on the integrity and indivisibility of human nature as assumed by the Word.

Since the Fall, however, flesh means sin, as we have discovered in the Lombard's discussion of the law of the flesh in book 2: *ipsum peccatum dicitur manere in carne*, he wrote there, "sin itself is said to dwell in the flesh."[14] And there is no indication that Master Peter shared the sophisticated understanding of the biblical concept of flesh that we find in more recent scriptural scholarship, which has shown, for example, that in his Letter to the Galatians, St. Paul uses "flesh" (Gr. σάρξ) to denote the human condition as a whole in its fallenness, and not merely the body (see Gal 5:13–26).[15] Given his medieval notion of the law of the flesh, Peter must show in distinction 3 that the conception of Christ did not taint Him with the sinfulness of the human flesh. Consequently, he maintains that, prior to the Incarnation, the Holy Spirit liberated the Virgin from all sin, purging the "tinder of sin" (*fomes peccati*) so effectively that henceforth her flesh no longer presented her with any temptations. Moreover, Christ's conception was not accompanied by lust, which is the hallmark of original sin, for, as Peter states in the words of John Damascene: "The self-subsistent Wisdom and Power of the most high God overshadowed her . . . like divine semen [see Lk 1:35 and 1 Cor 1:24], that is to say, the Son of God, homousian [that is, consubstantial] with the Father; and It united Itself with the flesh from the most holy and pure blood of the same Virgin, [flesh] animated by the rational and intellective soul of our old paste [see 1 Cor 5:7], not inseminating [*non seminans*], but creating through the Holy Spirit."[16] The Word, then, descended upon the holy Virgin through the Spirit, spiritually begetting or creating Jesus, the Son of God and of (wo)man, who was to share the same nature as all of humanity—assuming the old "paste," or dough, that was in need of the leavening of salvation. Only His freedom from sin, ensured by the purity of Mary's flesh and blood, distinguished Christ's human nature from that of humanity at large.[17]

The latter statement, however, calls for a qualification. It is not clear how Christ's assumption of the human body and soul could cure mankind from sin if indeed Christ took on all of human nature except precisely its sinfulness. What is more, Romans 8:3 asserts that God sent His Son "in the likeness of sinful flesh." Peter resolves the problem by introducing a distinction between guilt and punishment as two distinct aspects of sin. Christ, who was indeed free from any guilt, nonetheless assumed the punishment consequent upon sin, namely, the capacity for suffering and the mortality that characterize human nature.

Distinction 4 asks why the Incarnation, which was the work of the entire Trinity, is nonetheless often attributed to the Holy Spirit, even in Scripture. In responding, Peter reemphasizes the principle that the three persons of the Trinity always act as a whole and indivisibly; and still it is not illegitimate to identify the Incarnation, God's work of love *par excellence*, with the Holy Spirit, who is God's ineffable charity. By the same token, we must be careful not to misinterpret the expression according to which Christ was born of the Holy Spirit from the Virgin Mary. It does not mean that Christ is the Son of the Spirit, although He is the son of man. Rather, Christ's birth "of the Spirit" (*de Spiritu Sancto*) signifies the action of divine grace in the conception of the Word.

The Hypostatic Union

Having attempted to elucidate the mode of Christ's conception, Peter is ready to approach the being of Christ from a more radically metaphysical perspective. We have already seen the Lombard grapple with questions of the relationship between nature and grace—grace as the manifestation of God's reaching into the realm of nature to elevate it—in the preceding book of the *Sentences*. These questions stand at the center of the Christian faith, and perhaps of religion as such, if religion is the effort to make sense of the finitude and brokenness of human existence in relation to the perfection of the infinite. In the problem of the Incarnation, the challenge to understand the relationship between nature and grace, God and creation, the infinite and the finite comes to a head. Christians profess that in Christ, the Word has become flesh, that God, remaining truly God, has become fully human in order to bring broken human nature back to Him. In Christ, God and man are fully reconciled, yet their different natures are not canceled out. In more modern philosophical terms, we are dealing with the problem of an identity of identity and difference—and an identity of identity and difference that does not privilege identity over difference. But let us discover how Peter Lombard casts the problem. Distinction 5 broaches the issue in the following terms:

> **Whether a person or a nature assumed a person or a nature, and whether the nature of God became incarnate.** Since it is certain from the preceding [discussion] that the Word of God simultaneously assumed flesh and soul in the unity of its person, it is further necessary to inquire which of these [following positions] should preferably be conceded; namely, that [1] a person assumed a person, or [2] a nature a nature, or [3] a person a nature, or [4] a nature a person; and whether [5] it is thus fitting to say that the divine nature became incarnate, just as one can soundly say that God became incarnate and the Word became incarnate.—Following the testimony of the sacred authorities, this inquiry or course of questioning is partly implicit and complex, partly explicit and evident.[18]

It is not difficult to determine that it would be mistaken to say that the divine nature assumed a human person (4), or that a divine person assumed a human person (1). Peter Lombard quickly dismisses these possibilities by means of some quotations from Augustine. Indeed, it follows from the mode of Christ's conception, which we have discussed, that there was no human person to assume who existed before the conception. Rather, the second person of the Trinity assumed human nature (3), composed of body and soul, at the moment when Jesus was conceived through the Spirit: "The Word of God, therefore, did not take on a human person, but [human] nature, because that flesh and that soul did not constitute one human person that the Word could have taken on, but rather in taking on [flesh and soul,] it united [them], and in uniting [them] it took [them] on."[19]

Alternative (2) presents the most perplexing problems—not only, as Peter remarks, because the relevant authorities seem to contradict each other, but because they even contradict themselves. After several pages of to and fro, the Lombard decides in favor of the position according to which the divine nature itself can rightly be said to have assumed human nature. Again, it is in words from John Damascene that Peter finds the best formulation of the problem. In its unusual terminology, the passage he quotes retains something of its Greek flavor: "We say that in the humanation [*in humanatione*] of the Word of God, the whole and perfect nature of the Deity became incarnate in one of its hypostases, that is to say, it became united to human nature, and not part [of the divine nature became united] to part [of human nature]. For we say that the entire human nature was united to the entire nature or substance of the Deity."[20] In other words, the complete reconciliation of God and man does not exclude any aspect of either divine or human nature. A radical consequence follows: although the Father and the Spirit did not become incarnate, as the Eighth and Eleventh Councils of Toledo had emphasized, the divine nature itself did so (*incarnata est*) (5). Nonetheless, Peter Lombard stops short of affirming that the divine nature "became flesh" (*caro facta*)—not because the statement is intrinsically wrong, but because he considers it too expressive, suggesting as it might the "convertibility of nature into nature."[21] For in the Incarnation, God's nature did not become other than itself; God did not become another nature. Christ is a single (divine) person with two natures, divine and human.

Peter's analysis so far has certainly rendered our understanding of the hypostatic union more precise. It has not, however, managed to unravel the metaphysical mystery of the Incarnation—as Peter himself would have been the first to concede. The questions therefore continue, now focusing on the problem at its most profound and abstract metaphysical level: in taking on human nature, did God not have to become other than Himself? Let us consider the beginning of distinction 6:

> **On the understanding of these phrases: "God was made man," "God is man," whether by these phrases it is said, or is not, that God was made something else or is something else [*Deus factus esse aliquid vel esse aliquid*].** From the preceding [discussions], however, there emerges a question that contains much utility, but [also] enormous difficulty and perplexity. For, since it is certain from what has been said above and from many other witnesses, and [since] all Catholics unanimously confess that God was made man, and that Christ is true God and true man, it is asked whether by these phrases: "God was made man," "the Son of God was made the son of man," "God is

man" [*Deus est homo*], and "man is God" [*homo est Deus*], it is said
that God was made something else or is something else, or whether
something else is said to be God [*dicatur Deus factus esse aliquid vel esse
aliquid, vel aliquid dicatur esse Deus*], and whether it is thus fitting to
say: "Man was made God" [*Homo factus est Deus*] and "the son of man
was made the Son of God" [*filius hominis factus est Filius Dei*], just as
one says the converse; and [it is asked further] if by these phrases it is
not said that God was made something else or is something else, what
the [proper] understanding of these phrases and similar ones is.[22]

Unfortunately, some of the nuances of the original Latin text are difficult
to convey in translation. Two remarks seem in order. First, I have chosen
to render *aliquid* in English as "something else," and not simply as "something." *Aliquid* carries both these meanings (its etymology being *aliud
quid*, "another something," "something else"), and I do not see what sense
it would make, in our context, to ask whether God was "something." It
makes eminent sense, by contrast, to pose the question as to whether in
the Incarnation God was, or was made, something else, that is to say,
something other than God. Secondly, Latin is a heavily inflected language, whereas English has lost most of its inflections, hence indicating
differences in syntactic functions and semantic relations less through
modifications in the form of words than through their position within
the sentence. In our text, Peter Lombard raises a question that is related
to the convertibility of sentences. If it is true that *Deus factus est homo*,
that "God was made man," is it also true that *homo factus est Deus*, that
"man was made God"? In English, the converted form of the sentence
is less ambiguous than in Latin. This is because in Latin, *Deus* and *homo*
are in the nominative form in both sentences. Thus, *homo factus est Deus*
can be rendered both as "man was made God" and as "man [it is that]
God was made." This ambiguity is lost in the translation of *homo factus
est Deus* as "man was made God." The same remark holds good, *mutatis
mutandis*, for the case of *filius hominis factus est Filius Dei*, "the Son of
man was made the Son of God."

Such shades of meaning notwithstanding, the fundamental question
that Peter addresses in distinction 6 is clear: did God, in becoming man,
become other than Himself? The Lombard attempts to answer this question by means of the single most extended treatment of a particular point
in the entire *Book of Sentences*. In Brady's edition of the work, the treatise
on the "othering" of God in the hypostatic union occupies seventeen

pages. Its core is formed by a distinction of three different contemporary approaches to the union of the divine and human natures in the person of Christ, approaches whose authors, however, remain anonymous. Indeed, despite the detailed accounts that Peter provides, the three theories themselves are almost impossible to grasp in all their subtle qualifications and implications: "To present a clear exposition of the three famous theories of the Hypostatic Union recorded by Lombard is indeed extremely difficult," one commentator has admitted.[23] To complicate matters further, Peter's threefold distinction became the object of an influential contemporary commentary, John of Cornwall's treatise *Eulogium ad Alexandrum Papam tertium*, which was completed shortly before the Third Lateran Council in 1179. In the *Eulogium*, John of Cornwall adduced further authorities in support of each of the theories, identified some of their twelfth-century proponents, expressed his own preference, and urged Pope Alexander III to have the two approaches that he, John, considered heterodox condemned at the upcoming council.[24]

This is Peter Lombard's account of the first theory, which can be traced to Hugh of St. Victor's *De sacramentis christianae fidei*:

> **He relates the "sentence" of certain people.** Some people, in fact, say that in the Incarnation of the Word a certain human being was constituted from a rational soul and human flesh: out of which two every true human being is constituted. And that human being began to be God—not, however, the nature of God, but the person of the Word. . . . Not, however, by a migration of one nature into the other, but with the property of each of the natures being preserved did it come to pass that God was that substance, and that substance was God. . . . And although they say that that human being [that is, Christ] subsists from a rational soul and human flesh, nonetheless they do not confess that it is composed of two natures, divine and human; nor [do they confess] that the two natures are parts of that [human being], but only soul and flesh.[25]

The first theory, then, denies that a human and a divine nature were united in the person of Christ. Rather, it maintains that the specific property of human nature—namely, to be composed of a human body and a rational soul—was assumed into Christ, that is, into a divine person with a divine nature.

Now to the second *sententia* on the hypostatic union, which the *Eulogium* attributes to Gilbert de la Porrée. Peter Lombard summarizes it as follows:

> **The "sentence" of others.** There are, however, others as well, who agree partly with those [defenders of the first theory], but who say that that human being consists not only of a rational soul and of flesh, but of a human and of a divine nature, that is of three substances: divinity, flesh, and soul. This [human being] they confess to be Christ, and [they further confess] that He is only one person, who was simple only before the Incarnation, but in the Incarnation came to be composed of divinity and humanity.[26]

This second theory affords greater metaphysical consistency, one could say, to the human element in the person of Christ, which is no longer viewed as being present in Him only through its properties—body and soul—but through its very nature.

Finally, the third theory. John of Cornwall associates it with the name of Peter Abelard. As one might expect, the Abelardian position places even more emphasis upon the integrity of the human element in Christ, as well as upon the distinction between His humanity and divinity. The *Book of Sentences* characterizes the theory in the following terms:

> **A third "sentence" of others.** There are others, too, who deny not only that in the Incarnation of the Word a person was composed of natures, but also disavow that some true human being, or even some substance, was composed or made of soul and flesh here; but they say that these two—namely, soul and flesh—were united to the person or nature of the Word not in such a manner that from these two or from these three some substance or person was made or composed, but that the Word of God was clothed in these two as though in a garment so as to appear fittingly to the eyes of mortals.[27]

In other words, in the Incarnation God took on humanity not by wedding His nature to our nature, but by wearing human nature like a garment. While this *sententia* might appear to be the least likely candidate for orthodoxy among the three, there are strong authorities to corroborate it, most notably St. Paul's Letter to the Philippians: "But he emptied himself, taking the form of a servant, being made in the likeness of men, and in habit found as a man," *habitu inventus est ut homo* (Phil 2:7). In order to clarify this scriptural passage, Peter distinguishes four different senses of *habitus*, finding one that seems to elucidate the hypostatic union very well: Christ could be said to have assumed human nature like a garment that closely fits around someone's body, taking on and conforming itself to the shape of its wearer, without however losing its own identity. (Of course, the problem remains that the relationship between a body and a piece of clothing is entirely extrinsic.)

Ever since the days of John of Cornwall, there has been considerable debate on which of the three theories Peter Lombard himself advocated. John believed that the Lombard favored the third, Abelardian theory, albeit very tentatively. This opinion carries some weight, if only because John was one of Master Peter's own students. In a passage that we have already had an occasion to quote in chapter 2, the *Eulogium* attributes the *habitus* theory to the Lombard as a personal opinion, not an assertion claiming to represent the teaching of the Church: "Shortly before he was elected bishop of Paris, he declared to me and everyone attending his lecture that this was not his assertion but only an opinion, which he accepted from the masters. He also added these words: 'Never, God willing, will there be an assertion of mine unless it be [in correspondence with] the Catholic faith.' "[28]

From a reading of the *Sentences* themselves, it is not possible to determine with certainty which of the theories Peter preferred. Paul Glorieux has rightly adverted to the disproportionate amount of space that Peter accords to the second theory, which corresponds to the particularly careful treatment that he devotes to it. In fact, the text seems to hint gently at the privileged status of the second account: "The second *sententia* and its explanation have been laid out diligently. The authorities adduced in favor of the third *sententia* do not go against it at all, or [only] slightly."[29] Such vague gestures notwithstanding, the fact remains that the Lombard expressly refuses to decide. After weighing the pros and cons of each position, he once again humbly concludes that "**what has been said above does not suffice to understand this question.**"[30] He urges his readers to continue pondering the hypostatic union, and to do so in light of "other, perhaps better considerations and treatises."[31] A reaffirmation of the uncontroversial foundations of the Catholic faith in the Incarnation ends the discussion.

Christological Nihilianism

It is against the backcloth of the complex debates surrounding the hypostatic union that we now have to consider Peter Lombard's stance concerning Christological nihilianism. Book 3 of the *Sentences* takes up this issue in distinction 10.

"Is Christ, insofar as He is a human being, a person or [at least] something else [*aliquid*]?"[32] Peter concisely summarizes the arguments that must have led some contemporary theologians (including the same Master Roland Bandinelli who was later to become Pope Alexander III) to the seemingly ineluctable conclusion that Christ, qua human, was "nothing." For, if Christ (as man) is something (*aliquid*), He is either a person, a substance, or something else (*aliud*). But what else could Christ be, if not a person or a substance? Let us therefore assume that He is a substance. There are two kinds of substances: rational and irrational. Christ will hardly be an irrational substance, but rather a rational one. A rational substance, however, is precisely that in which Boethius understands a person to consist. Therefore, Christ, qua human, is a person. Now the argument continues. If Christ, insofar as He is man, is a person, this person is either going to be the third person of the Trinity or not. But Christ is a Trinitarian person. Therefore, if Christ qua human is the third person of the Trinity, Christ qua human is God. Qua human, however, Christ cannot also be divine. Hence, Christ, insofar as He is man, cannot be a person or even something else. He must therefore be nothing (*nec aliquid*).

Peter Lombard does not embrace this argument, identifying a twofold weakness in it. First, the argument suffers from a lack of precision with regard to the meaning of *secundum*, "insofar as" or "qua." "*Secundum*," Peter explains, "has a multiple meaning: for sometimes it expresses a condition or property of the divine or human nature, sometimes the unity of person; sometimes it indicates a *habitus*, sometimes a cause."[33] The implications of this statement for the validity of the nihilianist argument are not spelled out; perhaps Peter means that "Christ qua man" does not refer to Christ's human nature, but simply to the fact that Christ is one indivisible person, with a human nature that is capable of being conceived in various ways (as a *habitus*, for instance). Now if Christ qua man "has" a human nature (the *habitus* theory), as opposed to "being" human, the question concerning the constitution of that being (personal, substantial, or otherwise) would not arise. Secondly, if we concede that Christ qua man is a rational substance, it does not necessarily follow that He is also a person. According to a somewhat amusing etymology, the Lombard understands *persona* as *per se sonans*, "something that sounds through itself," that is to say, exists as a self-sufficient entity. Christ qua man, however, is not a self-sufficient entity, but an aspect of a self-sufficient entity. This, at least, is what I take this not entirely lucid passage to convey.

Peter cites another argument that could be advanced in support of Christological nihilianism, but refutes it as well, before moving on to other matters. Thus, an examination of the relevant texts in the *Sentences* must leave us puzzled as to why anyone would have accused Peter Lombard of nihilianism. Are the implications of his counterarguments not stated with sufficient clarity? Perhaps so, and of course we are not shown a viable alternative to Christological nihilianism, for all that distinction 10 accomplishes is a refutation of the arguments in its favor. We do not learn what Christ as man could be, positively. It is in a case such as this one that the drawbacks of the method of the sentence collection make themselves felt. The *Book of Sentences*, we have said, had the capacity to become such a success precisely because of its relative looseness as a work of systematic theology; the rich documentation and conceptual grid that it hands down to the tradition are not yet streamlined, as it were, in support of one rigorously argued theological "position." As a consequence, however, the *Sentences* frequently remain vague, which created room for misunderstandings.[34]

Furthermore, in the classroom, Peter Lombard seems to have experimented with views that he was hesitant to commit to paper, lest they cause scandal or be misconstrued by unsophisticated readers. He was thus following the contemporary principle *quedam tamen concedimus in legendo, que non concedimus in disserendo*, "we concede certain [positions] in lecturing that we do not concede in writing."[35] Just as John of Cornwall was under the impression that Master Peter entertained certain cautiously expressed sympathies for the *habitus* theory, so another student (possibly Peter Comestor) believed that the Master taught at least some version of Christological nihilianism:

When asked whether Christ, insofar as He is man, is something [*aliquid*], the Master . . . did not always deny this; in fact, he sometimes conceded it to external people. When he denied it, however, he spoke to safe ears, that is to say, to those whom he instructed. For he said that, although nouns of the neutral gender are usually taken to designate a nature, they are nonetheless very often taken to designate a person. For that reason, he conceded: "Christ, inasmuch as He is man, is something," that is, of a certain nature. He denied it, however, because "something" seems to be taken here to designate a person. For Christ, inasmuch as He is man, is not a person.[36]

According to his student, then, Peter Lombard taught future theologians that Christ, qua human, had better not be designated as *aliquid*, "something," for despite its neutral gender, the word *aliquid* might suggest that Christ, as man, was a person. Now Christ certainly was a person, but it would be wrong to call the human aspect of Christ a person. If, on the other hand, it is made clear that *aliquid* signifies a nature, then it is quite legitimate to consider Christ, qua man, as "something," namely, as possessing a certain nature.

In concluding this section on Christological nihilianism, I should stress that we have barely even scratched the surface of the complex debates in which Peter Lombard and the *Book of Sentences* were entangled—or indeed modern scholars' attempts to comprehend these debates. To cite only one example, there is disagreement as to whether the student's report just quoted really refers to Master Peter, or rather to some other contemporary master.[37] The degree of difficulty that is involved in understanding the hypostatic union comes as no surprise, however. With the question of how exactly to conceptualize the central tenet of the Christian faith— that God became man in Christ Jesus—we are indeed operating at the very limits of human intellection.

Related Christological Questions

After studying the Lombard's agonizingly hesitant metaphysics of the Incarnation, what a relief it is to turn to the next series of distinctions! They read as though Peter himself felt liberated from the weight of those unfathomable mysteries, for he now dispatches a series of questions quickly and unambiguously. "We respond," "it is evidently shown," "it can soundly be said"—these are the watchwords of the next few pages. Was Christ an adopted son of the Virgin (dist. 10, chap. 2)? No, any

form of adoptionism is incompatible with what we have already established concerning Christ's nature. Was Christ a creature, or can He be
considered to have been created or made (dist. 11)? Simply speaking,
Christ was not created, which is what the "perfidious" Arians have failed
to grasp. If, however, one is careful to specify that one is considering
Christ as man, it is permissible to speak of Him as a creature. Similarly,
Christ as man began to be, whereas the Word always was (dist. 12, chap.
1). Could God have assumed another human being than the historical
Jesus, even someone outside the race of Adam (dist. 12, chap. 2)? Yes,
certainly, and God could also have taken on the flesh of a woman, although "it came to pass more suitably and fittingly that He was born
from a female and took on a male, so that in this manner the liberation
of both sexes might be shown."[38] Distinctions 13 and 14 are devoted to
the wisdom, grace, and power that Christ possessed. Corresponding to
His two natures, we must distinguish a twofold wisdom in Christ,
namely, begotten and created. As Son of God, Christ Jesus was substantial
Wisdom: "He was wise in virtue of the begotten Wisdom that He is."[39]
As son of man, Christ was wise not substantially, but "according to his
soul,"[40] and possessed wisdom by the grace of the Holy Spirit. Concerning
the nature of this created, human wisdom, "it can soundly be said that
[Christ], as man, from his conception received such a fullness of wisdom
and grace that God could not have bestowed them upon him more
fully."[41] This answer is more subtle than might appear at first sight. Peter
does not maintain that the Father bestowed all His wisdom and grace
upon the man Jesus, but only so much wisdom and grace that He could
not possibly have given more. In other words, He gave precisely as much
as Jesus' human soul permitted. How much was that? Enough for Christ
to know just as much as the Father, albeit less "clearly and perspicu-
ously."[42] Lest he be misunderstood, Peter Lombard adds that God's own
wisdom remained "by far superior" (*multo dignior*) to that of Christ as
man[43]—no doubt because Christ's human soul placed limitations upon
the knowledge that he could receive through grace. Similarly, the human
Christ was not omnipotent because his nature as man would not have
been capable of such divine power.

I am not sure if it is fair to criticize the Lombard for his "quasi-
divinized view of Christ's human nature."[44] Even if Christ possessed a
fully human nature, the same person was also fully God. While the

distinction of His two natures is indeed necessary, we must not split the one person to whom these natures belonged. To be sure, Christ possessed a *gemina sapientia*, a twofold wisdom, divine and human, corresponding to His two natures. Yet Christ was not schizophrenic. I understand Peter's theory of Christ's human wisdom—which he takes to have the same breadth as the Father's, but not the same depth—as an attempt to minimize the distance between Christ's two wisdoms, precisely to avoid the impression that Christ's personality was less than unified: "And although there is a twofold wisdom in Christ, He is nonetheless one and the same person."[45]

Soteriology

Christ's actions reflect His human nature even more clearly than His being and attributes do. The next group of distinctions, 15 through 22, is centered upon Christ's saving work, its preconditions, essence, and modalities. The *Book of Sentences* first analyzes the human defects and weaknesses that Christ assumed, which were integral to His saving work. It distinguishes between passibility of the flesh and of the soul. Hunger and thirst fall into the first category, whereas sadness, fear, and pain are aspects of the soul insofar as it is subject to suffering.[46] In this context, Peter reiterates his previous discrimination between guilt and punishment. Christ assumed only those defects of human nature that came to affect it as a punishment for sin; by contrast, as He was not guilty of any sin, He was evidently free from the effects of guilt. Moreover, Christ was not subject to ignorance and weakness of the will, although these are integral parts of the human condition. What Peter Lombard is arguing, really, is that Christ assumed the defects of human nature to the extent that His mission required it. In distinction 15, he summarizes his position:

> Christ, then, took upon Himself all our defects except sin which it was fitting for Him and useful for us to take upon Himself. For there are several kinds of sickness and [several] imperfections of the body from which He was entirely free. Those defects that He did have, He took upon Himself either in order to show His true humanity (such as fear and sadness), or in order to complete the work for which He had come

(such as His capacity to suffer and His mortality), or in order to build up our hope from the state of desperation in regard to immortality (such as death).[47]

Further specifying the kind of afflictions to which Christ submitted Himself for our salvation, the *Sentences* emphasize the reality of His pain and fear, thus repudiating an argument according to which He underwent a mere similitude of suffering. Yet Christ did not experience exactly the same fear and sadness as ordinary human beings. It is necessary to introduce a distinction here between "passion" and "propassion." The emotional upheaval caused by fear and sadness can be so intense as to destroy the rectitude of the sufferer's will and turn him away from God. Not so in the case of propassion, which does not throw the soul into disorder. Thus, Christ Jesus did experience genuine fear and sadness, but in the mode of propassion.[48] Another difference between Christ's suffering and that of ordinary mortals consists in the fact that the former accepted the passibility of his body and soul freely, for our salvation, whereas we ordinary human beings are subject to physical and moral suffering as a necessary and inevitable consequence of the human condition.

Thus, Jesus' actions are indeed intelligible only as a result of His twofold nature as both Son of God and son of man. His will provides another example of how these two natures shaped His life. Matthew 26:39 reports Jesus as praying that He may be spared the suffering of the cross: "My Father, if it be possible, let this chalice pass from me. Nevertheless not as I will, but as thou wilt." In this scriptural text Peter Lombard discerns the presence of two distinct wills, divine and human. Christ, the Son of God, acted and prayed according to the divine will, but Christ, the son of man, felt the stirrings of the will as an affect (*affectus*) of the sensuality of the body, which did not want to die (although Christ's human will, qua affect of reason, did consent to the passion). Not that there was any tension in Christ between His divine and His human wills, for it was God's own will that Christ Jesus "should experience the truth of humanity within Him."[49]

In distinction 18, the *Sentences* embark upon the discussion of what exactly Christ accomplished through the passion. Peter states the following initial solution, upon which distinctions 18 and 19 elaborate:

Whether Christ earned [anything] for Himself and for us, and what [He earned] for Himself and for us. We must also not pass over

Christ's merit, of which some are accustomed to say that He earned nothing for Himself, but only for His members.

On the one hand, He earned for His members redemption from the devil, from sin, [and] from punishment, as well as the unlocking of the kingdom, so that, with the flaming sword [see Gn 3:24] removed, the entrance might be free without let. On the other hand, He also earned for Himself the glory of impassibility and immortality, as the Apostle says: "He humbled himself, becoming obedient unto death, even to the death of the cross. For which cause God also hath exalted him, and hath given him a name which is above all names" [Phil 2:8–9]. The Apostle plainly says that Christ was exalted by the glory of impassibility because He was humbled by the obedience of His passion. Thus, the humility of His passion was the merit that earned Him exaltation, and His exaltation was the reward for His humility.[50]

The passion, we learn from this text, earned Christ Jesus immortality and immunity from suffering in the hereafter; moreover, Christ qua human was given "a name above all names," which means that he was divinized. And we, Christ's members, were redeemed from the devil, as well as from sin and the punishment consequent upon it.

In distinction 13, Peter Lombard affirmed "that [Christ], as man, from his conception received such a fullness of wisdom and grace that God could not have bestowed them upon him more fully." It follows, then, that Christ could not grow in grace, which also means that the merits of the passion could not increase it. Peter is therefore thinking quite logically when he states, in chapter 2 of distinction 18, "Christ earned these [impassibility, etc.] not only when he, obeying the Father, submitted to the cross, but also from his very conception."[51] Marcia Colish brings out the meaning of this paradoxical position aptly when she comments that, according to the Lombard, "the passion of Christ was not, for Him, a critical event in His relationship with God the Father. The passion simply afforded Him another opportunity to display the perfect obedience that He had always possessed."[52]

"The passion of Christ was not, for Him, a critical event in His relationship with God the Father"—not for Him, but for us it was. Following the schema laid out at the beginning of distinction 18, Peter Lombard goes on to explain the significance of the passion for the redemption of humankind. It is fascinating to note, in this context, a modification in Peter's style, which, in its Scholastic flatness, is not ordinarily of great literary appeal. But suddenly, Peter's tone becomes warm and personal, as though the master had temporarily ceded his voice to the pastor. The following excerpt from the *Sentences* almost sounds like part of a homily:

> **On the cause of the death and passion of Christ.** For what [end], then, did He wish to suffer and die, if His virtues were sufficient for Him to earn these [graces]? For you, not for Him. How for me? So that His passion and death might be a form and cause for you: the form of virtue and humility, and the cause for your liberation and beatitude. For through His endurance of death and of the passion He earned for us what He could not have earned by what preceded [them], namely, access to paradise and redemption from sin, from punishment, [and] from the devil. And by His death we have been granted these, namely, redemption and adoption as sons of glory. For in dying, He was made the sacrifice [*hostia*] of our liberation.[53]

Peter Lombard's theory of the redemption combines a subjective and an objective component. On the one hand, the example of Christ's virtue and humility effects a change of heart in us, a turning away from sin that enables us to receive the grace of salvation. Expanding upon this idea, the Lombard explains that the charity which God manifested toward us, in giving up His Son for our sins, in turn arouses in our hearts the charity that saves.[54] Again, in somewhat different terms, which reflect the different traditions of soteriology flowing together in the *Book of Sentences*, "if . . . we look to Him who hung on a tree for us [see Gal 3: 13] with the look of right faith, we are delivered from the chains of the devil, that is, from [our] sins."[55] On the other hand, Christ's consummate humility in accepting death was the sacrifice that reconciled humanity with God, who had been offended by Adam's pride and transgression. This is the objective side of the Lombard's theory of salvation: due to original sin, in which we took something from God that belonged to Him (namely, our obedience), we are indebted to God, so that a sacrifice proportionate to our debt had to be made for us to be reconciled with Him.[56] There is even an echo of the old "rights of the devil" theory in the *Sentences*, for instance in the following quotation derived from the *Glossa ordinaria*: "For if it had not been man who defeated the devil, man—who freely subjected himself to him—would have seemed to be taken away from him not justly, but violently; but if man defeats him, he loses man with manifest justice. And so that man may win, it is necessary that God be in him, who renders him immune from sins."[57] Through Adam's transgression, man fell under the rule of the devil. In order to liberate himself, he had to overcome the devil's power, which resides in sin. Only the God-man, however, could accomplish the devil's ultimate defeat.

Even from our brief summary of the Lombard's soteriology, it is evident that the *Sentences* do not provide a rigorous synthesis of the heterogeneous elements which they inherited from the tradition.[58] But that is not to say that the soteriology of the *Sentences* is incoherent. In fact, the subjective and the objective aspects of the Lombard's theory of salvation represent the corollary of an account of original sin that takes seriously both the role of the devil in tempting Eve and the humans' inner assent to that external temptation.

Charity and the Virtues

According to Peter Lombard's soteriology, virtue plays a crucial role in our salvation. It is in emulating Christ's perfect humility that we render ourselves fit for salvation; it is in attempting to reciprocate God's charity that our hearts are raised to the love of God and neighbor that saves; and it is faith in the efficacy of Christ's death on the cross that tears us away from the sins standing in the way of virtue. The treatise on virtue, therefore, constitutes a logical extension of the *Sentences'* Christology and soteriology. Since Christ is the exemplar of virtue, Peter Lombard's treatment begins with the question of "**whether Christ had faith and hope just as [He had] charity.**"[59] The formulation suggests that Peter's reflections are guided by the belief that the theological virtues, and perhaps all virtues, form a close unity. But it also hints at the fact that charity and the virtues might not be situated at quite the same level.

The foundation of the moral life of the Christian is not virtue, really, but rather the person of Christ Himself—Christ who literally embodies God's love, which human beings are invited to return: "The foundation is Christ Jesus, that is to say, Christ's faith, namely, [the faith] 'that worketh by charity' [Gal 5:6], through which Christ dwells in [our] hearts."[60] "He had charity in His heart that He showed us through His work, so that, by means of the form in which He showed it, He might teach us to love."[61] In the Incarnation, God implanted His love in humanity, in order to allow us to participate in the return to Him of His Son, if only we recognize Christ for what He is and cling to Him with all our hearts. This recognition, this faith, is facilitated by Christ's works, which reveal His love to us; our love, in turn, will give rise to similar works of virtue in order to make itself known and to disseminate God's love further in space and time. Naturally, then, "charity is the cause and mother of all the virtues. **(Augustine, on John:)*** 'If it is absent, the others are possessed in vain; but if it is present, all are possessed.' For charity is the Holy Spirit, as has been argued in the preceding [parts of the work]."[62]

The dynamism of God's love and humanity's loving response to that love is the breath of the Holy Spirit. Again, both God's charity and man's charity express themselves in works or virtues, although these virtues are not of the same order in the two cases, for Christ's perfect virtues serve as the exemplars of our finite efforts. The virtues fall into four categories, which Peter treats one by one in distinctions 23–36 of book 3: the theological virtues of faith and hope (dist. 23–26), the cardinal virtues of prudence, justice, fortitude, and temperance (dist. 33), and the seven gifts of the Holy Spirit (wisdom, understanding, counsel, fortitude, knowledge, piety, and fear of God), which are considered virtues as well (dist. 34–35). A detailed treatise on charity is inserted between the theological and the cardinal virtues, in distinctions 27–32. At the end of book 3, the *Sentences* devote distinctions 37 through 40 to the Ten Commandments, which are to be understood as precepts urging love of God and neighbor.[63] The *Sentences'* teachings on virtue could be summarized as in figure 4.

Not only can the virtues not exist without charity, but they also come into existence together with it. In other words, Peter Lombard does not believe that it is possible to be filled with genuine charity and nonetheless lack any of the virtues: "Since charity is the mother of all the virtues, in whomsoever that mother exists, all her sons are rightly believed to exist as well."[64] Furthermore, the bond between charity and the virtues, and among the latter, is so close that a virtuous individual necessarily possesses all of them to the same degree, at least *in habitu*: thus, a virtuous person cannot be more faithful than prudent, or more courageous than wise. Admittedly, however, the possession (*habitus*) of a virtue is not always manifested in a person's exterior acts. Peter cites the case of a just man who, by engaging in the marital act, necessarily fails to be continent.

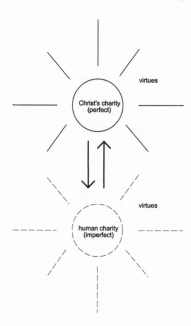

FIG. 4. Charity and virtues

Peter insists: "he does not have continence in act, which he nonetheless has *in habitu*."[65] In the final analysis, then, the author of the *Sentences* reduces all the virtues to charity.[66] Charity, however, is not a virtue, properly speaking. It is the Holy Spirit itself. Peter Lombard is very consistent in this teaching of his. Although he treats charity in the distinctions that are devoted to the theological virtues, he never calls it a virtue, not once.

The ethics of the *Book of Sentences* is a Christocentric ethics of love. Such an ethics naturally gives relatively short shrift to the law; neither does it spend much time on a careful distinction among theological virtues, cardinal virtues, and gifts of the Holy Spirit. They are all part of the same dynamism of charity. In the century after Peter Lombard, when Aristotle's ethics was rediscovered, Christian thinkers would emphasize the difference between cardinal and theological virtues, the former being defined as attainable through man's natural powers, without the gift of charity.[67] Prudence, justice, fortitude, and temperance (Aquinas would argue) are moral virtues that can be exercised locally, as it were, with regard to specific and limited objects independent of man's ultimate end, God.[68] By the same token, the gifts of the Spirit were demarcated from the theological virtues, as adding a supernatural degree of perfection to the latter. As an example, Aquinas cites the difference between the theological virtue of faith and the gift of understanding (*intellectus*): where faith in God remains dependent upon analogies and similitudes between the Creator and creation, understanding gives a foretaste of the future vision promised to man.[69] Logically, as the specificity of the virtues and gifts was thrown into relief, the distinctness of charity was underscored as well. In this process, charity was redefined as a virtue. In his commentary on the *Sentences*, Aquinas thus writes that *caritas est specialis virtus ab omnibus aliis distincta*, "charity is a special virtue, distinct from all the others."[70]

There is loss and gain in such differentiation. The gain no doubt consists in the ability to distinguish purely natural aspects of man's moral life from the moral perfection envisaged and encouraged by the Christian faith, and to appreciate both for what they are. Marcia Colish is right in pointing out that an ethics of the Lombardian type has little to say about the question of the virtuous pagan.[71] The loss is above all a spiritual one. The old ethics of love and imitation of Christ is overshadowed by a multiplicity of details, at the expense of simplicity and beauty.

But we must continue our analysis of the *Book of Sentences*. According to Peter Lombard, the human virtues are imperfect by comparison with Christ's because their root, charity, is but imperfectly realized in the human realm. Scripture enjoins us to love God with all our heart, all our soul, and all our mind. "This precept, however, cannot be fulfilled completely by man in this mortal life, but [only] in part; not totally, because we love in part, just as 'we know in part' [1 Cor 13:9]; in the future, however, it will be fulfilled totally."[72] The total love of God requires an emptying out and recentering of self that are not possible in this life. Only Christ fully achieved them, which is why He is our model. Paradoxically, Christ's perfect charity entails that the theological virtues— faith and hope—are canceled out in Him. If "faith is the virtue by which one believes what one does not see,"[73] and if hope consists in the "certain expectation of future beatitude,"[74] then Christ simply had no need for these virtues. Thanks to His divine nature, Christ knew what He believed and hoped for, namely, His resurrection. In this context, Peter

Lombard does not distinguish between Christ's human and divine natures. The cases of the saints and of the angels are similar.[75] In the presence of God, where love is at its most ardent, faith and hope disappear,
having become pointless. There is, therefore, no place for them in the
hereafter, in which, together with charity, the cardinal virtues and gifts
of the Holy Spirit will reach perfection.[76]

For an understanding of Peter Lombard's theological system, it is not
necessary to dwell upon his treatment of the Ten Commandments in
distinctions 37 to 40. As already indicated, he interprets the commandments as precepts meant to specify the modalities of charity in this life.
The first three commandments instruct us on the requirements of loving
God, while the last seven detail what (not) to do in loving our neighbor.
The only commandment that the *Sentences* examine in depth is the
eighth, which prohibits the bearing of false witness or lying (dist. 38).
This discussion is complemented by an entire distinction devoted to per-
jury (dist. 39), an emphasis explained by the fact that the feudal order of
medieval society was based upon the oath.

It is obvious that the commandments must stand at the periphery of
the Lombard's ethics of charity. In their predominantly negative mode,
they do nothing more than to indicate the "other" of charity, as it were,
its outside, the spaces of human conduct where it has broken down.

THE *SENTENCES*, BOOK IV, DISTINCTIONS 1–42

On the Doctrine of Signs

Christology and the theology of the sacraments are closely related, since the sacraments owe their salvific force directly to Christ's exemplary virtue and charity. The sacraments, Peter Lombard writes, were not given to us before the coming of Christ because they "are drawn from the power of His death and passion."[1] This connection is perhaps clearest in the case of the water of baptism and the wine of the Eucharist, which signify the water and blood that came from Jesus' side when one of the soldiers present at the Crucifixion pierced it with his spear (see Jn 19: 34).[2] Sacraments, then, are signs of God, of His charity, and of His determination to save us through His grace. The conception of sacraments as signs appropriately places them in the final part of the Lombard's theological system, governed as that is by the Augustinian distinction between things and signs. In the opening sentence of book 4, Peter reminds us of the structure of his work: "Having treated of those matters which pertain to the doctrine of things that are to be enjoyed [i.e., the Trinity], that are to be used [creation in general], and that are to be used and enjoyed [man, the angels, the virtues, and even Christ], we approach the doctrine of signs."[3]

Yet sacraments are more than signs of grace. In addition to signifying grace, they actively bestow it upon humanity, thus being sanctifying as well. This is why, in giving us the sacraments, God can be likened to the Good Samaritan binding the wounds of the wayfarer who had fallen prey to the robbers—a parable that, we may remember, the *Sentences* invoked earlier in book 2 in order to illustrate the effects of sin.[4] The sacraments, then, heal the wounds inflicted upon humanity by both original sin and actual sin.[5]

The Sacraments: Definition and General Questions

Peter Lombard summarizes his understanding of the sacraments in the following definition, which was to become classic:

> **Quid proprie dicitur sacramentum.** Sacramentum enim proprie dicitur, quod ita signum est gratiae Dei et invisibilis gratiae forma, ut ipsius imaginem gerat et causa exsistat. Non igitur significandi tantum gratia sacramenta instituta sunt, sed et sanctificandi.

> **What is properly called "sacrament."** We therefore properly call "sacrament" that which is a sign of the grace of God and the form of invisible grace, in such a way as to carry its image and to be its cause. Therefore, the sacraments were instituted not only for the sake of signifying, but of sanctifying as well.[6]

In this context, the word *form* simply means "visible appearance"; it should not be construed in the Aristotelian sense that it acquired in the century after Peter Lombard.[7]

God could, of course, have bestowed His grace upon us without the sacraments. This truth leads Peter Lombard to the question as to why the sacraments were instituted. In his answer he discerns three reasons. First, God uses the sacraments to humble us, for they make us seek our salvation through elements of creation that are naturally inferior to us, such as water and wine. Secondly, the sacraments are meant to instruct us, so that we may learn how to penetrate mentally through the outer appearance of things to their inner power, and ultimately to God Himself. Thirdly and finally, the sacraments provide salubrious exercise for us, thus preventing us from engaging in the kinds of vain and noxious activities that so easily give rise to temptation.

Each sacrament is composed of two elements: "words" (*verba*) and a "thing" (*res*). For example, the dispensation of a sacrament may involve the invocation of the Trinity, while sacraments may be administered through "things" such as water or oil. What distinguishes a New Testament sacrament (baptism, for example) from a sacrament of the old dispensation (circumcision, say)? This question constituted an important issue in Peter Lombard's day, when fellow theologians such as Hugh of St. Victor worked with an extremely broad notion of sacrament. Hugh, in fact, considered as a sacrament "anything manifesting God to man and anything helpful in man's restoration."[8] Conversely, Hugh employed the mystifying term *sacramenta diaboli*, or "sacraments of the devil," to designate obstacles to salvation. Along similar lines, some contemporaries spoke of the Incarnation itself as a sacrament, employing expressions like *sacramentum incarnationis* or *deitatis*.[9] Peter Lombard, however, will have none of this. From the beginning of book 4, he sets out to render the term more precise, discreetly but decidedly. As far as the "sacrament of the Godhead" (*sacramentum deitatis*) is concerned, he excludes it from consideration since it is not a sacred sign but the signified Godhead Himself.[10] Regarding the so-called sacraments of the Old Testament, some were simply signs of divine grace, not possessing any efficacy to justify. Sacrifices, offerings, and ceremonial observances belong to this category. The practice of circumcision presents a more complicated case, since important authorities—the *Sentences* cite Augustine and Bede—believed it to be an efficacious remedy for sin, similar in function to baptism. Peter is ready to concede this point, but at the same time he emphasizes that there remains a crucial difference between circumcision and baptism: though the former was efficacious in the remission of sin, it did not confer any additional grace, nor did it augment the virtues. On the other hand, Marcia Colish goes too far in claiming that Peter Lombard regards circumcision as plainly "superfluous."[11] He admits, after all, that the unfortunate children who died before being circumcised in accordance with the Law could not but be lost.[12]

The New Testament knows seven sacraments: baptism, confirmation, the Eucharist, penance, unction of the sick, ordination, and marriage. The *Sentences* treat the sacraments in this order, beginning with baptism in distinctions 2 through 6, then moving on to confirmation (dist. 7), the Eucharist (dist. 8–13), penance (dist. 14–22), unction (dist. 23), ordination (dist. 24–25), and ending with a long discussion of marriage (dist. 26–42).[13] Peter remarks that certain sacraments (he mentions baptism) rem-

edy sin and confer assisting grace; others (marriage is his example) function merely as a remedy for sin; while a last group of sacraments (such
as the Eucharist and ordination) strengthens us through grace and virtue.[14] In the final distinctions of book 4, at the very end of the *Sentences*
(dist. 43–50), we find the Lombard's treatise on Last Things—appropriately so, since they complete the cycle of human life. We will treat the
eschatological distinctions in the following chapter.

Baptism

Because the sacraments derive all their power from Christ, Peter begins
his discussion of baptism by stating, in distinction 2, that the baptism
administered by St. John was of a purely preparatory nature. It was a
sacrament only in the limited sense in which other pre-Christian rites
can be considered such. Its function was to call those baptized to penance,
for the ablution of the body in which the baptism of St. John consisted
remained outward in its significance, not being capable of remitting sin.

Turning in distinction 3 to the sacrament of baptism properly speaking, Peter offers the following definition: "We call 'baptism' the bathing,
that is, the exterior ablution of the body, performed under the prescribed
form of words."[15] As in all the sacraments, the combination of the
"thing"—in this case, water—with the appropriate words is crucial.
"Take away the word," the Lombard writes, using a quotation from
Augustine, "and what is water but water?"[16] On the other hand, the
appropriate thing together with the right words suffices for the validity
of each sacrament; further ceremonial provisions may enhance its dignity,
but do not belong to its substance.

Following Matthew 28:19, the Church baptizes in the name of the
Trinity: "Going therefore, teach ye all nations; baptizing them in the
name of the Father, and of the Son, and of the Holy Ghost." It is true
that the apostles used to baptize in the name of Christ alone, as Acts
reports happened on several occasions (see Acts 2:38, 8:12, and 19:5);
however, Peter decides that the entire Trinity is implicitly understood in
the name of Jesus. Similarly, as long as the person who conducts the
baptism has the intention to baptize and believes that he is doing so,
other forms are valid as well, such as baptisms in the name of the Father
alone or of the Spirit alone. A baptism "in the names" (*in nominibus*) of

the Trinitarian persons, however, would not be valid, straying too far from the prescribed form of the sacrament. Thus, it is safer to use the formula transmitted in the Gospel according to Matthew.

With regard to the matter, or thing, of baptism, the Lombard decides it is water that has to be used, and not any other liquid. Indeed, water is particularly appropriate for several reasons. Jesus himself said, "Unless a man be born again of water and the Holy Ghost, he cannot enter into the kingdom of God" (Jn 3:5). Furthermore—as we already know—the water of baptism symbolizes the water that came from Christ's side at the Crucifixion. Again, water is especially suitable because, just as in everyday life it serves to cleanse the body, so in baptism water signifies the cleansing of the soul from sin. And finally, water has the advantage of being universally available to all mankind, unlike wine or oil. It is inconsequential, however, whether the individual being baptized is immersed once or thrice—unless the baptizer, by performing the immersion only once, does so in disregard of the customs of the local Church or in order to affirm that the single immersion constitutes the only acceptable practice.

The sacrament was instituted at the time when St. John baptized Christ in the river Jordan. The reason Peter Lombard cites to support this position reminds us of the direct dependence of the sacraments upon the power of Christ: "It is more appropriately said, therefore, that the institution occurred when Christ was baptized by John in the Jordan— which He arranged not because He wished to be cleansed (for He was without sin), but because through the contact with His clean flesh He conferred upon the waters His regenerative power, so that someone who would subsequently be immersed while the name of the Trinity was being invoked might be purged from his sins."[17] Baptism was instituted, then, to give man a fresh start, allowing him to leave behind his old sinful self and equipping him with the virtues necessary so that he may "walk in the newness of life" (Rom 6:4).

Distinction 4 analyzes the problem of the relationship between the sacrament of baptism and its "thing" (res)—the meaning of the latter having shifted since Peter Lombard first employed the word to designate the external matter of the sacraments, such as water or oil.[18] Res now signifies the effects of the sacrament or, one could perhaps say, its content and power: "And this is the res of this sacrament, namely, interior cleansing. . . . Thus, the res of this sacrament is justification."[19] Some people receive both the sacrament and its *res;* some only the *res* without the sacrament; still others may receive the sacrament, but remain excluded from its salvific power. The standard case is that of children who are baptized and of faithful adults who receive baptism; in this case, sacrament and *res* go hand in hand. If, however, an adult is dishonest in receiving baptism, lacking true faith and genuine penance, the sacrament remains inefficacious and empty, as it were, not remitting the person's sins or conferring grace. This position makes sense, in that the sacraments are meant as assisting us in our limited efforts to emulate Christ's perfect virtue and charity—in the absence of such efforts, however, there is nothing to assist. It is logical, as well, to assume with Peter Lombard that martyrs, who have died for their faith and thus reenacted Christ's own passion, enjoy the justification that comes with baptism, even if they were never actually baptized. Yet Peter Lombard goes even further. Simple faith and contrition are able to justify people who honor the sacrament of baptism, but for some reason do not have access to it. Again, it is worth emphasizing that the sacraments do not work magic, but bestow the grace that is necessary for those striving to lead a Christlike life in order for them to reach their goal.

Distinctions 5 and 6 are devoted to questions at the intersection of theology and canon law. Who has the power to baptize? Is it legitimate to baptize a child in its mother's womb? What about the case of a priest so ignorant of Latin that he baptized people *in nomine Patria et Filia et Spiritu Sancta*—that is to say, using garbled and meaningless Latin ("in the name Fatherland and Daughter and through the Spirit Holy")? We need not examine these questions here. Not that they are insignificant; far from it. They demonstrate systematic theology in action, as it were. They show how the sacraments, in continuing and keeping present the charity that God extended to humanity in the Incarnation, penetrate right into the complicated details of everyday life.

Confirmation

The treatment of confirmation in the *Book of Sentences* is very brief, just over three pages in Brady's edition. The form of the sacrament poses no problems; it consists in the words that the bishop speaks as he marks the forehead of the confirmand with holy chrism. Curiously, the Lombard does not mention what these words are. On the subject of the power of confirmation, he is more precise: if in baptism the Holy Spirit is given for the remission of sins, the donation of the Spirit in confirmation conveys additional strength and virtue in the form of the seven gifts.[20] The custom according to which only the highest priests—that is, bishops—have the authority to confirm goes back to apostolic times, Peter Lombard relates, quoting a (spurious) letter by St. Eusebius, who was pope in the early fourth century. Confirmation is superior to baptism, because it is dispensed by superior priests, or perhaps because it is administered to a superior part of the body, namely, the forehead. Put differently, confirmation stands out in the augmentation of the virtues that it brings about, although baptism is of greater value for the remission of sins.[21] Just like baptism, confirmation must be administered by and to people who are fasting. It cannot be repeated.

All in all, the *Sentences'* treatment of confirmation is disappointingly thin. In the mid-twelfth century, confirmation was not a matter of much debate.[22]

The Eucharist

As the memorial, representation, and indeed sacramental reenactment of Christ's perfect sacrifice,[23] the Eucharist constitutes, in Peter Lombard's own words, "the fount and origin of all grace."[24] The sacrament of the altar is therefore the center and culmination of the sacramental life of the Christian, as the opening of distinction 8 affirms:

> **On the sacrament of the altar.** After the sacrament[s] of baptism and of confirmation, there follows the sacrament of the Eucharist. By baptism we are cleansed; by the Eucharist we are perfected in the good. Baptism extinguishes the fire of the vices; the Eucharist restores [us] spiritually. This is why it is excellently called "Eucharist," that is, good grace, because in this sacrament there is not only an increase of virtue and grace [as in confirmation], but He who is the fount and origin of all grace, is received entire.[25]

The philosophico-theological questions that the Eucharist raises are analogous to those we confronted in the case of the Incarnation. If God became man in Christ two thousand years ago, the bread and wine of the Eucharistic celebration become Christ's body and blood every day, thus allowing the believer to encounter the Savior in the course of his or her own life. To be sure, bread and wine lose their substance in this process, which means that the problem of the unity of two natures, divine and created, does not pose itself in quite the same terms as in the Incarnation. Or rather, the problem is now not one of the unity of two natures, but of the possibility of Christ's body and blood assuming the form of bread and wine.

After the opening remarks which we have quoted, the *Sentences* point out that the sacrament of the altar, just like baptism, is prefigured in the Old Testament in three ways. First, the Eucharist is a viaticum similar to the manna that the Israelites received after crossing the waters of the Red Sea (see Ex 16:4). The manna from heaven helped the children of Israel reach the promised land after their liberation from the Egyptians (who were submerged in the waters); analogously, the bread of the Eucharist helps us reach the Fatherland after the waters of baptism have liberated us by washing away our sins. Secondly, the blood of the paschal lamb that saved the Israelites as God killed all the firstborn of Egypt (see Ex 12:13) foreshadows the blood which flowed from Christ's side after His death, and which is symbolized by the Eucharistic wine. Thirdly and finally, the Eucharistic rite has a parallel in Melchisedech's offering of bread and wine to Moses in Genesis 14:18.

The Lombard now turns to the institution of the Eucharist, which occurred at the Last Supper, "when, after the manner of the lamb, [the Lord] offered the disciples His body and blood at supper."[26] Although the Church now requires us to show our reverence by fasting before we receive the Eucharist, Christ gave his body and blood to His disciples after the Passover meal. He did so "in order to show that the sacraments of the Old Law, among which the sacrifice of the paschal lamb was paramount, were terminated at His death, and the sacraments of the New Law were substituted, among which the mystery of the Eucharist is chief."[27] Thus, the institution of the Eucharist after the paschal meal was what we might call a gesture of sublation. The form of the sacrament of the Eucharist is taken from the very words Jesus spoke at the Last Supper: "This is my body" (Mt 26:26) and "this is my blood" (Mt 26:28). "For when those words are spoken, the conversion [*conversio*] of the bread and wine into the substance of the body and blood of Christ occurs; all the rest is said for the praise of God."[28] What Peter Lombard means is

that "this is my body" and "this is my blood" constitute the essential core
of the Eucharistic prayer; its other elements are useful for the purposes
of worship, without belonging to the heart of the sacrament.

Turning to the *res* of the sacrament of the altar (that is to say, its
content or power), the Lombard draws a twofold distinction:

> **On the "thing" of the sacrament, which is twofold.** Now the "thing"
> of this sacrament is twofold: namely, one that is contained and signi-
> fied, and another that is signified and not contained. The "thing" that
> is contained and signified is the flesh of Christ that He received from
> the Virgin, and the blood that He shed for us.—**Augustine, On John*:**
> The "thing" that is signified and not contained, on the other hand, is
> "the unity of the Church in those who are predestined, called, justified,
> and glorified." This is the double flesh of Christ.[29]

According to this text, the sacrament of the Eucharist unifies its recipients
with the body of Christ in a twofold sense, individual and ecclesial. In
the Eucharist, the faithful receive the body of Christ, the historical individual, and the body of Christ insofar as it is the mystical body of the
Church. The *Sentences* immediately restate this point in terms of the
relationship between the sacrament and its *res*:

> **On the three [elements] that can be distinguished here.** For there are
> three [elements] here that should be distinguished: one, which is the
> sacrament alone; a second, which is the sacrament and the "thing";
> and a third, which is the "thing" and not the sacrament. The sacrament
> and not the "thing" is the visible appearance [*species visibilis*] of the
> bread and wine; the sacrament and the "thing" [are] Christ's proper
> flesh and blood [*caro Christi propria et sanguis*]; the "thing" and not the
> sacrament [is] His mystical flesh [*mystica eius caro*].[30]

This last text envisages the relationship between the sacrament and its
res in terms of increasing spiritual power. The sacrament, pure and simple, consists in the appearance of ordinary bread and wine; the sacrament
considered at its first level of spiritual power contains Christ's "proper"
or real flesh and blood; and the sacrament taken at its most "mystical"
or spiritual level brings unity with the body of Christ that is the Church
herself.[31]

In accordance with Peter's general definition of sacrament, he must
show in what way the sacrament of the altar bears the image of the
graces that it confers. This image is, not unexpectedly, twofold. Just as

ordinary bread stands out among other food in restoring and sustaining the human body, so the body of Christ, more than any other gift of grace, restores and satiates the inner man. Insofar as the resemblance between the sacrament and its mystical *res* is concerned, the *Sentences* draw attention to the analogy that obtains between, on the one hand, the multitude of grains from which one loaf of bread is prepared and the large number of grapes that are necessary to make wine and, on the other hand, the unification of countless faithful individuals in the Church.

Another corollary of the fact that two "things" are conveyed in the sacrament of the altar consists in a corresponding duality in the reception of the Eucharist. Only those, in fact, who are "good," remaining in Christ in their moral conduct, receive His mystical body; or, as Peter Lombard puts it, only the good eat Him spiritually (*spiritualiter*).[32] Wicked people, by contrast, exclude themselves from the body of the Church by their behavior. As a consequence, they receive the body of Christ in a merely sacramental mode (*sacramentaliter*), which—Peter hastens to add—does not mean that in the case of the wicked, the Eucharist does not contain the real body of the Lord, the first *res* of the sacrament. Only people "enveloped in the darkness of error" could hold such an opinion.[33] Thus, although the Lombard acknowledges that the subjective disposition of its recipients plays a role in the celebration of the Eucharist, the *Sentences* strongly emphasize the objectivity of the sacramental presence of Christ's real body, the *caro Christi propria* from our earlier quotation. By the same token, the moral disposition and even orthodoxy of the celebrant is immaterial for the validity of the sacrament, as long as the priest is not cut off from the Church (through heresy or excommunication). In the latter case, he can no longer truthfully speak the words of the consecration "We offer"—we, the *persona Ecclesiae*, that is to say, the person of the Church as the mystical body of Christ.[34] Peter Lombard's theory of the sacrament of the Eucharist and its twofold *res* is summarized in figure 5.

Contemporary masters examined many other questions concerning the *res* of the Eucharist, some very Scholastic and subtle—yet all born out of a genuine concern to safeguard the dignity of the sacrament. In this context, there belongs the famous, bizarre, but at the same time real problem as to whether a mouse would partake in the real body of Christ if perchance it managed to snatch a crumb of the sacrament that had inadvertently been dropped from the altar. Artur Landgraf discovered

FIG. 5. The elements of the Eucharist and their relationship

five different types of solution to this much-debated issue in the theology of the twelfth century.[35] Peter Lombard, however, dispatches the mouse problem quickly: "What does the mouse receive? What does it eat? God knows."[36] Perhaps he regarded *Quid sumit mus?* as an example of the kind of theological curiosity that we have seen him treat with disdain on other occasions.

The Lombard's doctrine on the relationship between sacrament and *res* in the Eucharist has been the object of some lively theological debates—but not so much in the twelfth century as in the twentieth. In an article published in 1963, Ludwig Hödl, a well-known German historian of medieval theology, broke into exclamatory sentences of praise in describing the Lombard's achievement: "In Peter Lombard's version, the ternary theory of the Eucharist is characterized by a formal harmony and perspicuity that can hardly be surpassed. A polished element of the Scholastic doctrine of the sacraments! A tour de force of Scholastic, methodical thought!"[37]

In stark contrast to this laudatory assessment, Peter Lombard played the role of antihero in the late Cardinal de Lubac's second book, *Corpus mysticum*, a study devoted to changes in the conception of the Eucharist from patristic times to the Scholastic period.[38] In tracing the use of the term *corpus mysticum*, the cardinal found that its meaning underwent a significant reversal. Initially, in the writings of the Fathers, the Church herself was considered the "true body" of Christ, *corpus verum*, whereas the Eucharist was termed the "mystical body," *corpus mysticum*. From around the middle of the eleventh century, however, and as a consequence of the Berengarian controversy, increasing emphasis was placed upon the fact that the Eucharist itself is the true body of Christ, while the Church came to be viewed as His mystical body. De Lubac argued that this "Eucharistic realism" took place at the expense of the former "ecclesial realism"; in other words, the emphasis upon the real presence of Christ on the altar as distinct from, and presupposed by, His mystical presence as the Church privileged a new understanding of the Church as a corporate, hierarchical entity—and not as one body, one person. It was now no longer the Eucharist that made the Church, but the Church that made the Eucharist. At the same time, the hardening of the doctrine of the real presence, with its concomitant difficulties, made it increasingly necessary to subject the Eucharist to logical scrutiny, indeed to a kind of Christian rationalism and "indiscreet intelligence" that were "no longer capable of envisioning the understanding of the mysteries outside of their demonstration."[39] The *Book of Sentences*, according to de Lubac, was instrumental in cementing this shift: "If the expression [*caro mystica* as the Church] was not new, it nevertheless seems that one finds it nowhere with such a clear ecclesial meaning before the time of Peter Lombard."[40]

It is important to understand that de Lubac's argument was not directed against the doctrine of the real presence as such, but rather against the primacy of Eucharistic realism over ecclesial realism. According to the great French theologian, the two realisms should be indissociable.[41] Unfortunately for de Lubac, when *Corpus mysticum* first appeared, in 1944, its critique of the conception of the Church as *corpus mysticum* could be read like a direct response to Pope Pius XII's encyclical *Mystici corporis*, which, issued the previous year, had warmly embraced that same conception. The book and its theses therefore became one of the factors that led to de Lubac's suspension from teaching and exile in the 1940s and 1950s.

What *Corpus mysticum* demonstrates, above all, is the relevance of historical theology to contemporary debates. In order to evaluate our current situation and, possibly, imagine alternatives to it, it is indispensable that we know the genesis of this situation; in other words, that we understand the successive stages in history at which theologians and the Church stood at crossroads and, for one reason or another, were led to pursue, in thought and action, a certain path, eschewing other possibilities.

More concretely, however, what are we to think of de Lubac's theses on the role of Peter Lombard in (mis)shaping the Catholic understanding of the Eucharist? Do the latter's ideas amount to a triumph of Scholastic perspicuity, as Ludwig Hödl would have it, or did they rather pave the way for a misdirected Christian rationalism in which rigid demonstration suffocated genuine spirituality, while the living dynamism of grace was congealed in static structures of authority? I personally consider Peter Lombard to have achieved an admirable balance between the legitimate claims of reason in coming to understand the mysteries of faith, and the humble recognition of the shortcomings of rationality when it is faced with "the foolishness of God [that] is wiser than men"—an awareness that, I think, is always the hallmark of authentic spirituality. In truth, however, answering our question requires far more than a study of Peter Lombard and the *Book of Sentences*, for there is no disagreement between Cardinal de Lubac and his critics over what the Lombard's text *says;* the controversy concerns the question as to what the text *means* for the course of Christian theology and, indeed, the Western tradition. De Lubac himself was keenly aware of the fact that, behind the seemingly "objective" *étude historique* conducted in *Corpus mysticum*, there loomed an entire philosophy of history. In the preface to the second edition, he declared:

> One should not accept too lazily, right inside [the sphere of] theological speculation, a certain schema of progress that all of the forces of the century contributed yesterday to impose upon us (and it is not certain, some appearances notwithstanding, that they do not continue doing so today). In reacting against the "modern" self-importance which makes our contemporaries believe that they have more wits than their fathers, for the sole reason that they were born after them, we believe that we are returning to a more traditional assessment, from which not only the patristic era and the high Middle Ages, but the following centuries as well, must benefit.[42]

It is fascinating to note how quickly one is led to pass from a debate over sacrament and *res* in the *Book of Sentences* to the question concerning the status of the modern project. We, however, must now return to Peter Lombard's treatment of the Eucharist, several aspects of which we have yet to explore.

In distinction 10, Peter further examines the first *res* of the sacrament of the altar, that is to say, the real body of Christ. He is appalled that anyone should deny the reality of Christ's presence in the Eucharist—an

error even more pernicious than that committed by theologians who argue that only good people receive the Lord's sacramental body:

> **On the heresy of others who say that the body of Christ is not on the
> altar except in sign [*in signo*].** Again, there are others who, surpassing
> the insanity of those preceding, and measuring the power of God ac-
> cording to the manner of natural things, contradict the truth [even]
> more audaciously and dangerously: they assert that the body or blood
> of Christ is not [present] on the altar, and that the substance of the
> bread or wine is not converted into the substance of flesh and blood.
> Rather, [they assert that] Christ said, "This is my body" [Mt 26:26],
> just as the Apostle said, "The rock was Christ" [1 Cor 10:4]. For they
> say that the body of Christ is [present] there only in sacrament, that
> is, in sign; and that it is eaten by us only in sign.[43]

There is, evidently, no "philosophical" or "logical" way of proving the
real presence of Christ's body in the sacrament of the altar. The Lombard
therefore proceeds by first scrutinizing the evidence adduced by those
who deny the real presence, evidence that consists in numerous quotations
from Augustine where the bishop of Hippo seems to be propounding a
merely symbolic interpretation of the Eucharist. Finding this evidence to
be based upon misinterpretations of the texts, Peter in a second step cites
authorities that support the orthodox point of view. These range from
Scripture's "Take ye, and eat. This is my body" (Mt 26:26) to several
passages from Ambrose, Augustine, and Eusebius Emisenus.

In distinction 11, transubstantiation is addressed, or rather, "conversion" (*conversio*), for that is Peter Lombard's term for the Eucharistic
change of the substance of bread and wine into the substance of the body
and blood of Christ.[44] The Master exhibits his customary humility on the
subject of how exactly the conversion occurs: "If, however, it is asked of
what sort this conversion is—whether formal, or substantial, or of another kind—I am not capable of defining [it]."[45] Despite this declaration
of *definire non sufficio*, Peter excludes several possible theories and indicates his own preference. First, the Eucharistic *conversio* cannot be "formal"—in the pre-Aristotelian sense of the word, which we have encountered previously in the *Sentences*—since the external appearance of
the bread and wine, such as their taste and weight, remains the same
after the conversion as it was before. This exclusion focuses our attention
on the second possibility: that the conversion is of a substantial kind. This
theory, however, faces a ponderous objection in the idea that the body

and blood of Christ are somehow increased each time the words of consecration are spoken. The Lombard replies that the conversion of the
substances of bread and wine is not comparable with the conception of
the Word in the Virgin; that is to say, the body of Christ is not recreated
(or "reformed") each time the Eucharist is celebrated. Such a conversion
without augmentation is possible only through the will and power of
God Himself. Peter rejects the notion according to which the substances
of bread and wine continue to exist after the consecration, as though the
substances of Christ's body and blood had merely been added to them.
Such a theory of consubstantiation finds no support in the texts of the
Fathers.

At the beginning of distinction 12, Peter Lombard briefly discusses
the problem of the accidents of bread and wine, which patently do not
disappear after the *conversio*: the "bread" retains its original shape and
weight; the "wine" continues to taste like wine. The existence of the
bread and wine accidents along with the substances of the body and blood
of Christ, however, seem to necessitate a subject in which they can inhere.
Not so, the Lombard opines: since they are not appropriate as accidents
of Christ, they must be *sine subiecto*, "without subject." How precisely
this is possible obviously presents us with a mystery. The same remark
applies to the question of what exactly is broken when the priest divides
and distributes the bread of the Eucharist. Since Christ's body, which is
in heaven, is incorruptible, we are forced to admit that only the appearance (*species*) of the bread is broken. Peter seems to be slightly embar-
rassed by this conclusion: "Do not be amazed, however, or taunt if the
accidents seem to be broken, since they exist without subject here—
although some people assert that they are founded in air."[46]

Another interesting discussion is occasioned by the following point: if
Christ has given us His body and blood for our salvation, why did He
do so by using the external appearances of bread and wine? The *Sentences*
teach us that there are three reasons. First, the Eucharist as we know it
offers us the opportunity of proving our faith and thus earning merit.
Secondly, "we are not in the habit of eating raw flesh and blood";[47] such
a practice would not only horrify us, but it would be inappropriate to
devour Christ with our teeth if this act were not veiled in mystery.
Thirdly, the consumption of raw flesh and blood would expose the faith
to the mockery of unbelievers. If these reflections may strike us moderns
as strange, they certainly throw into relief how deep the medieval sense

of Christ's presence on the altar really was. Yet Peter Lombard does not conceive this presence as simply physical.

We shall pass over several minor questions that arise in distinctions 11, 12, and 13. These questions are mainly of two kinds. Some concern the symbolism of the Eucharist; for example, the bread refers to our bodies, and the wine to our souls, both of which Christ has liberated through His sacrifice. The water with which the wine is mixed stands for the faithful. On the other hand, the Lombard spends some time on canonical issues. What if the priest forgets to add water to the wine, or if a really confused priest distributes only wine: will the sacrament still be valid? (Yes.) And if only water is offered? (No Eucharistic celebration would occur in this case.) Can the bread be made from anything but wheat? (No, since Christ compared Himself to a grain of wheat in John 12:24.) How often should we communicate? (At least three times a year: at Easter, Pentecost, and Christmas.)

Penance

Peter Lombard's treatment of penance is—shall we say—convoluted. It is very detailed, too, occupying the Master in nine full distinctions, 14 through 22. The reason for the length and somewhat sinuous course of the Lombard's reflections lies in the fact that the sacrament of penance was undergoing a through theoretical and practical restructuring in the twelfth century. We shall speak of these developments momentarily.

The treatise on penance opens with some incisive thoughts on the place that this sacrament occupies within the overall sacramental system of the Church. Just as he did in the cases of confirmation and of the Eucharist, Peter defines the role of penance in relation to baptism, the first Christian sacrament:

> **On penance.** After this, we must treat of penance. Penance is necessary for those placed far away [from God], so that they may approach Him. For it is, as Jerome says, "the second plank after the shipwreck," because if someone has, by sinning, tainted the robe of innocence received in baptism, he can restore it through the remedy of penance. The first plank [upon which we can save ourselves after the "shipwreck" of sin] is baptism, where the old man is put off and the new one put on [see Eph 4:22–24]; the second [is] penance, through which we rise again

after the fall, while the old state, which had returned, is repelled and the lost new state resumed. Those who have fallen after baptism can be renewed by penance, but not by baptism; [for] it is lawful for man to do penance frequently, but not to be baptized [more than once].

Baptism is a sacrament only, but penance is said to be both a sacrament and a virtue of the mind [*virtus mentis*]. For there are inner penance and outer penance. The outer one is a sacrament; the inner one is a virtue of the mind; and both are the cause of justification and salvation.[48]

The tripartite distinction in the last sentence of the above excerpt reminds us of the threefold distinction in the relationship between sacrament and *res* that the Lombard had developed in his analysis of the Eucharist; and indeed, at the very end of his treatment of penance, in distinction 22, he will apply this distinction to penance as well. Thus, outwardly displayed acts of penance (*poenitentia exterior*) constitute the sacrament, that is, the sign and remote cause of grace. The corresponding inner penance (*poenitentia interior*), or contrition of the sinner, functions as both sacrament and *res*, in that it is already a first effect of grace, but also the sign and cause of yet another level of grace. Finally, the remission of sins is the second *res*, or ultimate effect of grace brought about by the two preceding sacramental levels. In the Lombard's own words: "For the inner penance is both the *res* of the sacrament, that is, of outer penance, and the sacrament of the remission of sins, which it signifies and brings about. But the outer penance is the sign both of the inner [penance] and of the remission of sins."[49] A schema might help us understand this conception (see figure 6).

Although the terminology of sacrament and *res* is not used systematically in the distinctions on penance, the *Sentences'* treatment of the subject matter largely focuses upon the relationships among outer penance, inner penance, and the remission of sins (or justification). Put more concretely, is the outward act of penance necessary for the forgiveness of sins? Do sins have to be confessed to a priest, or is the inner act of contrition sufficient for salvation? These questions are analogous to, but not the same as, the problem of the relation between sacramental and spiritual reception of the Eucharist.

Before turning to this issue, however, Peter Lombard addresses another problem that preoccupied contemporary masters of theology: can the penitential act be repeated?[50] In this question, we hear an echo of

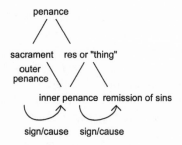

FIG. 6. The elements of penance and their relationship

the penitential practices of the early Church, practices that, by the mid-twelfth century, had largely fallen into disuse, but nonetheless had not yet been fully replaced by a fresh theoretical paradigm. In other words, between the seventh and the twelfth centuries, the penitential practices of the Latin Church had slowly moved away from earlier customs and theory, but it was not until the twelfth century that theologians began to catch up with the new customs, the subsequent theological definition and regulation of which culminated in the Fourth Council of the Lateran (1215). In fact, until the sixth century, the only form of canonical penance that the Church knew was public.[51] The sinner recognized his or her serious failings as an offense against God and the entire body of Christ; a public self-accusation followed, which the Church acknowledged by excluding the penitent from communion and placing him or her in a special "order of penitents" (*ordo poenitentium*). Subsequently, the penitent was expected to make satisfaction for his or her offenses, a task with which the community would assist through prayer and other, more practical forms of succor. The process of expiation eventually led to the penitent's readmission into the Eucharistic community, in a ceremony presided over by the bishop.

Evidently, this early form of penance involved much more than the sinner's feeling some vague regrets for his or her sins and saying a few prayers. It was a radical process of conversion, a kind of second baptism. Naturally, then, the Church developed the belief that canonical penance could not be repeated, but had to be a second—and now definitive—"yes" to God. Several consequences ensued. If penance could not be re-iterated, grievous sins committed after the canonical act of penance would have to remain without atonement. By reason of the seriousness of this situation, precautionary measures were imposed upon the penitent lest he or she be tempted to transgress again: the person "must not carry any weapons or engage in any sort of commerce. He must live in continence. That is why in many places canonical penance was not allowed to be imposed on married couples without the consent of both partners."[52] These rigors of penance precipitated a further modification of the Church's customs: penance came to be viewed as a preparation for death, and was delayed until such a time in the Christian's life when the risks of sinning were as minimal as the impact of the renunciations required by the penitential act.

This latter development created the need for new forms of penance, in addition to the old canonical rite, forms that could facilitate and strengthen the ongoing process of conversion during every believer's life. From the seventh century onward, therefore, we witness the slow evolution of penitential practices that gradually came to resemble what we would now recognize as the modern rite: private confession of one's sins is made to a priest, who imposes certain acts of penance, after the completion of which (or in anticipation of which) the penitent is granted reconciliation.

The complex analyses in distinctions 14 to 22 of the *Book of Sentences* are fully intelligible only against the backdrop of the historical situation just sketched. Peter Lombard's frequent hesitations, in particular, have everything to do with the fact that, in the middle of the twelfth century, a new doctrine of penance was taking shape in the Western Church.

Without discounting the "solemn and single penance" of the tradition, Master Peter limits its application to the "graver, horrible, and manifest offenses."[53] While this particular rite, which Peter imagines involves ashes and sackcloth, cannot be repeated, ordinary penance can, and should. The repeatability of penance must not be misconstrued as a license to take it lightly, as we learn in distinction 15. There is no such thing as partial penance for some sins; all sins have to be confessed together. By the same token, generous almsgiving cannot justify people who fail to do penance for their mortal sins. These points are discussed in considerable detail. In distinction 16, the Lombard introduces three aspects of penance: compunction of heart, confession of the mouth, and satisfaction by means of a "work." Further analysis of this distinction, however, is suspended for several pages of pastoral considerations. These include advice for the confessor, who needs to take the precise circumstances of each sin into account in determining what constitutes appropriate expiation; a paragraph or two on the importance of not dividing confession of one's sins among several priests; brief remarks on the mode of satisfaction for venial sins; and similar matters. In perusing these pages, one cannot help gathering the impression that Peter must have worked his way, step by step, through the issues as they occurred to him, without being guided by a plan conceived beforehand. It is not a coincidence that the crucial discussion of sacrament and *res*, in their application to penance, comes at the very end of the treatise.

In distinction 17, Peter finally returns to the three elements of penance: compunction of heart, confession of the mouth, and satisfaction. On this subject, he formulates a multipartite question: "Here a question with many parts arises. For first, it is asked whether a sin can be forgiven anyone without satisfaction and confession of the mouth, in virtue of the sole contrition of his heart. Secondly, whether it sometimes suffices to confess to God, without a priest. Thirdly, whether a confession made to a faithful layman is valid."[54] According to Marcia Colish, "Peter plans to answer each of these questions with a resounding 'yes,'" reducing confession and satisfaction "to desirable and recommended practices."[55] The eminent historian continues: "Of all the masters on the contritionist side of the debate, the Lombard is the only one who is truly and wholly faithful to the logic of that position, to the point of being willing to regard confession and satisfaction as optional."[56] Really? It seems to me that Professor Colish is exaggerating the decisiveness of the Lombard's stance on these matters, indeed to the point of misrepresenting his position. For Colish downplays a crucial aspect of Peter's theory: the penitent's intention or desire (*votum*) to complete his or her contrition, or inner penance, with the requisite outer acts, and to do so as soon as possible. Let us read some of the relevant texts:

> For just as inner penance is enjoined upon us, so too [are] both the confession of the mouth and outer satisfaction, if the opportunity [for them] exists [*si adsit facultas*]. Therefore, someone who does not have the desire to confess [*votum confessionis*] is not truly penitent. And just as the remission of sin is the gift of God, so the penance and confession by which sin is erased, cannot be but from God.... It is necessary,

therefore, that the penitent confess, if he has time [*si tempus habeat*]; and yet remission is extended to him before the confession by mouth occurs, if the desire is in his heart [*si votum sit in corde*].[57]

That it is not sufficient to confess solely to God if there is time [*si tempus adsit*]. But that it is necessary to make confession to priests, is proven not only by this authority of James: "Confess therefore your sins to one another," etc. [Jas 5:16], but also by the testimonies of many others. . . . From these and many other [authorities] it is indubitably shown that it is necessary to make confession to God first, and then to a priest; and that it is not possible to gain entrance to paradise otherwise, if the opportunity [for confession to a priest] exists [*si adsit facultas*].[58]

For what the second question contained—namely, whether it might be sufficient to confess to God alone, without confession [to] and judgment of a priest—has been disclosed, and it has been established by the aforementioned testimonies that it does not suffice to confess to God without a priest; neither is the penitent truly humble if he does not desire and seek out the judgment of a priest. But is it equally valid for someone to confess to a companion or to his neighbor, at least when a priest is not available?
    Solution*. It can soundly be said that the examination of a priest should be sought out eagerly [*studiose*], since God has granted the priests the power to bind and loose; and therefore those whom they forgive, God too forgives. Should, however, a priest not be available [*si tamen defuerit sacerdos*], confession should be made to a neighbor or companion.[59]

These three texts can hardly be interpreted as ringing endorsements of contritionism. Again and again, they emphasize the unity of the three aspects of penance: contrition of the heart, external manifestation of that contrition (shown in a confession made to a priest, together with works of expiation), and remission of sins. Peter's argument for the necessity of outer penance seems to be based upon commonsense pastoral experience. Genuine remorse is keen to show itself in external acts. A true penitent will be eager to consult a priest on the appropriate satisfaction required to atone for his or her misdeeds; to undo the damage, as it were. A truly remorseful person, moreover, will not be reluctant to humble him- or herself by accepting the priest's judgment.

Yet Peter Lombard is not prepared to sacrifice souls to rigid theological principles. He views the difficulties of ordinary life with compassion. Thus, we can imagine situations in which a person is genuinely contrite, feels the desire (*votum*) to confess, but lacks the time or opportunity to do so. The kind of persons of whom the Lombard is thinking here will hardly be "people with such busy schedules that, for perfectly legitimate reasons, they may be unable to go to confession."[60] It is more likely that he has in mind believers who live in outlying areas, hamlets in the middle of nowhere with no, or only difficult, access to a priest.

So much for the Lombard's "resounding 'yes' " to contritionism, which has turned out to be a qualified "no." And yet, despite this "no" to the temptation of belittling the importance of external acts of penance, Peter unambiguously declares that "sin is already canceled in contrition."[61] It is not the priest to whom confession is made who forgives our sins; it is God Himself. What, then, about the famous "keys" of Matthew 16:19, that is, the Church's power of binding and loosing? Just as genuine compunction seeks to externalize itself, in order to make a positive difference in the world of the now repentant sinner, so God's forgiveness has its external counterpart in the judgment of the priest. The confessor's function is to *show* God's forgiveness, as Peter explains in distinction 18:

> We can soundly say and teach this, that God alone forgives and retains sins, and [that] nonetheless He has granted the Church the power of binding and loosing. But He Himself binds and looses in one way, the Church in another. For He, through Himself only, forgives sin in such a way as to cleanse the soul from its inner stain and to free it from the debt of eternal death.
>
> **How priests loose and bind from sins.** However, He has not granted the priests this [power]. Rather, He has assigned them the power of binding and loosing, that is, of showing that people are bound or loosed [*ostendendi homines ligatos vel solutos*].[62]

At the very instant when the sinner begins to feel remorse for his or her offense, God has already forgiven it. The remorse, in fact, is nothing less than the presence of charity, and therefore of the Holy Spirit, in the repentant sinner's heart:

> For no one feels true compunction for his sins, possessing a "contrite and humbled heart" [Ps 50:19], unless [it be] in charity. But someone who has charity is worthy of life. No one, however, can at the same

time deserve both life and death; he is not, then, bound by the debt of eternal death. For he has ceased to be a "son of wrath" [see Eph 2: 3], from the moment that he has begun to love and to do penance; from that [moment], then, he is freed from wrath, which does not remain on someone who believes in Christ, but on someone who does not believe.[63]

We are now at the core of Peter Lombard's theology of penance. That Master Peter managed to penetrate to the theological heart of the sacrament, through thick layers of ancillary reflections, is a tribute to the remarkable achievement of the author of the *Book of Sentences*. Suddenly the meaning of penance is crystal clear: inner penance is a virtue of the mind because, like all the other virtues, it is an indissociable effect of charity, which, in turn, has its source in Christ, and in our adherence to Him in faith.[64] Penance is one of the "rays" emanating from the "sun" of charity in the diagram printed in figure 4.

Charity seeks to permeate the world of fallen man, in order to return him to God. True charity cannot, therefore, adequately express itself, and be contained, in an inner act of penance, but rather presses on into the external world. This is why the role of the priest, which is secondary in the remission of sins, is crucial in shaping the penitent's actions. Peter places much emphasis upon the fact that the apostolic keys, which every priest receives at the time of his ordination, are of twofold use: "the use of these keys, however, is multiple, namely, to discern those who are to be bound and loosed, and then to bind and loose."[65] The two functions are, of course, connected, in that the priest's decision to pronounce the penitent's sins to be forgiven—and under what conditions to do so—is dependent upon his judgment of the genuineness of the sinner's contrition, the gravity of the offense, and the appropriate satisfaction to atone for it. Unfortunately, confessors will often lack the wisdom that is necessary to advise their confessants with compassion, prudence, and justice, a fact that Peter Lombard deeply laments. In one of the rare passages of the *Sentences* where the Master allows us to catch a glimpse of his personality, his voice is tinged with emotion as he describes the unworthiness of many of his fellow priests: "It can soundly be said that not all priests have the second of these keys, that is to say, the knowledge to discern: which is to be deplored and lamented. For many, although lacking discernment [*indiscreti*] and devoid of the knowledge by which the priest

must distinguish himself, presume to accede to the grade of the priesthood, being unworthy of it in knowledge and life, [people] who neither
before nor after [being received into] the priesthood have the knowledge
to discern who is to be bound or loosed."[66]

Two consequences follow from the sad realization that many priests
are unworthy confessors. First, it is important to understand that "God
does not follow the judgment of the Church," but rather the other way
around, for the Church "sometimes judges with dishonesty and ignorance
[*per subreptionem et ignorantiam*]; but God always judges according to the
truth."[67] Secondly, the penitent must take the utmost care in selecting his
or her confessor; should a worthy and qualified priest not be available,
it is preferable to make one's confession to a layperson: *Quaerendus est
enim sacerdos sapiens et discretus, qui cum potestate simul habet iudicium;
qui si forte defuerit, confiteri debet socio*—"For one should seek out a priest
of wisdom and discernment, who possesses [good] judgment along with
the power [of binding and loosing]; should [such a priest] perchance be
unavailable, one must confess to a companion."[68]

Distinctions 20 through 22, dealing with such issues as penance de-
ferred to the end of one's life, remission of sins for the dying, purgatory,
and the seal of confession, add nothing to the substance of Peter Lombard's teachings. His ideas are summarized in figure 7.

As one can see in this diagram, the priest functions as a kind of
midwife, helping the process of penance to come to birth, to take shape—
the proper shape—as pangs of conscience, indicating the presence of
God's love and forgiveness in the penitent's heart, slowly manifest themselves in the words of a confession and are, finally, channeled into works
of satisfaction. Note that the causal order of our first schema of penance
has been reversed in light of our subsequent discussion. While it remains
true that outer penance is the sign of inner penance, which again is a
sign of God's forgiveness, the causal relationship among the sacrament
and its twofold *res* proceeds in the opposite direction: God's charity wipes
out our sins, and this forgiving love announces itself in inner remorse,
which in turn gives rise to the desire to make a confession and to engage
in works of atonement. Peter Lombard addresses this difficulty—the fact
that his general definition of sacrament does not appear to apply to penance—at the end of distinction 22. His answer remains somewhat hesitant, but it is clear that he does not consider the issue to raise much of

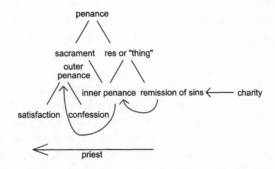

FIG. 7. Causal relationships in penance and the function of the priest

a difficulty. In the case of other sacraments, too (Peter must be thinking of baptism), the *res* sometimes precedes the sacrament itself; in other words, the sacrament serves only as a material confirmation of God's salvific action, which has already occurred in the soul. Then again, perhaps penance—together with marriage—is not governed by quite the same structures as baptism, confirmation, and the Eucharist, for the reason that only the latter are distinctive of the New Testament.

Unction of the Sick

Peter Lombard has little to say about unction, to which distinction 23 is devoted. He begins by pointing out that there are three kinds of unction, only one of which is a sacrament. "Principal unction," *principalis unctio*, is administered to kings and bishops, conferring an "abundance of grace" upon them through the Holy Spirit. Principal unction is celebrated by means of both oil and balsam, which stand for the strengthening of, respectively, the conscience and popular fame (*fama*) of their recipients. The second form of unction occurs in conjunction with baptism, when neophytes and catechumens are anointed on the chest and between the shoulders. "The third unction, however, is that which is called 'oil of the sick' [*oleum infirmorum*], of which we will treat now."[69]

Turning to the institution of this unction of the sick (*unctio infirmorum*), the *Sentences* find evidence for the existence of the sacrament in apostolic times. For St. James writes in his Epistle, "Is any man sick among you? Let him bring in the priests of the Church, and let them pray over him, anointing him with the oil in the name of the Lord. And the prayer of faith shall save the sick man: and the Lord shall raise him up: and if he be in sins, they shall be forgiven him" (Jas 5:14–15). From this passage, we learn that unction was instituted for two reasons: for the remission of sins and to alleviate physical sickness. Should God not judge it to be expedient that the recipient of the unction receive its physical fruits, he or she will acquire only the health of the soul. As in the case of penance, Peter Lombard distinguishes an interior and an exterior aspect of unction. The *unctio exterior*—the material act of anointing—constitutes the sacrament, while its *res* consists in an *unctio interior*, that is to say, in the remission of sins and strengthening of the virtues.

The bulk of Peter's short treatise on unction deals with the question of its repeatability, which was controversial at the time. Peter's own opinion is that unction is indeed repeatable, since diseases can be prolonged or occur more than once in a person's lifetime: "If the disease does not return, the medicine is not repeated; but if the disease cannot be stopped, why ought the medicine to be prohibited?"[70] The Lombard, therefore, does not seem to regard unction as "extreme unction," that is to say, as a sacrament for the dying. On the other hand, he does, at one point, refer to the administration of unction *in extremis*, that is, at the end of one's life.[71] Most likely, Peter simply failed to smooth over discrepancies among the sources that he was using in compiling the distinction on unction. According to Otto Baltzer, the same explanation would account for the fact that the Lombard does not mention physical healing in discussing the *res* of the sacrament.[72]

Finally, it might be useful to draw attention to an oddity in Colish's account of the distinction devoted to unction. Professor Colish believes that Peter Lombard held the "idiosyncratic" position of "insisting that this sacrament must be administered by a bishop."[73] But this is not so. Distinction 23 touches upon the role of the bishop on two occasions, on both of which the Lombard clearly states that the oil to be used in unction must be consecrated by a bishop—consecrated, not administered: ". . . unction of the sick, which is performed at the end of life, by means of oil consecrated by a bishop [*quae fit in extremis oleo per episcopum consecrato*]."[74] And again, "unction can be performed only with oil sanctified by a bishop [*de oleo ab episcopo sanctificato*]."[75]

Ordination

The seven ecclesiastical orders correspond to the seven gifts of the Holy Spirit, Peter suggests toward the beginning of distinction 24, although he does not spell out the exact correlation between individual gifts and spiritual offices. All seven ranks of clerical office stem from Christ Himself, who in His own person united the functions associated with them; but in the Church, His mystical body, these roles have come to be distinguished: doorkeeper (*ostarius*), reader (*lector*), exorcist (*exorcista*), acolyte (*acolythus*), subdeacon (*subdiaconus*), deacon (*diaconus*), and priest (*presbyter*).

After a short reflection on the need for worthy ministers of God, Peter explains the meaning of the tonsure, which marks all holders of clerical office. The tonsure can be interpreted as symbolizing a crown, since the ministers of the Church are people of high dignity and because "to serve God is to rule."[76] Moreover, the shaving of the top of one's head indicates an openness of the mind to contemplation and to the secrets of God. The *Book of Sentences* traces the tonsure, on the one hand, to an old custom of the Nazarites, referred to in the Old Testament (see Nm 6:18), and, on the other hand, to the apostles: "But Paul, when he had stayed yet many days, taking his leave of the brethren, sailed thence into Syria (and with him Priscilla and Aquila), having shorn his head in Cenchrae: for he had a vow" (Acts 18:18; also see 21:24).

The principal points of the discussion so far set the stage for Peter's description of the seven offices; in each case, he explains the office's Old Testament precedent, the function of its holder, and the manner in which Christ Himself instituted and performed it. Where necessary, a brief etymology serves to elucidate the Latin term for the office as well as its Greek equivalent. Let us limit ourselves to the gist of this discussion.

The doorkeeper, naturally, administers the keys of the Church, which he receives from his bishop at the time of his ordination. The reader is a minister of the word of God, being charged with the duty of reading from the "prophecies and lessons," that is to say, from the Old Testament. This task requires appropriate education, as Peter Lombard stresses. The exorcist expels unclean spirits, and as a symbol of that office receives a book of exorcistic formulae from his bishop when he is ordained. The acolyte is responsible for his Church's candles, as well as for the cruets that hold the water and wine for the Eucharistic celebration. With the office of the subdeacon, we move closer to the center of the divine offices, for the subdeacon's duties correspond to what we would now consider to be those of the server at mass: he brings the chalice and paten up to the altar, assists the celebrant to wash his hands before the consecration, and so on. The office of the subdeacon is the first ecclesiastical order to require celibacy: "the law of continence is imposed upon them."[77] The deacon's work is placed even more closely within the sphere of the sacraments: "It is incumbent upon the deacon to assist the priests and to minister in everything that is done in [connection with] the sacraments of Christ, namely, in baptism, in chrism [unction], in the paten and chalice [in the Eucharist]; [it] also [is their duty] to carry the offerings and place them upon the altar; to arrange the table of the Lord and to cover it; to carry the Cross; and to preach the Gospel and the Apostle."[78] When a deacon is ordained, the bishop places a stole on his left shoulder, to symbolize the "sweet yoke" of the Lord, and gives him a copy of the Gospel; both are signs of his office. Finally, we come to the office of the priest, whose central function is the celebration of the Eucharist: "It is the duty of the priest to perform the sacrament of the body and blood of Christ on the altar, to say prayers, and to bless the gifts of God."[79] To symbolize his duties, the priest receives a stole on both shoulders, as well as a chalice with wine and a paten with hosts, when his bishop ordains him.

Having treated of the seven clerical orders, Peter Lombard hastens to add that only the diaconate and the priesthood should be referred to as "holy orders," because the primitive Church knew only these two. A short paragraph is devoted to the definition of the orders as sacraments:

> **What it is that is called "order" here.** If, however, it is asked what it is that is called "order" here, one can soundly say that it is a certain sign [*signaculum*], that is, something sacred, by which the ordained [person] is entrusted a spiritual power and office. Therefore, the spiritual mark [*character spiritualis*] by which the bestowal of power occurs, is called "order" or "grade." And these orders are called "sacraments," because in their reception a sacred thing [*res sacra*]—that is, grace—is conferred, which those things that are carried here [during the ceremony] symbolize.[80]

We can see that Peter applies his general definition of sacrament to the ecclesiastical orders systematically and point by point. A sacrament is a sign of grace—not only a sign, however, but an efficacious sign, one that brings about what it signifies and resembles. For example, the ordination of a priest, as a sacrament, confers a certain spiritual power, divine grace, or thing (res) upon the ordinand. The sacrament is a sign of this grace in that it symbolizes it through the stole and the vessels of Eucharistic celebration that the ordinand receives from his bishop.

Apart from the seven ecclesiastical orders, Peter lists several other offices or "dignities" in the Church, which cannot however claim the status of sacraments. Peter mentions the offices of bishop, pope, seer (vates), and cantor. Interestingly, the role of the pope, which has become such a central definiens of Catholicism, is described in fewer than three lines: "**On the pope***. The pope is the head of the priests, like a way for those who follow [quasi via sequentium]. He is also called the 'high priest': for he makes the Levites and priests, and arranges all the ecclesiastical orders."[81] The category of seers includes priests, prophets, and poets— the latter perhaps understood as writers of liturgical hymns. Similarly, by cantors, Peter might well intend not only singers, but composers as well. Distinction 25 investigates the validity of orders received from heretical or simoniacal bishops, a question that, for our purposes, we need not pursue.

Marriage

The insight that sexual intercourse, which binds human beings together more closely than any other form of relationship, also, and perhaps paradoxically, orients them toward a dimension that transcends the purely human realm—this insight is by no means new or even specifically Christian. Plato already wrote, in the Symposium, that "it is a divine affair (θεῖον τὸ πρᾶγμα), this engendering and bringing to birth, an immortal element (ἀθάνατον) in the creature that is mortal."[82] Plato went on to explain the reasons for his high view of procreation:

> The mortal nature ever seeks, as best it can, to be immortal. In one way only can it succeed, and that is by generation; since so it can always leave behind it a new creature in place of the old.... Every mortal thing is preserved in this way; not by keeping it exactly the same for

ever, like the divine (τὸ θεῖον), but by replacing what goes off or is antiquated with something fresh, in the semblance of the original. Through this device, Socrates, a mortal thing partakes of immortality (ἀθανασίας μετέχει), both in its body and in all other respects; by no other means can it be done.[83]

For Peter Lombard, as well, the coming together of husband and wife in marriage is a divine affair, though of course he expresses this idea in the language of Christian theology. Thus, marriage for him is a sacrament—the visible sign and cause of something divine, of a particular grace. And it is not the least significant of the seven sacraments, despite its treatment at the very end of the portion of the *Sentences* that is devoted to sacramental theology. Marriage occupies the Master from distinctions 26 through 42, which cover almost a hundred pages in the most recent edition of the *Sentences*. Many of these distinctions are devoted to particular questions of canon law, with especially detailed discussions of impediments to marriage, such as consanguinity, and of legitimate grounds for separation and remarriage. We will focus our analysis on the points that are most central for understanding the Lombard's conception of marriage as a sacrament.[84]

Unlike the other sacraments, which were established "after sin and because of sin,"[85] marriage is coeval with the human race. In paradise, God instituted marriage not as a remedy for sin, but rather as a duty: "Increase and multiply" (Gn 1:28). After the Fall, marriage was reinstituted, but with a new purpose: it now became a way of channeling sexual desire into legitimate paths, of repressing vice and sin. "Since, as a result of sin, the law of deadly concupiscence has come to inhere in our members without which there is no carnal commixtion, sexual intercourse [*coitus*] is reprehensible and evil, unless it be excused by the goods of marriage."[86] But Peter adds a qualification to the idea of the twofold institution of marriage. The command to increase and multiply continued to be binding even after the Fall, "until the multiplication was achieved."[87] Only then did marriage become a voluntary matter, something permitted to those incapable of choosing better things: "For we have learned from the Apostle that marriage was allowed [*indultum*] to the human race to avoid fornication."[88] Peter is alluding to the First Letter to the Corinthians: "It is good for a man not to touch a woman. But for fear of fornication, let every man have his own wife, and let every woman have her own husband. . . . But I speak this by indulgence, not by commandment" (1 Cor 7:1–2 and 6).

It is not at all clear how Peter's presentation up to this point could possibly become the basis for a positive assessment of marriage, and indeed for a conception of marriage as a sacrament. But his discussion now takes a slight turn. He asks what it means that marriage is allowed, as St. Paul says, "by indulgence [*secundum indulgentiam*]." The answer is that "indulgence" may mean concession (*concessio*), remission (*remissio*), or permission (*permissio*). The Lombard continues: "And indulgence, in the New Testament, concerns minor goods, as well as minor evils. One of the minor goods is marriage, which does not deserve a palm, but is for remedy. One of the minor evils [that is, venial ones] is sexual intercourse that occurs because of incontinence. The former [that is, marriage] is allowed [that is, conceded]; but the latter [that is, sexual intercourse] is permitted [that is, tolerated], because it is not prohibited."[89] This passage makes a distinction between two ways in which sexual relations within marriage are allowed. Regarded strictly as a remedy for fornication, marriage is allowed as a minor good, and hence "conceded [*conceditur*]." On the other hand, sexual intercourse within marriage that pursues other than such remedial goals is allowed as a minor evil, and hence "permitted [*permittitur*]" or "tolerated [*toleratur*]."

Next, Peter has to accomplish the transition from minor good to sacrament. It occurs in the paragraph that follows the one just quoted. Suddenly, we learn "**that marriage is good.**"[90] God Himself instituted it, after all (see Gn 1:24); moreover, we know from John 2:2–11 that Jesus performed a miracle when he attended a wedding in Canaan; Jesus also forbade divorce, except in cases of fornication (see Mt 5:32 and 19:9). "It is certain, then," Peter concludes, "that marriage is a good thing. Otherwise it would not be a sacrament: for a sacrament is a sacred sign."[91]

We now approach the center of the Lombard's reflections on marriage as a sacrament, namely, his identification of the *res* of the marital relationship:

> **Of what "thing" marriage is the sacrament.** Since, therefore, marriage is a sacrament, it is also a sacred sign and [the sacrament] of a sacred thing, namely, of the union [*coniunctionis*] of Christ and the Church, as the Apostle says. It is written, he says [that is, St. Paul says, quoting Gn 2:24]: " 'For this cause shall a man leave his father and mother, and shall cleave to his wife, and they shall be two in one flesh.' This

is a great sacrament; but I speak in Christ and in the Church" [Eph 5:31]. For, just as between the consorts there is a union according to a concord of souls and according to a mingling of bodies; so the Church is joined to Christ [*Ecclesia Christo copulatur*] by will and by nature: because she wills the same as He, and [because] He took on form from the nature of man. Therefore, the bride is joined to the bridegroom spiritually and corporeally, that is, by charity and by a conformity of nature.—The symbol [*figura*] of both these unions [*copulae*] is in marriage: for the concord of the consorts signifies the spiritual union [*copulam*] of Christ and the Church that comes about through charity; but the commixtion of the sexes signifies that [union] which comes about through a conformity of nature.[92]

Marriage is a "great sacrament" indeed. The spiritual and physical relationship between husband and wife represents nothing less than the union between Christ and the Church, His mystical body. This union possesses two aspects. First, the incarnate Christ instituted the sacraments—above all, the Eucharist—through which He continues to live in and, indeed, to *be* His Church. Secondly, the Church of the faithful continuously responds in charity to Christ's giving of Himself (which is itself *the* act of charity). The relationship between husband and wife replicates the natural and spiritual union between Christ and the Church, through the sexual union of the consorts and through their bond of charity, respectively.

Note the parallel between the respective roles of the Church and the bride, on the one hand, and Christ and the bridegroom, on the other. Christ and the groom join themselves to the Church and the bride by a conformity of nature: the Word, with its divine nature, took on human nature, while the sexual complementarity of man and woman renders possible the marital act, in which (our text suggests) the husband takes the initiative. The Church and the bride respond to this initiative by reciprocating their respective bridegrooms' love. Thus, marriage functions as a church *in nuce*, or as an image, on a smaller scale, of the relationship between Christ and His spouse. This relationship is animated by an intense dynamism of mutual charity. It is worth adverting to the fact that the language of the paragraph on which we are commenting is suffused with sexual metaphors. The *Sentences* do not hesitate to use such terms as *coniunctio* or *copula* to depict the relationship between Christ and the Church. This choice of terms strongly emphasizes the dignity of marriage—worthy to serve as the source of metaphorical language to describe the dynamism occurring between Christ and His mystical body. It also highlights how far Peter Lombard has come since the first pages of the distinctions on marriage, pages in which marriage was presented as nothing more than a remedy for sin.

The sacrament of marriage is structurally analogous to penance: both the sacrament and its *res* form pairs of two. Toward the end of distinction 26 and throughout the following distinctions, the *Book of Sentences* attempts to arrive at a clearer understanding of the relationship between, and implications of, the two sacramental elements of marriage, that is to say, the spiritual union and the physical union of the married couple. The initial occasion for this discussion is furnished by the question of whether an unconsummated marriage is valid. In other words, is it the physical union or the spiritual union that is primary in the constitution of the marital bond? Two extremes need to be avoided in this context. If marriage were defined simply as the common life of two people (*cohabitatio*), "then brother and sister, father and daughter, [would be] able to contract a marriage."[93] On the other hand, if the marital bond resided primarily in the consent to engage in sexual intercourse (*consensus carnalis copulae*), then the marriage of Saints Mary and Joseph, Jesus' human parents, who lived together in complete chastity, would not have been a valid one! *Quod nefas est sentire*, Peter exclaims, "which it is impious to hold."[94] The marital bond requires a special kind of community, which is not sufficiently described as either the shared life of two loving people or as sexual union. "Consent of a shared life or of carnal union does not constitute marriage"; rather, it is the consent to live together in "conjugal fellowship [*consensus coniugalis societatis*]"[95] that creates the marital bond.

In order to elucidate further the nature of this conjugal fellowship, it is useful to turn to the Lombard's formal definition of marriage in distinction 27: marriage is "the marital union of man and woman, between legitimate persons, which places a limit upon the individual habit of life [*individuam vitae consuetudinem retinens*]."[96] Peter renders the last crucial phrase more precise. To be limited in the habits of one's individual life means, for example, that it is not licit for a married person to take a vow of chastity or to join a religious order without his or her partner's consent, or to have sexual relations with someone who is not his or her spouse. More positively, in their relationship with each other, married people are required to treat the other person with the same care that they would show toward their own well-being: *ut invicem alter alteri exhibeat quod quisque sibi*.[97] This requirement implies a recognition of equality between the consorts, for God made woman from man's side for the reason that He gave man "neither a servant nor a boss."[98]

Marriage, then, consists in a particular kind of union, the *coniugalis societas*. We must return for a moment to the role of sexual relations in this conjugal fellowship. Throughout his discussion of this problem, Mary and Joseph's marriage stands before Peter Lombard's mental eye. The marriage of Jesus' human parents serves the author of the *Sentences* as paradigmatic of the ideals to which every marriage should aspire, yet he must recognize that it was an exceptional marriage, in that Mary and Joseph did not have sexual intercourse. Peter resolves the dilemma by making a distinction: Mary and Joseph's marriage was perfect in sanctity, not in signification.[99] Since they did not have sexual relations, their marriage did, in fact, fall short of expressing fully the twofold union of Christ and the Church. On the other hand, their mutual vow of chastity made their marital bond all the more holy. Moreover, the marriage of Mary and Joseph instantiated the threefold good that should characterize all marital relations: faithfulness of the partners, the raising of offspring, and the sacramental indissolubility of the marital bond.

Distinctions 26 through 42 raise many further points of great interest. But we must break off here, having covered what is most essential to understanding Peter Lombard's conception of marriage. Commentators on the *Book of Sentences* have often pointed out that the Master fails to account for a crucial element in the sacramental nature of marriage for, according to his own definition, sacraments are efficacious signs, helping to bring about the grace that they signify. He remains silent, however, on the question of how the sacrament of marriage could cause its *res*.[100] According to Professor Colish, it would have been easy for the Lombard to extend his theology of marriage in this direction; for example, the physical union of the married couple could have been "envisioned as the external expression of the grace already received through their union of minds and hearts as mediated through their articulation of their vows."[101] Indeed, it would have been easy for Peter Lombard to spell out, explicitly, how the dynamism of charity obtaining between Christ and His mystical body flows into the married couple, animating their spiritual union and finally finding external expression in their sexual relationship. This is not, however, what is at stake in the problem of the causality of the sacrament

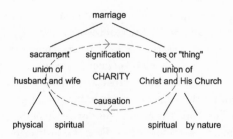

FIG. 8. The dynamism of charity in the sacrament of marriage

of marriage. It seems to me that the question Peter Lombard would have to answer, in order to bring his theology of marriage into alignment with his initial definition of sacrament, concerns the manner in which the spiritual-physical union between the consorts causes, or brings about, that which has been identified as its *res*, namely, the spiritual-natural union between Christ and the Church. But does this question have an answer? Would it not make more sense to assume—on the model of penance—a reversed order of causality, proceeding not from nature to grace, but from grace to nature? Thus, the sacrament of marriage would signify its *res*, which in turn would animate the sacrament (see figure 8).

In figure 8, the metaphorical marriage between Christ and His Church and the actual marriage between husband and wife appear as different aspects of one and the same dynamism of charity. It is the same Spirit that breathes in both, albeit in different ways. As a sacrament, human marriage symbolizes the marriage between Christ and His spouse, while the latter, conversely, serves as the paradigm and cause of the Christian marriage. Admittedly, this interpretation goes beyond the letter of Peter Lombard's text. Nevertheless, I hope that it captures its intention—even if problems do remain.

8

THE *SENTENCES*, BOOK IV, DISTINCTIONS 43–50

On the Resurrection and the Circumstances of Judgment

One short paragraph accomplishes the transition from Peter's theology of the sacraments to his eschatology. Its tone is matter-of-fact: "**On the resurrection and the circumstances of judgment.** Finally, we must briefly discuss the circumstances of the resurrection and the manner in which those rising will exist, as well as the nature of [God's] judgment and mercy."[1]

In the Christian tradition, there have always been those eager to paint the last judgment and the events leading up to it in sensational and lurid colors; Peter Lombard's days were no exception to this rule.[2] The *Sentences*' treatment of this topic, however, displays Master Peter's usual moderation and humility. Theology is too serious a matter for a responsible teacher to give free rein to curiosity and speculation. "I am not able to satisfy all the questions that are wont to be raised on this matter," Peter thus declares at the beginning of his distinctions on eschatology, in words borrowed from Augustine.[3] The Lombard's simple strategy in providing a reliable account of Last Things is to stay close to the scriptural evidence. Questions about which Scripture has nothing to say or which it does "not explicitly define [*non aperte definit*],"[4] he takes up with great reluctance and hesitation.

The structure of the *Sentences*' treatise on Last Things is as follows. Distinctions 43 and 44 address the resurrection of the dead, distinction

44 being devoted, in particular, to the condition of the bodies of the resurrected. Distinction 45 asks what prayers, alms, and burial ceremonies can accomplish on behalf of the deceased. Distinction 46 then moves on to a discussion of the relationship between God's justice and mercy. In distinctions 47 and 48, Peter turns to the judgment itself, distinguishing four categories among the people judged; seeking to clarify the roles that the saints, angels, and demons play in the last judgment; and discussing why it is qua man that Christ is going to judge us. In distinction 49, we learn about the rewards of the elect, while distinction 50 examines the condition of the damned. The *Sentences* end with an allegorical sentence, full of allusions to Scripture, which is meant to summarize the structure of the four books. We will attempt to unravel it.

The Resurrection

That the resurrection of the dead forms an integral part of the Christian faith is spelled out *praeclarissime*, "very clearly," in both the Old and the New Testaments, Peter Lombard affirms. In particular, he cites Isaiah 26:19 and 1 Thessalonians 4:13–17.[5] The Master interprets the trumpet that St. Paul mentions in his letter to the Thessalonians as Christ's own voice, or perhaps the voice of one or several archangels, which will be powerful enough to awaken the dead. References in Scripture according to which Christ's Second Coming will occur in the middle of the night (see Mt 25:6 and 1 Thes 5:2) are misunderstood as indications of a particular time, but are better taken to convey that "He will come when He will not be expected."[6] Thus, with the mainstream of the Christian tradition, Peter repudiates any attempts to calculate the precise moment when the world will come to an end.

How should we interpret the scriptural idea according to which all the books will be opened on doomsday? Peter believes that "the books are the consciences of the individual people, which will then be opened to others."[7] At last, we will appear to our fellow humans as the people who we really are, deep in our hearts and apart from all appearances that we may have contrived during our lifetimes. In the same way, individuals will no longer be able to deceive themselves about their own moral status, for on the day of judgment, each person will have a complete and immediate recollection of everything, good and bad, that he or she has ever done. "By this witness [man] will be saved or damned," Peter Lombard declares, indicating that God's judgment will not be extrinsic and utterly unexpected, but will correspond to what, deep down, we always knew about ourselves.[8] But what about those who will be saved: will they remember all their past sins, just like the damned? Yes, they will, Peter replies, with the difference that the saints will not be troubled by these memories, which will rather become an occasion for them to be grateful to God. By the same token, those sins of the elect already purged by temporal punishment will not become known to all.[9]

With regard to those people who will be alive at the time of Christ's Second Coming, the question can be asked whether they will first have to die before immediately rising again, or whether they will be transported from life to immortality without having to undergo death at all. Peter Lombard, after a brief presentation of the arguments for each side, opines that "it is not up to human judgment to decide which of these [positions] is more true."[10]

The Resurrected Body

In the First Letter to the Corinthians, as well as in the Letter to the Ephesians, St. Paul mentions the perfect state of the bodies of the resurrected, which will be incorruptible (see 1 Cor 15:52) and reflect the ideal age of Christ at the time of His death and resurrection (see Eph 4: 13). On the basis of this scriptural evidence, distinction 44 investigates further details concerning the bodies of the resurrected. The *Sentences* emphasizes that the distinction of the sexes will persist and that the perfection of the resurrected bodies does not imply equal height for everyone. However, everyone will be endowed with a body at the age of thirty-two years and three months, which is the age at which Christ died. This applies even to people who, in their mortal lives, passed away long before or long after reaching thirty-two. As for the problem of how God will accomplish the restoration of our decomposed bodies, Peter uses an analogy that he found in Augustine. If we imagine a sculptor faced with the task of recreating a statue that has been melted down or pulverized, it would be inconsequential for the integrity of the refashioned statue that all its material components be returned to their exact former locations, that hair become hair again, or nails nails. Thus, although "our" former matter will be returned to each of us, there is no need to assume that specific material components will be employed for the recreation of the same body parts that were constituted of them in our former lives. And "thanks to the providence of the Artificer," we need not fear "lest anything unbecoming might occur."[11] This remark, amusing as it might appear to us, reminds us of the deep suspicions that medieval theologians harbored toward the flesh and in particular toward human sexuality— not an unambiguous condemnation to be sure, as the Lombard's own reflections on marriage have shown us, but nonetheless a controlled fear. Perhaps "awe" would be the right word to characterize Peter Lombard's attitude toward sexuality: reverence coupled with abashed fear, in the presence of a phenomenon recognized in its both sacred and demonic dimensions.

Distinction 44 continues with a discussion of further issues concerning the resurrected body in its materiality—for it clearly is a material body that Peter Lombard is envisaging.[12] The saints, we are informed, will rise in bodies free from all imperfections, including "all such deformities as they had here [in this life]."[13] Whether this will be the case for the wicked as well is a question that Peter leaves open. It is certain, on the other hand, that their bodies will burn in hell without being consumed, causing the souls of the wicked interminable suffering. Corresponding to the materiality of the resurrected body, the Lombard decides that the fires of hell must be material as well, although he is unwilling to speculate upon the precise nature or location of Gehenna. He does not doubt, however, that even before the resurrection of their bodies, the souls of the reprobate are subject to torments caused by the fires of hell. The fact that in dreams the soul sees itself as walking or even as flying demonstrates its affinity to bodily action and passion.

Prayers for the Deceased

This last point naturally leads, in distinction 45, to the problem of the effectiveness of prayers, alms, and masses offered for the souls of the deceased. In this connection, a threefold distinction is necessary: "Now when sacrifices—be it [sacrifices] of the altar, be it [sacrifices] of whatever kind of alms—are offered for all the baptized, for the very good ones they are actions of grace; for the not very wicked ones, propitiations; but for the very wicked ones, even if they are no help for the dead, at least they are some kind of consolation for the living. Those, however, whom they benefit, they either help that there might be full remission [of their sins] or surely that their very damnation might be more tolerable."[14] To this quotation from Augustine, Peter Lombard adds a distinction of his own in order to shed further light upon the benefits that the "not very wicked ones," *non valde mali*, might derive from our prayers and sacrifices. Unlike the saints, who do not need our prayers, and the damned, whose conduct during this life renders our actions on their behalf pointless for them after they have died, a large group of people directly benefits from our prayers and sacrifices. The "moderately wicked" (*mediocriter mali*) might be granted mitigation of their punishment, while we may hope that our supplications will move God to grant the "moderately good" (*mediocriter boni*) complete absolution of their sins.

The next point that arises in this distinction concerns the offices for the dead. Peter asks us to ponder the case of two people, both "moderately good," but one of whom is wealthy, while the other is poor. For the rich person, the funeral arrangements are elaborate, including not only the regular prayers for the dead, but additional prayers and copious alms. For the poor deceased, on the other hand, only the regular prayers are said. The problem to be considered is this: if the two men are of equal moral standing, it is difficult to defend the idea that the wealthy person should be assisted more by the prayers offered for his soul than the poor man. Yet if a man's merits and demerits in the eyes of God depend solely upon his actions during this life, what is the point of offering special prayers and alms for anyone? Peter suggests two possible answers, between which he does not decide. Either we can say that the special prayers and alms do not confer any advantage upon the wealthy man, without however denying their usefulness—for the same gain may well be the result of different causes. Perhaps what Peter Lombard means is that the elaborate prayers offered for the wealthy person produce the same effect in the eyes of God as the simple prayers made for the poor man, but that it is nonetheless appropriate for the affluent man's family to go to greater expense in the funeral of their relative. The second answer is less ambiguous: "It is possible, however, to say that those more numerous means of assistance confer faster absolution upon the wealthy person, albeit not a fuller one."[15]

The role of the angels and saints in interceding for us represents another interesting topic that Peter addresses in distinction 45. Again, the problem presenting itself in this context requires a reconciliation of religious practice with doctrinal truth. For, if we imagine the intercession of the angels and saints to whom we pray as though they brought our supplications to God's knowledge, we are making a fundamental theological mistake: God, being omniscient, has nothing to learn. Indeed, the opposite holds good: the angels and saints learn of our prayers from God, whom they see face to face. For the same reason, they understand which of our desires it is in God's will to fulfill. Subsequently, the angels, in their function as messengers, "either clearly or in a hidden fashion report to us" what God has decided before all time.[16] If we nonetheless speak of the angels as though they convey human prayers to God, we do so for a reason that one could call psychological or spiritual for, as the Lombard puts it in words borrowed from Augustine, "the rational creature has the need to trace temporal causes back to the eternal truth."[17] God always already knows what is in our hearts, but we need the opportunity to view the world around us in light of God's eternal truth, and this opportunity is afforded us in the contemplation of prayer.

At the end of this discussion, which appears to have undermined intercession as it is commonly—and naïvely—understood, Peter Lombard presents a compromise formula, a way of conceiving of intercession that neither offends the religious sensibilities of the ordinary faithful nor violates the principles of sound dogmatic theology. Thus, he declares: "The saints, then, intercede with God on our behalf, and [they do so] through their merit (when their merits support us) and through their sympathy [affectu] (when they wish that our desires be fulfilled)—which, however, they do only when they have learned that it is in God's will that [our desires] be fulfilled. We pray, therefore, that they might intercede for us, that is, that their merits might support us; and [we pray] that they themselves might will our good, because if they will it, God wills it, and in this manner it will be brought to pass."[18] This passage demonstrates a new aspect of the humility that pervades Peter Lombard's theology, an aspect that we have not yet examined, but that is nevertheless relevant for a proper understanding of the flavor and tone of the *Book of Sentences*. The Lombard is prepared to admit to the shortcomings of philosophico-theological rationality not only when it is measured by the incomprehensible sublimity of the Trinity, the Incarnation, and similar objects of faith; he is also humble enough not to permit the legitimate insights of theoretical reason to overturn religious practice, which possesses its own, different kind of wisdom. In the *Book of Sentences*, theological theory does not simply overrule religious practice; it elucidates and—where necessary—gently corrects it.

God's Justice and Mercy

A similar issue arises in distinction 46, which opens with the question of whether even the very wicked experience God's mercy, in that they are punished less than their transgressions—and hence God's justice—would require. Peter approaches this question on two levels. First, he cites authorities in favor of each of the two possible answers (yes, even the very wicked benefit from God's mercy, and no, they do not), attempting to reconcile them in his own "determination." On this level, Peter does not question the legitimacy of the naïve assumption according to which justice and mercy indeed represent two different aspects of God's judgment. But then, Peter moves on to a deeper level of theological analysis: "**On the justice and mercy of God.** But in what way did Cassiodorus say above that God's justice and piety [that is, mercy] are 'two things,' which 'are always attached to God's judgment'? For God's justice and mercy are not two things but one thing, namely, the divine essence—as has been shown above [in book 1] by means of several authorities. . . . Why, then, does Scripture say of the works of God that some are [works] of mercy, others [works] of justice?"[19]

Peter's answer respectfully interprets popular belief and scriptural texts in light of the insights of fundamental theology. When we distinguish between God's justice and His mercy, he writes, such parlance should be understood as referring to different effects and manifestations, in creation, of God's one and undivided essence. Perhaps one could go a step further, however, and maintain that even in its effects, God's essential justice-cum-mercy remains indivisible: "for there is no work of God in which there is not an effect or sign of equity and clemency, either in a hidden or in an open way. Sometimes, however, the clemency or benignity is manifest, while the equity is hidden; sometimes [it is] the other way around."[20]

The Judgment

In the last judgment, Christ will be assisted by the saints, although the Lombard is reluctant to pronounce himself on details concerning their precise function. In distinction 47, he declares: "If it is asked what will be their power or authority in judging, I believe that this cannot be known before it is seen—unless someone should have learned it through divine revelation."[21] Four categories of people need to be distinguished in connection with the last judgment. Peter articulates this insight in terms derived from Gregory the Great, who draws a distinction between the elect and the reprobate, and then again between those among the elect who will be judged and will rule, and those who will not be judged and will rule; similarly, among the reprobate, some will be judged and will perish, while others will not be judged and will perish.

The wicked people who will be damned without judgment are those who do not believe in Christ, for "he that doth not believe, is already judged" (Jn 3:18). But why will there be no judgment passed upon unbelievers? The answer is not, as Marcia Colish suggests, "because they have openly condemned themselves to damnation as unrepentant sinners in this life."[22] Peter Lombard's argument is different. He writes, "Those who did not subscribe to [*tenuerunt*] the sacraments of the faith, will not hear the chiding [*increpationem*] of the Judge arise in them, because, prejudged by the darkness of their infidelity, they will not be worth being rebuked by the invective of Him whom they have disdained."[23] It seems to me that Peter's point here is the same as one already made earlier, in connection with the meaning of the opening of the books. God's judgment upon us will not be at all extrinsic, but will rather consist in the exterior manifestation and revelation of the state of our own consciences. This is why people who have no faith in Christ will be unable to hear His judgment: they have not sufficiently developed their inner sense of hearing, that is to say, their consciences. Their interior darkness is such that they will sink into damnation without even knowing why.

As for those who will be judged and will perish, these are people who professed faith in Christ during their lives here on earth, but only verbally, without putting it into practice: "Those will at least hear the words of the Judge, because they have held at least a verbal faith in Him."[24] Moving on to the elect, Peter speaks of believers who "wipe away the blemishes of life with tears and hide them by erasing them with alms."[25]

In this group, we recognize sinners who have repented of their transgressions and performed the requisite works of expiation to atone for them. Finally, a last group of faithful will be saved without requiring any kind of judgment, namely, the saints, who "go beyond the precepts of the law through the virtue of perfection."[26] Those who have lived a life of consummate charity will not be subjected to any judgment, but will rather, along with Christ Himself, judge the two preceding groups.

The last judgment will involve several steps. In His Second Coming, Christ will be preceded by a huge fire, which will consume the wicked, while leaving the good people alive and, where necessary, purging them. This fire, Peter adds, will change heaven and earth, without however destroying them substantially. Then, Christ will call for the resurrection of the dead. Through the ministry of the angels, the good people will be gathered from the four corners of the earth and carried away "to meet Christ, into the air" (1 Thes 4:16), whereas "the reprobate will remain on the earth that they have loved."[27] Next, Christ will pronounce His judgment (although the *Sentences* leave open whether this will be uttered vocally). Subsequently, those found to be wicked will be ushered by the angels to hell, where demons will torture them.

In distinction 48, Peter goes on to specify that Christ will preside over the last judgment in the form of His glorified human body. He rules out the possibility of Christ's appearing at the last judgment in the form of God, "since the Divinity cannot be seen without joy."[28] The wicked, however, will not react with joy upon beholding their judge, but rather with fear: "for He will be terror for the wicked and light for the just."[29] Another reason why it will be particularly appropriate for Christ to appear qua man at the last judgment is that His resurrection is what renders ours possible.

It is "puerile" to believe that the last judgment will take place in the valley of Josaphat (see Jl 3:7). Against such a "frivolous" opinion, Peter affirms that the judgment will not occur anywhere on earth, but rather in heaven. After the judgment, the sun and the moon will continue to exist, although they will no longer rise and set, shining permanently. Moreover, their strength will be restored to their prelapsarian condition, "for the light of the sun and the moon and the other stars was diminished by the sin of the first man; but then, the sun will receive the wages of its labor, because it will shine sevenfold."[30] A side effect of the arrest of the heavenly bodies will be to deprive the wicked of any light. For, if hell is located beneath the disk of the earth, and the sun and moon will no longer perform their circular motions around it, then the space under the earth will be condemned to eternal darkness.

After this rather graphic description of the condition of the earth following Christ's Second Coming, Peter avows that he is at a loss as to why exactly humanity will still require the light of the sun and moon: "if it is asked, however, what will then be the use of the light of the sun and the moon, I confess not to know, because I do not remember reading [about this] in the Scriptures."[31] What is perhaps most interesting for us, in the present context, is the very material way in which Peter Lombard is imagining the condition of the resurrected body and its earthly environment. We tend to think of kingdom come in abstract and spiritual categories, in terms of souls in spiritual bodies floating in empty space. For the author of the *Sentences*, the world following the resurrection and the last judgment will be transfigured and brought to perfection, but not abolished in its materiality.

The Beatific Vision

The two principal questions that Peter Lombard investigates in distinction 49 concern the beatific vision insofar as it is common to all the blessed and in its individual differences. Indeed, one could go further and maintain that, in a certain sense, the beatific vision is common to all human beings, blessed *and* damned—not, to be sure, in the sense of both groups experiencing it, but insofar as even the damned have a desire to be completely happy and fulfilled. The philosophico-theological problem of humans' universal desire for happiness is a very old one, going back at least as far as Aristotle's *Nicomachean Ethics*. For who would deny that even cruel and wicked people live in order to be happy? No one becomes a thief or a murderer in order to be wretchedly unhappy, but rather because the results of their actions appear as something desirable to the perpetrators of such crimes. In a theological perspective, the paradox that it is possible to pursue Go(o)d perversely, and thus literally go to hell in the quest for heaven, is even more striking. In the *Book of Sentences*, Peter Lombard employs classical reflections from Augustine's *De Trinitate* in order to shed light upon this problem. With the bishop of Hippo, he suggests that there must be a difference between the desire for happiness and the knowledge of what true happiness consists in, namely, "to live according to virtue."[32] All humans possess the former, but many people sadly lack the latter. So is the universal desire for happiness a matter of the will, while the failure to reach the goal of happiness is due to some defect of the intellect? Thomas Aquinas would later suggest this to be the case,[33] but Augustine and Peter Lombard would not agree. They argue that "no one is capable of loving something of which he knows neither what nor how it is; neither can he ignore what it is that he knows he desires; it follows that all know the happy life."[34] Ultimately, then, wickedness and the consequent failure to be happy are not a matter of tragic ignorance, but rather of unwillingness to live a virtuous life. We already know, of course, that for Peter Lombard the virtues cannot be separated from charity, which in turn is impossible without faith in Christ. Therefore, "desiring to be happy belongs to all human beings; all see in their heart[s] that they desire to be happy; however, not all have the faith through which one attains happiness."[35]

Let us turn to the beatific vision that the blessed will enjoy in the hereafter.[36] The elect will all "live happily in eternal life," without any desire to sin.[37] Nevertheless, "some will be more distinguished than others," in accordance with the scriptural saying that there exist "many mansions" in the Father's house (Jn 14:2).[38] Peter explains:

> For, just as the lighting up [*clarificatio*] of bodies will be different, so the glory of souls will be different [as well]. "For star differeth from star," that is, one elect [differs] from the other, "in glory" of mind and soul [1 Cor 15:41]. For some will contemplate the appearance of God [*speciem Dei*] more closely and more clearly than others, and the very difference in contemplating [God] is called the diversity of mansions. The house, in fact, is one; that is, the denarius is one [see Mt 20:1–16]; but the diversity is [one] of the mansions here; that is, [it is] a difference of clarity. [This is so] because both the beatitude and the life of all is one and the highest good, namely, God Himself. All the elect will enjoy this good, but some more fully than others. They will, however, have the enjoyment by seeing by means of the appearance [*per speciem*], and not "through a glass in a dark manner" [1 Cor 13:12].[39]

This passage does not explain upon what basis the elect will enjoy different degrees of physical and spiritual glorification. We may reasonably conjecture, however, that the various levels are understood to cor-

respond to the kinds of lives that the elect have lived here on earth—
lives of greater or lesser purification of the body, and of greater or lesser
spiritual intensity perhaps.[40] The word *species*, incidentally, is not easy to
translate. Literally, it means "something that is seen." Most likely, Peter
does not wish to imply that the beatific vision, the vision face to face,
involves an intermediary or theophany in which God clothes Himself in
order to appear to the human eye—this would be the traditional Eastern
position on this subject. On the other hand, some early commentators on
the *Sentences* have interpreted *species* in precisely this sense. Thus, Pseudo-
Peter of Poitiers paraphrases *videndo per speciem* as *contemplando eius
potestatem* or *maiestatem*, that is, "seeing [God] by means of the appearance" becomes "contemplating His might" or "majesty."[41]

On the same subject of differences in the way in which the elect
contemplate God, the Lombard further specifies, "All the elect will know
in common everything about God that pertains to beatitude, but differently." Again, "all will see the whole of what serves the cognition of
beatitude; but they will differ in the manner of seeing [it]."[42] Will these
diverse ways of contemplating God occasion different levels of enjoyment? Peter is uncertain, offering two possible answers. Perhaps "everyone will have equal joy [*par gaudium*], although unequal clarity of cognition, because through charity, which will be perfect in the individuals,
each and every one will rejoice in the good of the other just as much as
he would rejoice if he had it in himself."[43] In this answer, the Master is
envisaging a loving community of the blessed in which the joy of living
in the presence of God will be shared without a hint of jealousy—despite
differences in the clarity of contemplation that individual members will
enjoy, due no doubt to differences in mental capacity. According to this
conception, we may imagine St. Thomas Aquinas and St. Jean-Marie
Vianney—the saintly but simple *curé d'Ars* who was hardly able to complete his studies for the priesthood—as sharing their joy in contemplating
God, although Thomas's depth of understanding, and hence individual
enjoyment, would by far surpass the understanding (and therefore joy)
of which Jean-Marie Vianney would be capable, again as an individual.
Put differently, the intellectual quality of the beatitude experienced by
Thomas Aquinas would be superior to Jean-Marie Vianney's beatitude,
but the latter would partake in the greater joy of the former due to their
bond of perfect charity.

If in his first answer, Peter Lombard insists on the equality of joy among all the blessed despite cognitive differences, in the second answer he appears ready to concede that not all the blessed will experience an equal level of joy. In fact, he writes: "It is also possible to understand 'equal joy' in such a way that it does not relate the equality of enjoyment to the intensity of the affect of those experiencing it [*ad intensionem affectionis gaudentium*], but rather to the whole of the things in which they will rejoice: for in all the things in which one will rejoice, all will rejoice."[44] What Peter means in this sentence is that all the blessed will share "equal joy" insofar as they will rejoice in contemplating the same divine objects, but not with regard to the intensity of each individual's subjective level of enjoyment. Nonetheless, even if we accept this solution, St. Thomas Aquinas's and St. Jean-Marie Vianney's enjoyment would still remain, in a very real sense, equally perfect—not only inasmuch as both are contemplating God, but also insofar as each contemplates God in such depth as is appropriate for him. Jean-Marie Vianney's beatitude would be perfect for Jean-Marie Vianney, just as the level of Aquinas's beatific vision would perfectly suit Aquinas's brilliant theological mind.

Hell

In hell, the wicked will no longer be capable of sinning, which does not mean, however, that they will have been purged of their wickedness. On the contrary, their "malignant will is going to serve, for them, as the culmination of their punishment."[45] Thus, as we have learned previously, the wicked will certainly be subject to torture, even physical torture administered by demons; yet the *cumulum poenae*, the height of their punishment, will consist in nothing but their own malignancy. Let us note, once again, the symmetry between interiority and exteriority that we have encountered so frequently in Peter Lombard's theology—in sacraments such as penance or marriage, but also in the last judgment, which we have interpreted as the exteriorization of people's interior moral state.

Next in distinction 50, the *Sentences* address the darkness that will envelop the wicked in hell: **"Why the darkness is said to be exterior."**[46] Peter Lombard explains: "[This is] because then [in hell] the wicked will be utterly without corporeal and spiritual light; that is, [without] God. Now, however, in spite of the fact that they suffer darkness in their blindness of mind, they are nevertheless not utterly without the light of

God, nor are they deprived of corporeal light."[47] The darkness of hell represents the permanent objectification and culmination of the subjective blindness that is, already in this life, at the heart of the moral perversity of bad people. Marcia Colish aptly speaks of an "eternalization" in the hereafter of the moral state that characterizes people in this life.[48] The Lombard's further description of the mental state of the reprobate is worth quoting at greater length:

> The "exterior darkness" [Mt 8:12] can soundly be understood as some kind of malignancy of hatred and of the will, which will then rise up in the minds of the reprobate, and some kind of oblivion of God, because they will to such a point be affected and perturbed by the pains of their exterior and interior torments, that they will hardly and rarely, or never, call their minds back from [these pains] to understanding something of God. . . . In this life, however, no one is evil to such a point that he is totally cut off from understanding God, and no one loses his desire for happiness and a certain love of the good, which the rational creature possesses naturally.[49]

Again, this extract confirms that hell constitutes a radicalization and eternalization of the moral condition of the sinner. In this life, no one— not even the perpetrators of the worst crimes—are completely and definitively separated from God, insofar as there always remains in them an inextinguishable love of the good and desire to be happy. In hell, this flame of love will die forever, primarily because the (self-inflicted) psychological and physical torture of the wicked will prevent them from focusing their attention upon anything but their own pain. In this description, one is reminded of Plato's characterization of the tyrant in book 9 of the *Republic*: a man whose oppression and terrorization of others eventually returns upon himself, so that he who craved total domination is in the end forced to live a life dominated by boundless fear. On the other hand, since the damned will be utterly oblivious of God and—as Peter Lombard adds—incapable of seeing the blessed, one may wonder to what extent they will be able to grasp what is happening to them. Just as unbelievers will not be able to hear Christ's judgment, the damned will not be in a position to compare their own fate with that of the blessed, nor to measure their malevolent misery against any spark of goodness remaining in their own souls. The blessed, by contrast, will be aware of the ineffable wretchedness of hell, but recognizing in it God's justice, they will feel no compassion for its inhabitants and rather "give thanks for their own liberation."[50]

The Allegorical Conclusion and the Structure of the *Sentences*

The last sentence of Peter Lombard's *magnum opus* is so dense as almost to defy translation: "These [points] it suffices for the writer, even if not for the reader, to have related about the feet of Him who is seated 'upon a throne high' [Is 6:1], [and] which the seraphim covered with two veils [see Is 6:2]—[for the writer] who, having begun with the face of Him who is seated, has through those that are in the middle, arrived right at the feet, by means of the guiding Way."[51] By the "feet" of God, who is seated upon His high throne, Peter must be referring to the blessed and the damned, whose respective fates in the hereafter have formed the subject matter of book 4 of the *Sentences*.[52] These Last Things are appropriately symbolized by God's furthest extremities, that is to say, His feet. God's feet are said to be veiled, because we are not allowed to come to a complete understanding of life in the hereafter.

In the second part of the allegory, the Lombard sketches out the structure of the *Book of Sentences*. In book 1, the work started with an investigation of "the face of Him who is seated," that is, with a discussion of the divine essence and the Trinity, which constitute God as He is seen face to face by the blessed. The *media*, "things in the middle," are the elements of creation to which book 2 was devoted. In book 4, the *Sentences* arrived at the "feet," but only after having discussed the Way—Christ—in book 3. In this manner, the *Sentences*, as Aquinas has pointed out, describe a complete circle: from God, through creation, back to God. In fact, the literary structure of the greatest textbook of theology in the West mirrors the rhythm of the cosmos itself. Brought into being by God, the Creator, the world witnesses first the Fall of man, and then his salvation through the Mediator, who through the sacraments enables those who believe in Him to return to their Maker.

Conclusion

THE SIGNIFICANCE AND TRADITION OF THE *SENTENCES*

In the preceding chapters, I have endeavored to take the *Book of Sentences* seriously as a work of theological reflection. I have therefore spoken little of the sources from which the Master derived particular ideas, of the way in which he adapted these sources, and of the manner in which his own more or less synthetic theories were in turn received and transformed by later generations of theologians. Rather, I have placed emphasis upon the internal coherence of the *Sentences*, highlighting the intrinsic interest of Peter Lombard's teachings. It is now time to look back on this presentation, in order to draw some conclusions about Peter Lombard, the "great medieval thinker."

There can be no doubt about the greatness of the Lombard in terms of his accomplishment in pulling together, and reorganizing, the strings of the tradition of Christian thought that preceded him. Peter Lombard discharged this task so brilliantly as to become the leading theologian of his day. Neither can there be any doubt in regard to the sheer influence of his *magnum opus*. Indeed, the present chapter will elaborate upon Peter Lombard's heritage by attempting to present a broad sketch of the history of *Sentences* commentaries in the Middle Ages and beyond. Before embarking upon this outline, however, we must address another question, one that I think we owe Master Peter: what—if any—is the value of

Peter Lombard's theology, above and beyond its indisputable historical significance?

The Theology of the *Sentences*:
Attempt at an Assessment

There is no denying that there are loose ends, gaps, and even inconsistencies in Peter Lombard's account of the Christian faith. Most patently perhaps, Peter fails to develop a coherent theory of the central mystery of Christianity—the Incarnation. In fact, the Master simply refuses to decide among the three theories of the hypostatic union that he analyzes in book 3 of the *Sentences*. In a similar, and related, case of indecisiveness, his refutation of Christological nihilianism remains so ambiguous in its lack of an alternative theory that contemporaries came to consider him a supporter of this doctrine, which was anathematized in 1177.

On the other hand, the Lombard's tendency toward a certain theoretical vagueness does not always produce problematic results. Sometimes, the impression created is one of an attractive openness to a multiplicity of approaches; such is the case, for example, in the *Sentences'* various ways of explaining the image and likeness of God in man. On other occasions, however, Peter provides no viable theory at all, oftentimes simply declaring that the subtlety of the problem under consideration surpasses the capacity of the human mind. The important issue of God's presence to creation "presentially, potentially, and essentially" is a case in point.

The most notable inconsistencies in the *Book of Sentences* occur in connection with its understanding of grace. Did humanity enjoy any special kind of grace, beyond the *gratia creationis*, before the Fall? Peter Lombard seems to vacillate here. With regard to the sacraments, it remains unclear whether such sacraments as penance and marriage both signify and *cause* grace. Is it the remission of sin that brings about contrition (as Peter seems to be suggesting in his treatment of penance), or does contrition effect the grace of forgiveness (as one would expect from Peter's general definition of sacrament)? Further on the issue of the sacraments, the *Sentences* do not manage to reconcile the view of human sexuality as tainted, indelibly, by original sin, with the conception of marriage as a sacrament that images the union of Christ and His Church.

The list of weaknesses in the theology of the *Book of Sentences* could be extended. Let us admit, then, that Peter Lombard's theology is not perfect—owing not so much to defects in the Master's theological acumen as to the historical situation in which he was writing. For Peter Lombard was a pioneer of systematic theology, a trailblazer whose path proved to lead in the right direction, but not without calling for future improvements.

Upon closer inspection, however, some of the weaknesses of the Lombard's *chef d'oeuvre* might turn out to be hidden strengths. We have spoken of Peter Lombard's frequent hesitations, as well as his tendency to declare himself unable to solve crucial theological problems. *Horum autem quod verius sit, non est humani iudicii definire*, "it is not up to human judgment to decide which of these [positions] is more true"—how often have we encountered sentences such as this one in our discussion of Peter's theology! But is such an attitude of humility not, in fact, extremely appropriate with respect to the deepest mysteries of human existence: the nature of God, sin, and salvation? In our postmodern age, we have grown weary and suspicious of those pretending to offer us seamless systems of "absolute knowledge." Much of contemporary philosophy is nothing but an attempt to deconstruct such proud rationalism, in order to rediscover the mystery of existence beneath the tightly woven structures of knowledge that have enabled us to master our world ever more efficiently. But mastery at what price! Peter Lombard's humility, his hesitations, and perhaps even his inconsistencies are important and attractive reminders of the radical finitude of human thought and existence.

Indeed, some of the inconsistencies of the *Book of Sentences* may hold out the chance for us to rethink our own answers—perhaps facile answers—to some of the great questions of life. Let me take the example of sexuality. As Michel Foucault has so brilliantly shown, the modern age has, first through Victorian prudery and then through the "liberation" following it, sought to defuse the mystery of human sexuality: it has dissolved sex by "transforming [it] into discourse."[1] It is irrelevant, in the last analysis, whether this discourse is one of rigid regulation or of libertarian license. The result is the same: the trivialization of sex in endless talk. The modern age is, Foucault would say, thoroughly obscene. Compare Peter Lombard's reflections on the flesh, sex, and marriage with this modern attitude. Peter seems profoundly uncertain about the meaning of human sexuality: is it the vehicle for the transmission of original sin, so that even marriage can do no more than "excuse" the "reprehensible and evil" sexual act? Or is it an integral part of the beautiful sacrament of marriage, which is pervaded by the same charity that also binds Christ to His Church? Prima facie, Peter's indecision appears as just another unfortunate inconsistency in the theology of the *Sentences*. But perhaps it is much more, namely, the refusal to belittle the mystery of sexuality, in both its terrible and beautiful dimensions. In the sexual act, nothing less than the very limits of human subjectivity are at stake; indeed, these limits break down physically. Sexuality involves a terrible, awesome sacrifice of self, awakening Dionysian forces of self-annihilation. As such it is deeply dangerous, irrational, and potentially destructive. Yet the physical union of the married couple is also a sacramental reenactment of the love between God and His Church. I believe that Peter Lombard must have understood the complex, ambiguous character of human sexuality, and that the tensions in his thought on this subject reflect the complexity of reality, rather than an inability on his part to synthesize his sources.

I have referred to problems in the *Sentences'* theology of grace. Ultimately, these tensions are due to the fact that Peter Lombard's conception of the relationship between nature and grace either lacks certain mediating concepts, or has not yet defined them with complete accuracy. The epitome of such a relatively unmediated understanding of how God works in creation is the Lombard's very deliberate identification of charity with the Holy Spirit. For the author of the *Sentences*, charity is not a created virtue or habit of the soul, but the presence of the Spirit itself. Charity subsequently becomes the key to the Lombard's soteriology and ethics and also to his theology of the sacraments. Christ was born from the Virgin Mary "of the Spirit," because the Incarnation was a work of God's ineffable love. Christ's life, especially His passion, was a life of consummate charity—a life that we, in turn, are called to emulate. There is no room, in the *Book of Sentences*, for a consideration of "natural" virtue, that is, virtue independent of the love with which the Christian responds to Jesus' giving of Himself for our salvation. To be sure, the absence of a concept of natural virtue raises questions, for we would hardly want to deny the possibility that people of no faith or of other faiths can, in a very real sense, be virtuous in their conduct. Yet there is a precious intuition in the Lombard's move of tying ethics so closely to virtue, virtue so closely to charity, and charity so closely to Jesus: the Christian life is a life not, in the first place, in accordance with some "law" (even the natural law), but in the fellowship of Christ. The most important way of enacting this fellowship is through participation in the sacraments. Each sacrament reflects a crucial aspect of Christ's life—from His baptism in the river Jordan to the Last Supper—and reinforces the dynamism of charity that commits us to following the Way ever more perfectly. The absence of such concepts as natural virtue and natural law may be problematic from the point of view of a philosophy that, in the Aristotelian tradition, stresses the autonomy of the created order. The idea that a life in the fellowship of Christ is a life in, and indeed of, the Spirit belongs to a different strand of Christian thought, to an older spirituality, the insights of which are worth reconsidering.

The Tradition of the *Sentences*

In the introduction to this book, I quoted Marcia Colish's inspiring suggestion according to which the tradition of commentaries on the *Book of Sentences* could serve as an ideal guiding thread for the study of later medieval (and even early modern) thought. However, brilliant as this idea might appear, Colish quickly adds a "sobering reflection" to her enthusiastic remarks: given the staggering number of *Sentences* commentaries, as well as the fact that most of them remain unedited, it would take a "large international équipe of medievalists with unlimited funding" to pursue the promising project of studying their tradition.[2]

Against the background of both the potential of Colish's idea and the difficulties of putting it into practice, I would like to devote the final pages of this book to the task of outlining a viable methodology that would allow us to begin studying the tradition of *Sentences* commentaries in a systematic manner. In pursuing this line of research, I am indebted to some promising recent scholarship,[3] but also to much older studies; above all, Artur Landgraf's pioneering work on the reception of the *Sentences* in the twelfth century.[4] It is obvious that, in addressing this task, one has to steer clear of overly specific questions that would require detailed textual comparisons among dozens or even hundreds of commentaries. It is equally obvious that my suggestions will have to remain provisional, subject to correction as our knowledge of the *Sentences* commentaries becomes more complete. However, even the relatively small number of edited commentaries would overwhelm us by their wealth of material if we did not have categories of research at our disposal that enabled us to structure this material. In short, what are the most fruitful questions that we can ask in attempting to approach the tradition of *Sentences* commentaries in the current state of research?

Patterns in the Development of Medieval Commentary Traditions

As a textual tradition, the tradition of commentaries on the *Sentences* is not unique. Textual traditions tend to develop around core texts in concentric circles—successive layers of elucidation that build upon each other. The Christian tradition is centered around the Gospels. In chapter 1, we saw how these were first commented upon in the apostolic letters. The writings of the Church Fathers constituted the next layer of elucidation; upon their basis, as well as in dialogue with the biblical texts themselves, later Christian thinkers continued to develop the tradition. Over the centuries, other texts judged to be helpful in explaining Scripture were drawn into the circle of Christian thought—Neoplatonic and Aristotelian works, for instance. In the early Middle Ages, two texts of Aristotelian logic were particularly influential in shaping the debate, namely, the *Categories* and *De interpretatione*, which were available to medieval thinkers in Boethius's translations.

In an article that was originally published in 1993, the Cambridge medievalist John Marenbon devised a conceptual framework to analyze the medieval tradition of glosses and commentaries upon these treatises.[5] Marenbon argues that in the first stage of the reception of Aristotelian logic—in Carolingian times—authors such as Alcuin and his pupils "worked by abbreviating, extracting, and compiling their authoritative texts."[6] Later, through the eleventh century, the gloss became the typical form of commentary. Both Carolingian and later thinkers, however, more frequently worked with Porphyry's *Isagoge* and a pseudo-Augustinian paraphrase of the *Categories*, the *Categoriae decem*, than with the *Categories* and *De interpretatione* themselves. And when glossators had the courage to tackle Aristotle, their glosses were mostly adapted from Boethius's commentaries.

This situation changed in the twelfth century, when there was an increasing number of close literal commentaries on Aristotle. Moreover, these commentaries became gradually more independent of Boethius. Marenbon distinguishes three types of commentaries from the twelfth century:

1. "Literal" commentaries provide a close reading of Aristotle's text; in doing so, they use a variety of patterns and techniques to throw into relief the structure of Aristotle's argument. These range from simple phrases such as, "Having said X, Aristotle now turns to Y," to detailed topical analyses.

2. "Composite" commentaries combine the approach of the literal commentaries with sections devoted to "discursive treatment of problems,"[7] often in the literary form of the *quaestio*.

3. Finally, "problem-question" commentaries take a further step away from literal exegesis, concentrating upon the discussion of the philosophical issues raised in Aristotle's texts, rather than on the letter of the texts themselves.

From Marenbon's description, "there emerges a definite pattern of development in earlier medieval logic."[8] In fact, the tradition begins by abbreviating, extracting, and compiling texts related to Aristotelian logic. Subsequently, it turns to a closer reading of this propaedeutic material, such as the *Isagoge* and the *Categoriae decem*. At this stage, Aristotle's own works are glossed only rarely, and if they are, the glosses rely heavily upon Boethius's commentaries. Finally, the tradition is ready for literal exegesis of the *Categories* and *De interpretatione* themselves, literal exegesis that rapidly combines with more independent philosophical reflection. In the end, such independent reflection supersedes the literal commentary.

Another important aspect of Marenbon's analysis concerns the introductions to the commentaries. These introductions, which are meant to situate the work under consideration within the curriculum, exhibit definite patterns as well. Often, they follow these six points, which are derived from Boethius's first commentary on the *Isagoge*: intention of the author, utility of the work, its place in the order of study, its authenticity, its title, and the branch of learning to which it belongs.[9]

There are indications that a pattern similar to the one described by Marenbon also characterized the development of intellectual practices at the early universities, when the Christian tradition was faced with the task of digesting another wave of Aristotelian texts.[10] However, the question to which I would like to turn now is whether Marenbon's pattern is able to help us in our task of analyzing the tradition of *Sentences* commentaries. Do they follow similar lines of development? If so, Marenbon's categories of analysis would provide a viable methodology for a first understanding of the tradition of *Sentences* commentaries.

The Literary Form of the
Commentaries on the *Sentences*

Peter Lombard "read" the *Sentences* twice during his teaching career at Notre Dame, namely, in the academic years 1156–1157 and 1157–1158. Discussion of his work naturally began among his own students, but as recognition of the value of the *Sentences* increased, interest rapidly spread to other centers of learning. The earliest reception of the work, until the end of the twelfth century, took place in the form of abbreviations and glosses.

The abbreviations were elementary study aids, among which Père Raymond Martin has distinguished no fewer than eight kinds.[11] Most of the abbreviations of the *Sentences* were written in prose, but some manuscripts preserve abbreviations composed in verse. Some offer an abridgment of the entire text, while others limit themselves to parts. Again, certain abbreviations provide a kind of dictionary of technical terms employed in the *Sentences* (*verborum significationes*). There are also synoptic tables, as well as analytical or alphabetical tables of content. Martin Grabmann has drawn attention to the fact that some abbreviations were later themselves abridged.[12] Finally, in a development in which the literary genre of the abbreviation began to move beyond its original limits, some abbreviations incorporated other masters' opinions, or critiques of Peter Lombard's positions.

While abbreviations were employed from the very beginning of studies of the *Sentences*,[13] some continued to enjoy great popularity in later centuries. One of the last, but also most widespread abridgments—modestly entitled *Filia Magistri*, "Daughter of the Master"—was copied right into the fifteenth century.[14] Created sometime between 1232 and 1245, most likely by Hugh of St. Cher,[15] *Filia Magistri* reworked an older abbreviation, bringing it up to date by incorporating notes from Hugh's own commentary on the *Sentences*. Given their nature as study aids, abbreviations tended to undergo constant revision in function of the needs of their users. *Filia Magistri*, for example, is preserved in numerous manuscripts of unequal length.

Another early form of reflection upon the *Book of Sentences* was the gloss. Two kinds need to be distinguished: marginal glosses and keyword glosses.[16] The boundaries between these two forms remained fluid, since marginal glosses often furnished the material for the more developed and independent keyword glosses. The first users of Master Peter's *Sentences* annotated copies of the work in the margins of the manuscripts in which they circulated. These annotations, which have been examined by Joseph de Ghellinck,[17] served a variety of purposes. Some identify Peter Lombard's biblical and patristic sources; others draw attention to textual variants between the two "editions" of the *Book of Sentences* or offer brief critical discussions of its content; still others, going further, indicate parallel reflections in contemporary works. It is important to note that such marginal remarks were not limited to the period immediately following the publication of the *Sentences*, but continued to be added to manuscripts of the work right into the fifteenth and sixteenth centuries. Nonetheless, de Ghellinck considered the earliest annotations to represent "le stade primitif," as he said, of more fully developed commentaries.[18]

For such marginal annotations often spawned more elaborate glosses that were conceived as continuous works in their own right. In the marginal glosses, the word or phrase commented upon was indicated by means of a sign placed within the text and repeated in the margin. When such glosses were incorporated into a continuous work, keywords replaced the signs to indicate the portion of the *Sentences* being explicated. However, the continuous glosses did not content themselves with simply copying, in a mechanical way, marginal annotations from existing manuscripts of the *Sentences*. Rather, they created a selection of glosses considered particularly relevant, as well as adding fresh material from other sources, namely, other contemporary works of theology. These additions, which could not but draw attention to doctrinal problems and disagreements among different masters and schools, then occasioned small units of discussion. In this manner, first *quaestiones* arose within the *Sentences* literature.

The earliest known continuous gloss of the *Sentences* is also the one that found the widest dissemination in later times.[19] Composed before 1175, it is an anonymous work that used to be attributed, though mistakenly, to Peter of Poitiers.[20] The prologue of this so-called Pseudo-Poitiers gloss was adapted from an even earlier work, an introduction to the *Sentences* authored by Peter Comestor, whom we have encountered in previous chapters of this book as a student of the Lombard's at Notre Dame.[21] This early prologue inaugurates what was to become a long tradition: for centuries, the prefaces of *Sentences* commentaries were to function as the *locus classicus* of reflection upon the meaning, limits, and method of theology as a branch of knowledge. As for the length of the Pseudo-Poitiers gloss, it occupies folios 2 through 70 in its earliest known manuscript, namely, MS. *Naples, Biblioteca nazionale, VII C 14.*

Our rapid examination of the two main literary genres in which the *Book of Sentences* was first received exhibits marked parallels to the patterns that John Marenbon discerned in his studies on the early tradition of Aristotelian logic.[22] In both cases, the early reception of the authoritative text (or texts) is characterized by a slow process of familiarization in which the works are approached by means of simplifying study aids (such as paraphrases and abbreviations). Glosses, too, do not yet address the texts in their entirety—as complete projects, as it were—but rather aim to explain or question isolated passages and ideas. It is only at the next stage, that of the commentary, that the authoritative works are appropriated and subjected to critique as a whole, in all their foundations and ramifications.

In the case of the *Sentences*, Landgraf has argued that the beginning of this stage is marked by the commentary of Stephen Langton († 1228). The newly holistic character of this commentary is thrown into relief by the fact that the keywords in Langton's *Commentarius in Sententias* are no longer employed to identify individual words and phrases, but rather identify entire sections of the *Sentences*.[23] Indeed, Langton's commentary seems to presuppose a reading and understanding of Peter Lombard's work, for it tends to create its own emphases in function of the author's personal interests, as well as the state of contemporary debates. For instance, Stephen Langton summarizes the Lombard's controversial identification of charity with the Holy Spirit in exactly one sentence, refuting it in the next: " 'This however.' The Master was of the opinion that charity was not some kind of virtue, and that charity is nothing but the Holy Spirit, and that we love God and neighbor through the Holy Spirit only. We are not of this opinion, since charity is a virtue through which we love, just like faith."[24]

Instead of examining the *Sentences'* doctrine on charity, which takes up all six chapters of distinction 17 in book 1, Langton focuses his discussion on the problem of the missions of the Son and of the Spirit—a corollary of Peter Lombard's original point. Some distinctions are dispatched in one sentence, others ignored entirely. All in all, Landgraf's edition of the *Commentarius in Sententias* from the only extant manuscript (which lacks most of book 4) runs to just 153 pages. Thus, Langton's commentary on the *Sentences* represents a rather primitive example of the new genre.

Alexander of Hales is well known as the first Scholastic to use the *Book of Sentences* as the basis of his theology lectures. Let us begin our discussion of his *Glossa in quatuor libros Sententiarum Petri Lombardi* with the most obvious point.[25] Composed between 1223 and 1227, the work fills four thick volumes in its modern edition. In other words, in the fifty or sixty years that elapsed since the first abbreviations and glosses, the tradition learned how to read Peter Lombard closely, through commentary that takes its users through every step of the argument. But more than that, the commentators of the *Sentences* have come to an understanding of the structure of the work as a whole. We may remember from a previous chapter that Alexander's *Glossa* contains an important innovation: it bundles Peter Lombard's chapters into "distinctions," that is to say, it introduces divisions in between the chapter and the book levels that lend additional structure to the contents of the *Sentences*.[26] With a similar goal, Alexander inserts *divisiones textus* into his commentary—paragraphs in which he explains the line of thought that ties together several distinctions.[27] The commentary itself exhibits a level of reflection in which a basic comprehension of the text is presupposed. With rare exceptions,[28] Alexander does therefore not explain difficult words or paraphrase Peter Lombard's ideas. Rather, he discusses issues the text raises, attempts to resolve difficulties, and replies to objections. In fact, much of the commentary foreshadows the format of later Scholastic *quaestiones*. In his own *Introitus* to the work, Alexander sketches out the four books of the *Sentences* and the theological project as he understands it, on the basis of a scriptural quotation—a practice that was to become standard procedure.

Bonaventure, too, uses it in his *Prooemium* to the first book of the *Sentences*, but with an important addition.[29] The Seraphic Doctor combines the scriptural quotation with a presentation of the *Book of Sentences* in terms of the Aristotelian four causes: material, formal, final, and efficient. In this way, Bonaventure manages to marry a biblical approach with more "scientific" Aristotelian analysis of the theological project. At the end of his proem, he poses four *quaestiones*, structured according to the classic Scholastic format. The questions deal with the status of theology as a science, addressing its *subiectum* and *modus procedendi;* they ask whether it is a speculative or a practical science; and they examine the meaning of authorship in theology.[30] Bonaventure then turns his attention to Peter Lombard's own preface, to which he devotes close literal commentary that combines three *divisiones textus* with nine *dubia circa litteram*. Bonaventure's entire work—composed between 1253 and 1257—follows a similar pattern: the logical structure of the text of each distinction is first analyzed in a *divisio textus;* then several *quaestiones* of a more speculative kind are raised; and finally we get *dubia circa litteram*, that is, discussions of specific questions concerning Peter Lombard's own meaning. Bonaventure's commentary represents a stage in the reception of the *Book of Sentences* where Peter Lombard's text is subjected to close literal study, while at the same time serving as a point of departure for much more independent theological reflection. Many of the questions that Bonaventure raises reflect contemporary theological discussions, rather than issues arising directly from the *Book of Sentences*. In other words, Bonaventure's commentary both supports exhaustive study of the *Sentences* themselves and functions as a vehicle for the expression of the Seraphic Doctor's own thought—two central characteristics of the *Sentences* commentaries in the middle of the thirteenth century.[31]

We need not spend a lot of time on Thomas Aquinas's *Sentences* commentary, for its literary form is very much like that of Bonaventure's work.[32] Indeed, the two commentaries were composed almost simultaneously while their respective authors lectured at the University of Paris. What is worth noting, however, is this: we know from Tolomeo of Lucca that, in 1265–1267, Aquinas undertook a second, now lost, redaction of the first book of his *Sentences* commentary.[33] Yet after book 1 he gave up, presumably because the structure of the *Book of Sentences* did not enable him to articulate his own vision of systematic theology. Subsequently, Thomas embarked on the composition of the *Summa theologiae*, which allowed him to create a new order for his theological material. In other words, it would seem that, at the time of Thomas Aquinas, the *Book of Sentences* already begins to be viewed as an insufficient means for systematic theological reflection. Theologians start to create other genres.

Nonetheless, and interestingly, the commentaries continue. But they are no longer properly commentaries, moving away as they do further and further from the letter of the Lombard's text—just like the mature commentaries on Aristotle's *Categories* and *De interpretatione* examined by Marenbon. We can see this "taking off" of the *Sentences* commentaries impressively in Duns Scotus and William of Ockham. Scotus's massive *Ordinatio*, the fruit of many years of teaching courses based upon the *Sentences*, was composed between 1305 and 1307—or, rather, as the title suggests, during that period Scotus "arranged" different courses he had given on various books of the *Sentences* in one work.[34] We have already discovered that, since the time of the earliest glosses, the prologue tended to take on a life of its own, growing into a brief treatise on theological methodology. The prologue of the *Ordinatio* goes much further, however, filling 237 pages in the modern critical edition.[35] It falls into five *partes*, which respectively discuss the necessity of revealed doctrine, the sufficiency of Sacred Scripture, the object of theology, theology as a science, and theology as a practical science. Each of the *partes* is further subdivided into questions (though parts 1 and 2 have only one question each). These *quaestiones* are of a more complex literary structure than the "classical" ones of the thirteenth century, a fact that Russell Friedman attributes to the shift from an "argument-centered" to a "position-centered" approach.[36] In other words, as the theological debate advanced, arguments that used to be relatively straightforward—so straightforward that they could be handled satisfactorily in classical-style pro and con *quaestiones*—spawned positions of increasing complexity and sophistication. These positions then needed to be examined one by one, and in a detailed fashion, by any theologian attempting to develop his own solution and to define it over against the competing theories.

Duns Scotus's treatment of the first distinction of book 1 epitomizes the relationship between the *Ordinatio* and the text of the *Book of Sentences*. It is a very loose relationship. Scotus takes inspiration from some of the themes Peter Lombard discusses, but develops them without much reference to the *Sentences*. Thus, distinction 1 is devoted to the nature of enjoyment, or *fruitio*, a topic inspired by the Lombard's Augustinian distinction between use and enjoyment. Scotus, however, focuses on *fruitio* alone, dealing with *usus* very briefly in one sentence at the very end.[37] In other words, the *uti-frui* distinction no longer serves as a structuring principle in Scotus's theology, as it had in Peter Lombard's. One cannot but agree with the judgment expressed by the learned editor of the *Ordinatio*: "Whoever closely examines Duns Scotus's *Lectures* [on the *Sentences*] will immediately see that the Subtle Doctor has composed neither glosses nor commentaries properly speaking, but rather his own writing, a work of his own, occasioned by the text of the master. This is to be asserted with even greater certainty of the *Ordinatio*."[38]

William of Ockham put together his *Scriptum* on the *Sentences* only a few years after Scotus, in the years from 1319 to 1324, but the tendencies we already observed in Scotus's *Ordinatio* appear even more strikingly in Ockham's work. Again, the *Prologus* constitutes an independent treatise on the status of theology as a science and on theological method, a treatise developed in function of Ockham's own philosophico-theological options. This prologue runs to 370 pages in the critical edition.[39] The literary form of the twelve *quaestiones* that make up the *Prologus* has mutated beyond recognition; in fact, the complexity of Ockham's *quaestiones* resembles that of a modern chapter, in which the arrangement of arguments is not governed by any set pattern but is entirely at the author's discretion. Ockham's treatment of the first distinction consists of six *quaestiones* which (unlike Scotus's) do address the *frui-uti* distinction.

After Ockham, Peter Lombard's text fades even further into the background, although the *Book of Sentences* remains the occasion for a significant amount of theological writing. Yet the general importance of the genre seems to be diminishing: after the monumental productions of the first half of the fourteenth century, *Sentences* commentaries now become shorter. Moreover, many theologians no longer bother to publish their lectures on the *Sentences*.[40] Like most of his contemporaries,[41] Marsilius of Inghen, who composed his *Quaestiones super quattuor libros Sententiarum* between 1392 and 1396, gives up the division into distinctions, arranging his material only according to his own *quaestiones*. Sometimes, the subject matter of the questions corresponds to one or several distinctions, but like Scotus and Ockham, Marsilius feels no obligation to cover all of them.[42] Indeed, "only seldom is the content of the distinctions referred to briefly."[43] Before Marsilius, Robert Holcot († 1349) had already taken much greater liberties with the arrangement of theological material in the *Book of Sentences*, opting to shift issues originally belonging to the first book into the second.[44] What we witness in the fourteenth century, thus, is the fact that the *Book of Sentences* no longer provides anything but a basic structure for the discussion of theological matters, a basic structure in the sense of a rough grid that suggests an order for the arrangement of questions. This grid, however, is itself subject to modification.

Until the fourteenth century, then, the medieval reception of the *Sentences* appears to follow a logical and predictable course similar—let me stress it again—to the pattern described by John Marenbon. The earliest approaches to the work occur in literary genres that, defining themselves closely in relation to the authoritative text, serve propaedeutic and ancillary functions. From these abbreviations and glosses, there gradually grow more exhaustive treatments of the *Sentences* in commentaries, which not only display a command of individual passages and questions, but serve as elucidations of the Lombard's theological project as a whole. At the same time, the most mature of the commentaries—best exemplified by the works of Bonaventure and Thomas Aquinas—use the *Sentences* as a foil for the development of their own visions of theological knowledge, its method, structure, and contents. This balance, however, is quickly lost when fourteenth-century theologians first explode the boundaries of the *Sentences* commentary in runaway discussions of ever-increasing detail that submerge the structure of the original work, and then lose interest in the genre, which by the end of the century seems to have exhausted its usefulness as a vehicle for theological discussion.

The little research that exists on the *Sentences* literature of the fifteenth century indicates a fascinating reversal of this trend. It is almost as though, once the textual tradition of the *Sentences* had expanded to its extreme limits and moved further and further away from its center, it contracted again, returning to the text of the Lombard's work in a renaissance of interest in the Master himself. Indeed, in an excellent contribution on the *Sentences* in the fifteenth century, John Van Dyk has remarked that "the spirit of 'back-to-the sources,' so characteristic of the humanists, may well have pervaded the minds and hearts of the fifteenth-century *Sentences* commentators."[45] Thus, the commentaries of this period once again cover the whole of the Lombard's book. In a centripetal move balancing the centrifugal tendencies of the innovators of the fourteenth century, their fifteenth-century successors frequently content themselves with the task of recording and cataloging the positions of their predecessors, taking stock, as it were, of the tradition. Nonetheless, the great

Sentences commentaries of this time are not devoid of individual flavor and orientation. Denis the Carthusian combines the two tendencies in his commentary, composed between 1459 and 1464, which illustrates and expounds on the Master's ideas by means of extensive references to the great authorities of the tradition, while giving the whole work a mystical bent.[46] In the fifteenth century, the genre is also resurrected as "a key vehicle for theological dialogue"[47] between and among different schools. Such is the case, for example, in the commentaries of John Hus with their Wyclifite influence, or in the *Defensiones* of Thomism which John Capreolus presented in the form of a *Sentences* commentary.[48]

Before concluding this rapid overview, it will be interesting to cast a glance on the work of one of the last great theologians who commented upon the *Book of Sentences*: Martin Luther. Luther lectured on the *Sentences* at the University of Erfurt from 1509 to 1511, using a copy of the work printed in 1489 by Nicolaus Kesler of Basel. This copy has survived; it carries copious and careful marginal annotations.[49] The theological import of Luther's glosses has been the subject of several studies.[50] I will only say a few words here about their literary form and then add a brief reflection on the Reformer's preface.

There are three kinds of marginal remarks in Luther's copy of the *Sentences*, remarks, by the way, that were clearly meant not just as notes for their author's own use, but for other readers as well. Some of these glosses explain difficult words and phrases in Peter Lombard's text; for example, Luther glosses *compegimus* in the Lombard's preface with *compilavimus*, "we have compiled." Other glosses provide references to Scripture and the Fathers; for instance, Luther helps the reader of the preface by explaining that, "for the most part, this prologue is Hilary, book ten, and Augustine, book 3 [of] *On the Trinity*."[51] A third group of glosses represents brief theological and exegetical reflections. There is evidence that Luther must have consulted several contemporary glossed books of the *Sentences* in drawing up his own notes. By contrast, he does not appear to be familiar with the tradition of the great commentaries; for example, there is no reference to Bonaventure or Aquinas. Thus, at the beginning of the sixteenth century, the *Sentences* seem to have been studied quite naïvely, at least in certain quarters; and I do not mean this judgment in a pejorative sense. One could also speak of a fresh approach to the Master, one taking his text seriously, rather than allowing it to be overshadowed by hundreds of years of commentary. Before Luther formulated his famous principle of *Sola Scriptura*, he seems to have applied a similar approach to Peter Lombard: *Solis Sententiis*.

Luther's prologue shows that, paradoxically, the Reformer regarded the author of the *Sentences*—the work that developed into the greatest textbook of Scholastic theology—as a fellow traveler in his struggles against the influence of philosophy upon theological studies. As we know from our own examination of the *Sentences*, this assessment is not totally without foundation. After all, does Peter Lombard not declare, quite explicitly, that *fidei sacramentum a philosophicis argumentis est liberum*, "the sacrament of faith is free from philosophical arguments"?[52] In his prologue, Luther writes:

> Although I feel that the spoils of philosophy are not to be utterly rejected as of advantage to sacred theology, nevertheless the prudent restraint and unsullied purity of the Master of the *Sentences* wins my strongest approval in the fact that in every respect he so relies upon the lights of the Church, and especially of Augustine (whose radiance is the most brilliant and whose praise is never sufficient), that he seems to hold in suspicion whatever is anxiously explored but not yet known by the philosophers. And certainly to concern oneself with too much dedication with these thorn bushes, wrappers, and what approaches mere trifles—what else does this involve, I ask, but to build oneself labyrinths of irreversible error, to dig under the sand, and, to put it more pointedly, to push the rock of Sisyphus and to turn the wheels of Ixion? What will be the end of opinions and most pugnacious sects? The world is full of Chrysippus, yes even Chimeras and Hydras! The poets could devise nothing more expressive and humorous to laugh at the struggles, battles, and sects of the philosophers, than such monsters as these; they are certainly laughable, yet also appropriate and most acute in their witty pungency.
>
> Therefore, love authors of integrity, fidelity, and purity, or at least (if necessarily it must be so) acquire an ordinary familiarity with them, the philosophers I mean, that is to say, the opinionated doubters.[53]

A great thinker is an author whose works are sufficiently broad and rich, containing enough layers of meaning, to bear almost infinite reading and rereading by generations of interpreters. Peter Lombard's *Book of Sentences* has been the object of such fecund interpretation for more than eight hundred years, serving Christian thinkers again and again as a useful foil for their own understanding of who they are, and what their faith is. Even this small book is part of the tradition of the *Book of Sentences*, which Peter Lombard's students started sometime in the middle of the twelfth century, at the cathedral school of Notre Dame in Paris. In this sense, there cannot be the slightest doubt that Peter Lombard was, indeed, a great medieval thinker.

NOTES

INTRODUCTION

1. See Martin Grabmann, *Die Geschichte der scholastischen Methode*, vol. 2, *Die scholastische Methode im 12. und beginnenden 13. Jahrhundert* (Freiburg, Germany: Herder, 1911; reprint, Berlin: Akademie-Verlag, 1988), 392.

2. See Friedrich Stegmüller, *Repertorium commentariorum in Sententias Petri Lombardi*, 2 vols. (Würzburg: Schöningh, 1947). In truth, not all 1,407 entries are commentaries on the *Sentences*, though the bulk of them are. Stegmüller, however, also includes literature that is related to the *Sentences*, such as the works of Peter Abelard and Thomas Aquinas's *Summa theologiae*. Several updates to Stegmüller's *Repertorium* have appeared; the first one was Victorin Doucet, *Commentaires sur les Sentences: Supplément au Répertoire de M. Frédéric Stegmueller* (Quaracchi: Typographia Collegii S. Bonaventurae, 1954). For an up-to-date assessment of efforts to complete and correct Stegmüller's work, see Steven J. Livesey, "*Lombardus electronicus*: A Biographical Database of Medieval Commentators on Peter Lombard's *Sentences*," in *Mediaeval Commentaries on the* Sentences *of Peter Lombard: Current Research*, vol. 1, ed. G. R. Evans (Leiden/Boston/Cologne: Brill, 2002), 1–23, esp. 1–3.

3. See, most recently, Josef Wieneke, *Luther und Petrus Lombardus: Martin Luthers Notizen anläßlich seiner Vorlesung über die Sentenzen des Petrus Lombardus, Erfurt 1509/11*, Dissertationen, Theologische Reihe 71 (St. Ottilien: EOS Verlag, 1994). The well-known medievalist Paul Vignaux devoted a book to "Luther as commentator of the *Sentences*" in 1935: *Luther commen-*

tateur des Sentences (livre I, distinction XVII), Études de philosophie médiévale 21 (Paris: Vrin, 1935).

4. Colish, *Peter Lombard*, 1.

5. Martin Anton Schmidt calls the *Sentences* "ein Sammelbecken der bisherigen scholastischen Arbeit"; see his article "Die umfassende Bestandsaufnahme durch Petrus Lombardus," in *Die Lehrentwicklung im Rahmen der Katholizität*, vol. 1 of *Handbuch der Dogmen- und Theologiegeschichte*, ed. Carl Andresen (Göttingen: Vandenhoeck & Ruprecht, 1982), 594–605, at 594.

6. On the evaluation of Peter Lombard in modern scholarship, see Ermenegildo Bertola, "Pietro Lombardo nella storiografia filosofica medioevale," *Pier Lombardo* 4 (1960): 95–113.

7. Joseph de Ghellinck, S.J., *Le mouvement théologique du XIIᵉ siècle. Sa préparation lointaine avant et autour de Pierre Lombard. Ses rapports avec les initiatives des canonistes. Études, recherches et documents*, 2d ed., Museum Lessianum, Section historique 10 (Bruges: Éditions de Tempel; Brussels: L'Édition universelle; Paris: Desclée de Brouwer, 1948), 2: "une œuvre... dont la célébrité dépasse la valeur."

8. Grabmann, *Geschichte der scholastischen Methode*, 2:369.

9. Ibid., 406.

10. See Philippe Delhaye, *Pierre Lombard. Sa vie, ses œuvres, sa morale*, Conférence Albert le Grand 1960 (Montreal: Institut d'études médiévales; Paris: Vrin, 1961).

11. Ibid., 9.

12. Ibid.: "Son époque a connu des théologiens plus profonds: Abélard ou Hugues de Saint-Victor, des philosophes plus avertis."

13. Colish, *Peter Lombard*, 3.

14. Ibid., 77f. Earlier scholars, such as Joseph de Ghellinck, were not oblivious to the genuine superiority of the *Sentences* by comparison with its contemporary rivals: "On le voit," de Ghellinck wrote in his long article on Peter Lombard in the *Dictionnaire de théologie catholique*, "la suite logique des matières et un programme des questions aussi complet que possible donnent à l'œuvre de Pierre Lombard une réelle supériorité!" ("Pierre Lombard," in *DTC* XII/2 [1935], cols. 1941–2019, at 1980). It is strange that de Ghellinck nonetheless came to the negative judgment quoted earlier.

15. Several instances of such misrepresentations of Peter Lombard's teachings have been adverted to by reviewers. See, in particular, the review by W. Becket Soule, O.P., in *The Thomist* 61 (1997): 317–20; and Constant J. Mews's extended discussion of the work in *The Medieval Review* 95.07.03, downloaded August 28, 2002, from www.hti.umich.edu/t/tmr/.

16. See, for instance, *Medieval Commentaries on the* Sentences *of Peter*

Lombard: Current Research, vol. 1, ed. G. R. Evans (Leiden/Boston/Cologne: Brill, 2002).

17. David E. Luscombe, *The School of Peter Abelard: The Influence of Abelard's Thought in the Early Scholastic Period*, Cambridge Studies in Medieval Life and Thought, 2d ser., 14 (Cambridge: Cambridge University Press, 1969), 262.

18. Colish, *Peter Lombard*, 34.

I. FROM STORY TO SYSTEM

1. On the rationality of traditions, see Alasdair MacIntyre, *Whose Justice? Which Rationality?* (Notre Dame, Ind.: University of Notre Dame Press, 1988), chap. 18. Also see the interesting remarks in Paul Moyaert, *Ethiek en sublimatie: Over "De ethiek van de psychoanalyse" van Jacques Lacan* (Nijmegen: SUN, 1994), 121–25.

2. See François Picavet, *Esquisse d'une histoire générale et comparée des philosophies médiévales* (Paris: Alcan, 1905), 49: "La philosophie théologique du moyen âge commence au 1er siècle avec saint Paul, chez les chrétiens." On this topic, also see Martin Grabmann, *Die Geschichte der scholastischen Methode*, vol. 1, *Die scholastische Methode von ihren ersten Anfängen in der Väterliteratur bis zum Beginn des 12. Jahrhunderts* (Freiburg, Germany: Herder, 1909; reprint, Berlin: Akademie-Verlag, 1988), 55–65; and André Léonard, *Foi et philosophies: guide pour un discernement chrétien*, Chrétiens aujourd'hui, n.s., 4 (Namur: Culture et Vérité, 1991), 11–24.

3. On St. Paul and Hellenism, see Abraham J. Malherbe, *Paul and the Popular Philosophers* (Minneapolis, Minn.: Fortress Press, 1989).

4. Henrik Ljungman, *Das Gesetz erfüllen: Matth. 5,17 ff. und 3,15 untersucht*, Lunds Universitets Årsskrift, N.F. Avd. 1, vol. 50, no. 6 (Lund: Gleerup, 1954), 94.

5. Adolf von Harnack, "Geschichte eines programmatischen Wortes Jesu (Matt. 5,17) in der ältesten Kirche," in idem, *Kleine Schriften zur Alten Kirche: Berliner Akademieschriften 1908–1930*, Opuscula IX, 2 (Leipzig: Zentralantiquariat der Deutschen Demokratischen Republik, 1980), 166–89, at 189.

6. See ibid., 188. More recently, James McEvoy has explored the biblical origins of what he calls "a genuine, original Christian dialectic" (p. 2) in his article "The Patristic Hermeneutic of Spiritual Freedom and Its Biblical Origins," in *Scriptural Interpretation in the Fathers: Letter and Spirit*, ed. Thomas Finan and Vincent Twomey (Blackrock, Co. Dublin: Four Courts Press, 1995), 1–25. Also interesting in this connection is Rémi Brague's thesis on the structural "eccentricity" or "secondary" of Christianity in its relation to

Judaism; see Rémi Brague, *Eccentric Culture: A Theory of Western Civilization*, trans. Samuel Lester (South Bend, Ind.: St. Augustine's Press, 2002), esp. 43–64.

7. See Grabmann, *Geschichte der scholastischen Methode*, vol. 1, esp. 62–63.

8. See Tertullianus, *Adversus Praxean*, ed. A. Kroymann and E. Evans, Corpus Christianorum, Series Latina 2 (Turnhout: Brepols, 1954), 1157–1205.

9. See Tertullianus, *De praescriptione haereticorum*, ed. R. F. Refoulé, Corpus Christianorum, Series Latina 1.1 (Turnhout: Brepols, 1954), 7.9–12, p. 193, ll. 32–34 and 36–39: "Quid ergo Athenis et Hierosolymis? quid academiae et ecclesiae? quid haereticis et christianis? . . . Viderint qui Stoicum et Platonicum et dialecticum christianismum protulerunt. Nobis curiositate opus non est post Christum Iesum nec inquisitione post euangelium."

10. Tertullianus, *De fuga in persecutione*, 4.1, ed. J. J. Thierry, Corpus Christianorum, Series Latina 2, pp. 1133–55, at p. 1140, ll. 13–14.

11. Tertullianus, *De carne Christi*, 5.4, ed. A. Kroymann, Corpus Christianorum, Series Latina 2, pp. 871–917, at p. 881, ll. 28–29.

12. Recent debates on the distinction between things and signs, and between use and enjoyment, are summarized in Hubertus R. Drobner, "Studying Augustine: An Overview of Recent Research," in *Augustine and His Critics: Essays in Honour of Gerald Bonner*, ed. Robert Dodaro and George Lawless (London and New York: Routledge, 2000), 18–34, esp. 25f. (with bibliography).

13. Augustine, *De doctrina christiana*, 1.84, ed. and trans. R. P. H. Green, Oxford Early Christian Texts (Oxford: Clarendon Press, 1995), 49. For a collection of recent research on the work, see *De Doctrina Christiana: A Classic of Western Culture*, ed. Duane W. H. Arnold and Pamela Bright, Christianity and Judaism in Antiquity 9 (Notre Dame and London: Notre Dame University Press, 1995). Pages 247–60 proffer a "Bibliography of *De doctrina christiana*" by Lewis Ayres.

14. Augustine, *De doctrina christiana*, 1.86, p. 49.

15. See Grabmann, *Geschichte der scholastischen Methode*, 1:134.

16. See Augustine, *De doctrina christiana*, 2.30–58.

17. Ibid., 2.143, p. 125.

18. Ibid., 2.144–48, pp. 124–27.

19. On the dialogue in antiquity, see the classic work by Rudolf Hirzel, *Der Dialog: Ein literarhistorischer Versuch*, 2 vols. (Leipzig: Hirzel, 1895; reprint, Hildesheim: Olms, 1963). Pages 366–80 of vol. 2 are devoted to ancient Christian literature. More recently, see the useful article by J. Gruber et al., "Dialog," in *Lexikon des Mittelalters*, vol. 3 (Stuttgart and Weimar: Metzler, 1999), 946–65.

20. Grabmann, *Geschichte der scholastischen Methode*, 1:83.

21. See Origen, *De principiis* (Περὶ ἀρχῶν) ed. Paul Koetschau, Origines Werke 5/Die griechischen christlichen Schriftsteller der ersten Jahrhunderte 22 (Leipzig: Hinrichs, 1913); English translation: *On First Principles*, trans. G. W. Butterworth (New York: Harper & Row, 1966). For a good introduction, see Lothar Lies, *Origenes' Peri Archon: Eine undogmatische Dogmatik. Einführung und Erläuterung*, Werkinterpretationen (Darmstadt: Wissenschaftliche Buchgesellschaft, 1992).

22. See Joseph de Ghellinck, S.J., *Le mouvement théologique du XIIᵉ siècle: Sa préparation lointaine avant et autour de Pierre Lombard, ses rapports avec les initiatives des canonistes. Études, recherches et documents*, 2d ed., Museum Lessianum, Section historique 10 (Bruges: Éditions de Tempel; Brussels: L'édition universelle; Paris: Desclée de Brouwer, 1948), 6.

23. See John of Damascus, Ἔκδοσις ἀκριβὴς τῆς ὀρθοδόξου πίστεως, ed. Bonifatius Kotter, Die Schriften des Johannes von Damaskos 2/Patristische Texte und Studien 12 (Berlin: de Gruyter, 1973); English translation: St. John of Damascus, *Writings*, trans. Frederic Henry Chase, The Fathers of the Church 37 (New York: Fathers of the Church, 1958).

24. See John Damascene, *De fide orthodoxa: Versions of Burgundio and Cerbanus*, ed. Eligius M. Buytaert (St. Bonaventure, N.Y.: Franciscan Institute, 1955).

25. See Prosperi Aquitani, *Liber sententiarum*, ed. M. Gastaldo, Prosperi Aquitani Opera 2/Corpus Christianorum, Series Latina 68A (Turnhout: Brepols, 1972), 215–365.

26. See Grabmann, *Geschichte der scholastischen Methode*, 2:21–23. Grabmann cites the following definition of *sententia* from a sentence collection of the first half of the twelfth century: "Ut ex diversis praeceptis et doctrinis Patrum excerperem et in unum colligerem eos flores quos solemus, quasi singulari nomine, sententias appellare."

27. See *The New Shorter Oxford English Dictionary*, ed. Lesley Brown (Oxford: Clarendon Press, 1993), vol. 2, s.v. "sentence," 4.

28. See Isidori Hispalensis Episcopi, *Etymologicarum sive originum libri XX*, ed. W. M. Lindsay (Oxford: Clarendon Press, 1911; reprint, 1985); partial edition and translation: Isidore of Seville, *Etymologies: Book II*, ed. and trans. Peter K. Marshall (Paris: Les Belles Lettres, 1983); also see Ernest Brehaut, *An Encyclopedist of the Dark Ages: Isidore of Seville* (1912; reprint, New York: Franklin, 1964).

29. See Isidorus Hispalensis, *Sententiae*, ed. Pierre Cazier, Corpus Christianorum, Series Latina 111 (Turnhout: Brepols, 1998).

30. See Grabmann, *Geschichte der scholastischen Methode*, 1:145–46.

31. Boethius's famous announcement of this project is contained in A. M. S. Boetii, *Commentarii in Librum Aristotelis ΠΕΡΙ ΕΡΜΗΝΕΙΑΣ*, ed.

Carolus Meiser, vol. 2 (Leipzig: Teubner, 1880; reprint, New York and London: Garland, 1987), 2.3:79–80.

32. Discussion about the authenticity of the *opuscula sacra* has recently been reopened by Alain Galonnier, *Anecdoton Holderi, ou, Ordo generis Cassiodororum: Éléments pour une étude de l'authenticité boécienne des Opuscula sacra*, Philosophes médiévaux 35 (Louvain-la-Neuve: Éditions de l'Institut supérieur de philosophie; Louvain/Paris: Éditions Peeters, 1997).

33. Grabmann speaks of *Stoffzufuhr;* see the indexes of both volumes of *Die Geschichte der scholastischen Methode*.

34. See Iohannis Scotti Eriugenae, *Periphyseon (De Diuisione Naturae)*, ed. and trans. I. Sheldon-Williams et al., vols. 1–4 (vol. 5 is yet to appear), Scriptores Latini Hiberniae 7, 9, 11, and 13 (Dublin: Dublin Institute for Advanced Studies, 1968–1995). This edition is superseded by Iohannis Scotti seu Eriugenae, *Periphyseon*, ed. Édouard Jeauneau, vols. 1–4 (vol. 5 is yet to appear), Corpus Christianorum, Continuatio Mediaevalis 161–64 (Turnhout, Belgium: Brepols, 1996–2000). A complete English translation of all five books is available in Joannes Scottus Eriugena, *Periphyseon: The Division of Nature*, trans. I. Sheldon-Williams and John J. O'Meara, Cahiers d'études médiévales, Cahier spécial 3 (Montreal: Bellarmin, 1987). For an excellent introduction to the *Periphyseon*, see Deirdre Carabine, *Eriugena*, Great Medieval Thinkers (New York/Oxford: Oxford University Press, 2000).

35. *Periphyseon*, book I, 441A.

36. Ibid., 524B.

37. See ibid., 441B.

38. See, for instance, ibid., 513A: "For authority proceeds from true reason, but reason certainly does not proceed from authority. For every authority which is not upheld by true reason is seen to be weak, whereas true reason is kept firm and immutable by her own powers and does not require to be confirmed by the assent of any authority."

39. Ibid., 509A.

40. See Hugh of St. Victor, *Didascalicon*, book IV, chap. 2; PL 176: 778f.

41. See Henri de Lubac, S.J., *Medieval Exegesis*, vol. 1, *The Four Senses of Scripture*, trans. Mark Sebanc, Ressourcement (Grand Rapids, Mich.: Eerdmans; Edinburgh: Clark, 1998), esp. 225–67.

42. Robert Somerville and Bruce C. Brasington, *Prefaces to Canon Law Books in Latin Christianity: Selected Translations, 500–1245* (New Haven, Conn., and London: Yale University Press, 1998), 105.

43. See Bernold von Konstanz, *De excommunicatis vitandis, de reconciliatione lapsorum et de fontibus iuris ecclesiastici (Libellus X)*, ed. Doris Stöckly and Detlev Jasper, Monumenta Germaniae historica, Fontes iuris Germanici antiqui in usum scholarum separatim editi 15 (Hanover: Hahnsche Buch-

handlung, 2000). Also see Johanne Autenrieth, *Die Domschule von Konstanz zur Zeit des Investiturstreits: Die wissenschaftliche Arbeitsweise Bernolds von Konstanz und zweier Kleriker*, Forschungen zur Kirchen- und Geistesgeschichte N.F. 3 (Stuttgart: Kohlhammer, 1956); and Grabmann, *Die Geschichte der scholastischen Methode*, 1:234–29.

44. Bernold, *De excommunicatis*, p. 179, ll. 10–11: "Harum autem sententiarum diversitatem facile concordabimus."

45. See Grabmann, *Geschichte der scholastischen Methode*, 1:238.

46. See Peter Abailard, *Sic et Non: A Critical Edition*, ed. Blanche B. Boyer and Richard McKeon (Chicago and London: University of Chicago Press, 1976–1977), 617–34 ("The Textual Relationship of Ivo and Abailard") and 635–45 ("Parallel Passages of Abailard, Ivo, Gratian and Lombard").

47. See Yves de Chartres, *Le prologue*, ed. and trans. Jean Werckmeister, Sources canoniques 1 (Paris: Cerf, 1997). For an English translation, see Robert Somerville and Bruce C. Brasington, *Prefaces to Canon Law Books in Latin Christianity*, 132–58. An extensive study of Ivo's methodology in the prologue is contained in vol. 2 of Bruce C. Brasington's unpublished UCLA thesis: "The Prologue to the Decretum and Panormia of Ivo of Chartres: An Eleventh-Century Treatise on Ecclesiastical Jurisprudence" (Ph.D. thesis, University of California at Los Angeles, 1990), 3 vols. I would like to thank Professor Brasington for assistance with the Ivo bibliography.

48. See de Ghellinck, *Le mouvement théologique au XIIe siècle*, esp. chap. 5: "Théologie et droit canon au XIe et au XIIe siècle" (416–510).

49. Grabmann, *Geschichte der scholastischen Methode*, 1:258. The designation "Father of Scholasticism" has its origins in the breviary prayers for April 21.

50. Epistola 77, in S. Anselmi Cantuarensis Archiepiscopi, *Opera Omnia*, ed. F. S. Schmitt, O.S.B., vol. 3 (Stuttgart-Bad Cannstatt: Frommann, 1968), 199.

51. The late Sir Richard Southern acknowledged Augustine's influence on the *Proslogion*, but emphasized Anselm's originality in formulating the final argument; see R. W. Southern, *Saint Anselm: A Portrait in a Landscape* (Cambridge: Cambridge University Press, 1990), 127–29.

52. See Augustine, *De doctrina christiana*, 1.7.

53. For the useful distinction between *System der Anordnung* and *System der Entwickelung*, see Adolf Trendelenburg, *Logische Untersuchungen*, 3d ed., vol. 2 (Leipzig: Hirzel, 1870; reprint, Hildesheim: Olms, 1964), 446–47.

54. Reinhold Seeberg, quoted in Grabmann, *Geschichte der scholastischen Methode*, 1:269.

55. R. N. Swanson provides an excellent general introduction to the twelfth century, written primarily for the intellectual historian, in his book

The Twelfth-Century Renaissance (Manchester, England, and New York: Manchester University Press, 1999). The theological landscape of the twelfth century is the subject of the excellent essay by Jean Châtillon, "La Bible dans les écoles du XIIe siècle," in *Le Moyen Âge et la Bible*, ed. Pierre Riché and Guy Lobrichon, Bible de tous les temps 4 (Paris: Beauchesne, 1984), 163–97. Still useful, as well, is Artur Michael Landgraf, *Einführung in die Geschichte der theologischen Literatur der Frühscholastik unter dem Gesichtspunkte der Schulenbildung* (Regensburg: Gregorius-Verlag, 1948).

56. See Marcia L. Colish, "From the Sentence Collection to the *Sentence* Commentary and the *Summa*: Parisian Scholastic Theology, 1130–1215," in *Manuels, programmes de cours et techniques d'enseignement dans les universités médiévales*, ed. Jacqueline Hamesse, Université catholique de Louvain, Publications de l'Institut d'études médiévales, Textes, Études, Congrès 16 (Louvain-la-Neuve: Institut d'études médiévales, 1994), 9–29. Although he does not use the word "professionalization," M.-D. Chenu describes the phenomenon magisterially in his essay "The Masters of the Theological 'Science,'" in idem, *Nature, Man, and Society in the Twelfth Century: Essays on New Theological Perspectives in the Latin West*, trans. Jerome Taylor and Lester K. Little (Chicago and London: University of Chicago Press, 1968), 270–309. Another excellent study of the changing academic climate in the twelfth century is C. Stephen Jaeger, *The Envy of Angels: Cathedral Schools and Social Ideals in Medieval Europe, 950–1200*, Middle Ages Series (Philadelphia: University of Pennsylvania Press, 1994), esp. parts 2 and 3.

57. Chenu speaks of a movement "from sacred text to sacred doctrine"; see "The Masters of the Theological 'Science,'" 279.

58. Ibid., 276 and 280.

59. Karlfried Froehlich and Margaret T. Gibson, *Biblia latina cum Glossa ordinaria: Introduction to the Facsimile Reprint of the Editio Princeps, Adolph Rusch of Strassburg 1480/81* (Turnhout: Brepols, 1992), xi. Also see Guy Lobrichon, "Une nouveauté: Les gloses de la Bible," in *Le Moyen Âge et la Bible*, 95–114; Margaret T. Gibson, "The Place of the *Glossa ordinaria* in Medieval Exegesis," in *Ad litteram: Authoritative Texts and Their Medieval Readers*, ed. Mark D. Jordan and Kent Emery, Jr., Notre Dame Conferences in Medieval Studies 3 (Notre Dame, Ind./London: University of Notre Dame Press, 1992), 5–27; and E. Ann Matter, "The Church Fathers and the *Glossa ordinaria*," in *The Reception of the Church Fathers in the West: From the Carolingians to the Maurists*, ed. Irena Backus (Leiden/New York/Cologne: Brill, 1997), 1:83–111.

60. A facsimile of the first printed edition was published in 1992 in four volumes (see previous note). It will remain the standard reference until the

completion of a critical edition, of which so far one volume has appeared: *Glossa ordinaria*, vol. 22: *In Canticum Canticorum*, ed. and trans. Mary Dove, Corpus Christianorum, Continuatio Mediaevalis 170 (Turnhout: Brepols, 1997).

61. See Beryl Smalley, "Glossa ordinaria," in *Theologische Realenzyklopädie*, vol. 13 (1984), 452–57, at 455; also see Froehlich and Gibson, *Biblia latina cum Glossa ordinaria: Introduction*, ix.

62. Froehlich and Gibson, *Biblia latina cum Glossa ordinaria: Introduction*, vii.

63. See Colish, "From the Sentence Collection to the *Sentence* Commentary and the *Summa*," 9.

64. See Henri Cloes, "La systématisation théologique pendant la première moitié du XIIᵉ siècle," *Ephemerides theologicae lovanienses* 34 (1958): 277–329; and Marcia L. Colish, "Systematic Theology and Theological Research in the Twelfth Century," *Journal of Medieval and Renaissance Studies* 18 (1988): 135–56, at 142–56.

65. Grabmann, *Geschichte der scholastischen Methode*, 2:259.

66. Hugonis de S. Victore, *De sacramentis christianae fidei*, prologus, chap. 2, PL 176, 183A–B (my translation). An English translation of the work is available: Hugh of St. Victor, *On the Sacraments of the Christian Faith (De sacramentis)*, trans. Roy J. Deferrari, Mediaeval Academy of America, Publication No. 58 (Cambridge, Mass.: Mediaeval Academy of America, 1951; reprint, 1976).

67. See *De sacramentis*, chap. 3.

68. For a discussion of further weaknesses of the *De sacramentis*, see Colish, *Peter Lombard*, 58–63.

69. For the critical edition of *Sic et non*, see n. 46 above.

70. See *Sic et non*, prologus, p. 103, l. 330–p. 104, l. 350.

71. A good discussion of these rules is to be found in de Ghellinck, *Le mouvement théologique au XIIᵉ siècle*, 489–94. For an incisive recent analysis, see Cornelia Rizek-Pfister, "Die hermeneutischen Prinzipien in Abaelards *Sic et non*," *Freiburger Zeitschrift für Philosophie und Theologie* 47 (2000): 484–501.

72. See John Marenbon, *The Philosophy of Peter Abelard* (Cambridge: Cambridge University Press, 1997), 62: "The purpose behind this arrangement is ... to order the material which he wishes to use in his theological investigations."

73. See *Sic et non*, "Description of the Manuscripts," 7–80.

74. Petri Abaelardi, *Opera theologica*, vol. 3, *Theologia "Summi boni"*— *Theologia "Scholarium,"* ed. E. M. Buytaert, O.F.M., and C. J. Mews, Corpus

Christianorum, Continuatio Mediaevalis 13 (Turnhout: Brepols, 1987), 203. For a list of passages Peter Lombard borrowed from the *Theologia "Scholarium,"* see 264–65.

75. *Theologia "Scholarium,"* capitula 1, p. 317, ll. 1–3.

76. See ibid., liber 1.1, p. 318, ll. 1–2.

77. See Grabmann, *Geschichte der scholastischen Methode*, 2:221–29.

78. The following biographical sketch is based upon the "Esquisse biographique" to be found in *Œuvres de Robert de Melun*, ed. Raymond M. Martin, O.P., vol. 1, *Quaestiones de divina pagina*, Spicilegium Sacrum Lovaniense 13 (Louvain: Spicilegium Sacrum Lovaniense, 1932), vi–xii.

79. Raymond M. Martin, O.P., "Introduction," in *Œuvres de Robert de Melun*, vol. 3.1, ed. Raymond M. Martin, O.P., Spicilegium Sacrum Lovaniense 21 (Louvain: Spicilegium Sacrum Lovaniense, 1947), v–xxi, at xiv.

80. Robert of Melun, *Sententie*, prefatio, in *Œuvres de Robert de Melun*, vol. 3.1, p. 49, ll. 16–20. Also see ibid., p. 45, ll. 11ff.

81. Peter Abelard sometimes includes hope (*spes*) in his schema of faith-charity-sacraments.

82. See Robert of Melun, *Sententie*, prefatio, p. 49, l. 26–p. 56, l. 20.

83. Colish, *Peter Lombard*, 73.

84. See Robert of Melun, *Sententie*, prefatio, p. 47, l. 16–p. 48, l. 27.

85. See ibid., 59–156 (table of contents), together with Martin's introduction, ix–x.

86. "Capitula secunde partis principalis enumerationis," ibid., 106.

87. Namely, the work done by Marcia Colish in her two-volume study, *Peter Lombard*.

2. PETER LOMBARD: LIFE AND WORKS

1. The manuscript is *Florence, Biblioteca laurenziana (olim S. Crucis), Plutei XXV, dext. 1*, fol. 1r. My account of Peter Lombard's life and works is indebted to the research of Ignatius Brady, O.F.M., summarized in the introduction to his edition of the *Book of Sentences*: Magistri Petri Lombardi, *Sententiae in IV libris distinctae*, vol. 1, part 1: *Prolegomena*, Spicilegium Bonaventurianum 4 (Grottaferrata: Editiones Collegii S. Bonaventurae Ad Claras Aquas, 1971). Additions in vol. 2 of the same edition: *Sententiae in IV libris distinctae*, vol. 2, Spicilegium Bonaventurianum 5 (Grottaferrata: Editiones Collegii S. Bonaventurae Ad Claras Aquas, 1981), 7*–100*. Joseph de Ghellinck's older work can still be consulted with profit, although certain aspects are out of date; in particular, see his "La carrière de Pierre Lombard: Quelques précisions chronologiques," *Revue d'histoire ecclésiastique* 27 (1931):

792–830, and "La carrière de Pierre Lombard: Nouvelle précision chronologique," *Revue d'histoire ecclésiastique* 30 (1934): 95–100.

2. See Ignatius Brady, O.F.M., "Pierre Lombard," in *Dictionnaire de spiritualité* 12 (1986), cols. 1604–12, at 1605.

3. Epistola CDX, in *St. Bernardi Opera*, vol. 8, ed. J. Leclercq, O.S.B., and H. Rochais (Rome: Editiones Cistercienses, 1977), 391. All translations from Latin texts in this chapter are my own.

4. See Patricia Stirnemann, "Histoire tripartite: Un inventaire des livres de Pierre Lombard, un exemplaire de ses *Sentences* et le destinataire du Psautier de Copenhague," in *Du copiste au collectionneur: Mélanges d'histoire des textes et des bibliothèques en l'honneur d'André Vernet*, ed. Donatella Nebbiai-Dalla Guarda and Jean-François Genest, Bibliologia 18 (Turnhout, Belgium: Brepols, 1998), 301–33, esp. 307. I owe this reference to Constant Mews.

5. See John R. Williams, "The Cathedral School of Reims in the Eleventh Century," *Speculum* 29 (1954): 661–77, and idem, "The Cathedral School of Reims in the Time of Master Alberic, 1118–1136," *Traditio* 20 (1964): 93–114.

6. See de Ghellinck, "La carrière de Pierre Lombard: Quelques précisions," 800; and Brady, *Prolegomena*, 9*.

7. Father Brady doubts that Peter Lombard ever formally followed Peter Abelard's lectures; see *Prolegomena*, 17*.

8. Quoted in Ignatius Brady, O.F.M., "Peter Lombard: Canon of Notre Dame," *Recherches de théologie ancienne et médiévale* 32 (1965): 277–95, at 280.

9. See ibid., esp. 288.

10. Quoted in Brady, *Prolegomena*, 28*.

11. See Franz Pelster, S.J., "Petrus Lombardus und die Verhandlungen über die Streitfrage des Gilbertus Porreta in Paris (1147) und Reims (1148)," in *Miscellanea lombardiana*, 65–73.

12. See Brady, *Prolegomena*, 121*.

13. Quoted ibid., 33*, from Monumenta Germaniae historica, Scriptores VI, 509–10. For background on the episcopal elections in France under Louis VII, see Marcel Pacaut, *Louis VII et les élections épiscopales dans le royaume de France*, Bibliothèque de la Société d'histoire ecclésiastique de la France (Paris: Vrin, 1957). Peter Lombard is mentioned only in passing.

14. See Paul Glorieux, "Le *Contra Quatuor Labyrinthos Franciae* de Gauthier de Saint-Victor: Édition critique," *Archives d'histoire doctrinale et littéraire du moyen âge* 19 (1952): 187–335. The "four labyrinths of France" are Peter Abelard, Peter Lombard, Peter of Poitiers, and Gilbert de la Porrée. The invectives against Peter Lombard start in the very first line of the prologue and continue throughout the work.

15. Only one serious modern scholar has argued that Walter of St. Victor may have been right in suspecting "irregularities" in Peter Lombard's election; see R. Seeberg, "Lombardus," in *Realencyclopädie für protestantische Theologie und Kirche*, ed. Albert Hauck, vol. 11 (Leipzig: Hinrichs, 1902), 630–42, at 632.

16. On the controversies surrounding the *Book of Sentences*, see Joseph de Ghellinck, S.J., "Pierre Lombard," *Dictionnaire de théologie catholique* XII/2 (1935): 1941–2019, at 2003–11; as well as idem, *Le mouvement théologique du XIIᵉ siècle. Sa préparation lointaine avant et autour de Pierre Lombard. Ses rapports avec les initiatives des canonistes. Études, recherches et documents*, 2d ed., Museum Lessianum, Section historique 10 (Bruges: Éditions de Tempel; Brussels: L'Édition universelle; Paris: Desclée de Brouwer, 1948), 250–67.

17. Quoted by Brady, *Prolegomena*, 43*. August 13 in the Julian calendar corresponds to July 20 according to the Gregorian reckoning.

18. See Colin Morris, *The Discovery of the Individual, 1050–1200*, Medieval Academy Reprints for Teaching 19 (Toronto: University of Toronto Press, 1987).

19. Quoted in Brady, *Prolegomena*, 19*f. A *statio* is either a procession or a meal/distribution of food paid for by a public figure (such as a bishop). According to this text, the anniversary of Peter Lombard's death was commemorated by a procession or meal paid from an endowment that was funded by the rent of Peter's former house, which he had bequeathed to the chapter of Notre Dame. For help in interpreting this passage, I am grateful to my colleague Dr. Francis Swietek and to Madame Caroline Heid, of the Institut de Recherche et d'Histoire des Textes, Paris.

20. For the history of the church of St. Christopher, see Émile Raunié, *Épitaphier du vieux Paris*, vol. 3, *Histoire générale de Paris* (Paris: Imprimerie nationale, 1901), 107–16. Page 107 has a drawing of the church and its surroundings on the Île de la Cité, and p. 115 contains a map of the immediate vicinity of the edifice. Both the drawing and the map, however, reflect the situation after the construction of the new cathedral of Notre Dame.

21. On the cathedral schools in the twelfth century, see Philippe Delhaye, "L'organisation scolaire au XIIᵉ siècle," *Traditio* 5 (1947): 211–49.

22. Quoted in Ignatius Brady, O.F.M., "Peter Manducator and the Oral Teachings of Peter Lombard," *Antonianum* 41 (1966): 454–90, at 472.

23. Ibid., 473.

24. See Artur Michael Landgraf, "Schwankungen in der Lehre des Petrus Lombardus," *Scholastik* 31 (1956): 533–44, at 534. On the subject of oral teachings of the Lombard, also see Landgraf, "Die Stellungnahme der Frühscholastik zur wissenschaftlichen Methode des Petrus Lombardus," *Collectanea franciscana* 4 (1934): 513–21, esp. 519–21.

25. Brady, "Peter Manducator and the Oral Teachings of Peter Lombard," 476.

26. Ibid., 478.

27. Ibid., 473. The quotation is from John of Cornwall's treatise *Eulogium ad Alexandrum papam tertium*, edited by N. M. Häring, S.A.C., "The Eulogium ad Alexandrum papam tertium of John of Cornwall," *Mediaeval Studies* 13 (1951): 253–300, at 265.

28. For the following discussion, see Stirnemann, "Histoire tripartite," esp. 307–13.

29. A fact of which Peter Lombard was very much aware; see his glosses on the First Letter to the Corinthians, PL 191: 1560Cff.

30. See *Sententiae*, ed. Brady, 2:19*–52*. Some fragments from Peter's lost glosses are printed in Beryl Smalley and George Lacombe, "The Lombard's Commentary on Isaias and Other Fragments," *The New Scholasticism* 5 (1931): 123–62.

31. The text printed in PL 191: 55–1296 is based upon an edition that Richard of Mans, O.F.M., originally published in 1541. This latter edition and, hence, the text that appears in the *Patrologia latina* are unreliable, containing additions by Richard of Mans as well as other errors. (See Brady, "Pierre Lombard," 1606.)

32. Quoted in H. H. Glunz, *History of the Vulgate in England from Alcuin to Roger Bacon: Being an Inquiry into the Text of Some English Manuscripts of the Vulgate Gospels* (Cambridge: Cambridge University Press, 1933), 343, with commentary on pp. 219–21 and 226. Also see de Ghellinck, "La carrière de Pierre Lombard: Nouvelle précision chronologique," 98. There is disagreement among the commentators as to whether Bosham's passage applies only to the Gloss on the Psalms, or to that on the Epistles of St. Paul as well. The passage occurs in a preface that Bosham composed for his edition of the Lombard's Gloss on the Psalms, yet he refers to Peter Lombard's works in the plural: *hec opera/dicta opera*. I have translated these phrases in the singular because the characterization that Bosham offers of "these works" does not fit what we know about the Gloss on the Epistles.

33. Brady, *Prolegomena*, 57*.

34. Colish, *Peter Lombard*, 188.

35. The *Collectanea* is printed in PL 191: 1297–1696 and 192: 9–520.

36. See Brady, *Prolegomena*, 85*–88*. Marcia Colish (*Peter Lombard*, 23) has recently suggested a date of 1139–1141 for the first redaction of the *Collectanea*, but Brady's reasoning remains compelling. Colish offers the most thorough discussion to date of Peter Lombard's Gloss on the Pauline Epistles (see *Peter Lombard*, 192–225).

37. On the *Expositio epistolarum beati Pauli*, see Célestin Charlier, "La

compilation augustinienne de Florus sur l'Apôtre: Sources et authenticité," *Revue bénédictine* 57 (1947): 132–67.

38. See Brady, *Prolegomena*, 90*–93; and *Sententiae*, 2:53*–87*.

39. See Brady, *Prolegomena*, 90*–93*.

40. In the original version of the Gloss on the Letter to the Romans, the treatise occurred between the words *lucet Trinitas* and *Nam propter hoc naturam;* see PL 191: 1495C. Colish points out that "however long an excursus he may make, Peter always guides the reader firmly back to Paul's argument" (*Peter Lombard*, 224). I would suggest that the shortening and elimination of some of the treatises served precisely this goal.

41. On this point, de Ghellinck wrote: "on est amené de se demander si l'enseignement théologique de Pierre Lombard a pris d'abord comme matière le texte de la Bible..., avant de commencer l'espèce de synthèse contenue dans les *Livres des Sentences*" (de Ghellinck, "Pierre Lombard," *DTC*, col. 1958).

42. Edited in *Sententiae*, ed. Brady, 2:54*–77*.

43. "Ambrosius in libro Quaestionum veteris et novi testamenti, qui ab ignorantibus praetitulatur Augustini" (ibid., 56*).

44. Ibid., 57*.

45. Ibid., 63*.

46. The steps just described are found ibid., 62*f.

47. For a discussion of evidence that Peter himself engaged in disputations, see Artur Landgraf, "Notes de critique textuelle sur les *Sentences* de Pierre Lombard," *Recherches de théologie ancienne et médiévale* 2 (1930): 80–99, esp. 96–98. On this point, also see de Ghellinck, "Pierre Lombard," *DTC*, col. 1958.

48. *Sententiae*, ed. Brady, 2:68*.

49. See the list in Brady, *Prolegomena*, 99*–112*, with the additions in *Sententiae*, ed. Brady, 2:33*–35*. Twenty-six of Peter's sermons are printed in PL 171, where they are falsely attributed to Hildebert of Lavardin. On the chronology of the sermons, see also Damien Van den Eynde, O.F.M., "Essai chronologique sur l'œuvre littéraire de Pierre Lombard," in *Miscellanea lombardiana*, 45–63, esp. 58–60.

50. See Félix Protois, *Pierre Lombard, évêque de Paris, dit le Maître des Sentences: Son époque, sa vie, ses écrits, son influence* (Paris: Société générale de librairie catholique, 1881), 123–48, esp. 124f.

51. Ibid., 125. Jean Longère, author of a more recent comparative study of the oratorical works of the twelfth-century masters, agrees with this judgment. In his sermons, Longère writes, Peter "appears as a man of doctrine, rather than as a pastor. One cannot reproach him for appealing more to reason than to the emotions, yet his preaching lacks some warmth" (Jean

Longère, *Œuvres oratoires de maîtres parisiens au XIIe siècle: Étude historique et doctrinale* [Paris: Études augustiniennes, 1975], 1:295).

52. On this point, see *Sentences* 4, dist. 24, chap. 10, no. 2 (p. 402): "Nam sicut lectoribus vetus Testamentum, ita diaconibus novum praedicare praeceptum est."

53. C. F. R. de Hamel, *Glossed Books of the Bible and the Origins of the Paris Booktrade* (Woodbridge, Suffolk: Brewer, 1984), 9.

54. See ibid., esp. 14–27 (chap. 2).

55. Ibid., 17.

56. Ibid., 20.

57. Ibid., 23.

3. THE *BOOK OF SENTENCES*: STRUCTURE, METHOD, AND THEOLOGICAL VISION

1. See Brady, *Prolegomena*, 122*–29*, together with Artur Landgraf, "Notes de critique textuelle sur les *Sentences* de Pierre Lombard," *Recherches de théologie ancienne et médiévale* 2 (1930): 80–99.

2. Much controversy surrounds this manuscript. Unlike previous editors of the *Sentences*, Father Brady considered the date 1158 in MS. 900 to refer to the time when Peter Lombard completed the work, not when Michael of Ireland copied it (see *Prolegomena*, 130*f.). Interesting in this context is Brady's article "The Three Editions of the 'Liber Sententiarum' of Master Peter Lombard (1882–1977)," *Archivum franciscanum historicum* 70 (1977): 400–11. Patricia Stirnemann's arguments, however, have turned the scales again in favor of the interpretation that regards MS. 900 as dating from 1158; see Patricia Stirnemann, "Histoire tripartite: Un inventaire des livres de Pierre Lombard, un exemplaire de ses *Sentences* et le destinataire du Psautier de Copenhague," in *Du copiste au collectionneur: Mélanges d'histoire des textes et des bibliothèques en l'honneur d'André Vernet*, ed. Donatella Nebbiai-Dalla Guarda and Jean-François Genest, Bibliologia 18 (Turnhout: Brepols, 1998), 301–33, esp. 307–13.

3. See Brady, *Prolegomena*, 118*–22*, as well as Jacques-Guy Bougerol, "The Church Fathers and the *Sentences* of Peter Lombard," in *The Reception of the Church Fathers in the West: From the Carolingians to the Maurists*, ed. Irena Backus (Leiden/New York/Cologne: Brill, 1997), 113–64.

4. On the Lombard's use of Augustine, see Ferdinand Cavallera, "Saint Augustin et le *Livre des Sentences* de Pierre Lombard," *Archives de philosophie* 7, no. 2 (1930): 186–99 = [438]–[451]; and Bougerol, "The Church Fathers," 115–33.

5. See N. Wicki, "Das *Prognosticon futuri saeculi* Julians von Toledo als

Quellenwerk der Sentenzen des Petrus Lombardus," *Divus Thomas* (Fribourg) 31 (1953): 349–60.

6. The *Summa sententiarum* has been identified as a work by Master Otto of Lucca; see Ferruccio Gastaldelli, "La *Summa sententiarum* di Ottone da Lucca: Conclusione di un dibattito secolare," *Salesianum* 42 (1980): 537–46.

7. See Joseph de Ghellinck, S.J., "Pierre Lombard," *Dictionnaire de théologie catholique* XII/2 (1935): 1941–2019, esp. 1985–87.

8. Ibid., 1985.

9. On this subject, see A. J. Minnis, *Medieval Theory of Authorship: Scholastic Literary Attitudes in the Later Middle Ages*, 2d ed. (1984; reprint, Aldershot, Hamps.: Wildwood House, 1988).

10. Colish, *Peter Lombard*, 86.

11. See Philippe Delhaye, "L'organisation scolaire au XIIᵉ siècle," *Traditio* 5 (1947): 211–68, esp. 217–23.

12. Interestingly, the preface to the *Book of Sentences* contains an extended reflection on the connection between will and reason, and a warning against tendencies to bend doctrine to the whims of an undisciplined will: "Quorum professio est magis placita quam docenda conquirere, nec docenda desiderare, sed desideratis doctrinam coaptare" (*Sentences*, preface, no. 3, p. 4). One wonders whom Peter had in mind when writing these words.

13. *Sentences* 1, dist. 1, chap. 1, no. 1 (p. 55). In his edition, Brady uses bold characters to indicate rubrics—text written in red in order to help the reader find his way through the argument, to indicate the sources of quotations, etc. These rubrics often appear within the columns of text, but some of them are marginal, in which case an asterisk (*) is added.

14. See Augustine, *De doctrina christiana*, ed. and trans. R. P. H. Green, Oxford Early Christian Texts (Oxford: Clarendon Press, 1995), bk. 3, nos. 29–32, pp. 145–47.

15. *Sentences* 1, dist. 1. chap. 1, no. 9 (p. 60).

16. Ibid., chap. 3, no. 10 (pp. 6of.).

17. This is a quotation from *De doctrina christiana*, bk. 1, no. 84, p. 48.

18. *Sentences* 1, dist. 1, chap. 3, no. 11 (p. 61).

19. *De doctrina christiana*, bk. 1, nos. 23–24 (pp. 22f.).

20. *Sentences* 4, p. 231.

21. On this point, see the remarks in de Ghellinck, "Pierre Lombard," 1980–82; and Carl Andresen et al., *Die Lehrentwicklung im Rahmen der Katholizität*, Handbuch der Dogmen- und Theologiegeschichte 1 (Göttingen: Vandenhoeck & Ruprecht, 1982), 595. Colish, *Peter Lombard*, does not address this issue.

22. *Sentences* 3, prol. (p. 23).

23. See M.-D. Chenu, O.P., *La théologie comme science au XIIIe siècle*, 3d ed., Bibliothèque thomiste 33 (Paris: Vrin, 1969).

24. *Sentences*, preface, nos. 4 and 5 (p. 4).

25. Ibid. 1, dist. 2, chap. 3 (p. 63). Also see ibid., dist. 4, chap. 1, no. 2 (p. 78).

26. Ibid., dist. 9, chap. 3, no. 2 (p. 105).

27. Ibid., dist. 43, no. 1 (p. 298).

28. Ibid., dist. 44, chap. 1, no. 2 (p. 304).

29. Ibid. 3, dist. 22, chap. 1, no. 3 (p. 136).

30. Ibid. 1, dist. 32, chap. 1, no. 2 (p. 233).

31. Ibid., chap. 6, no. 2 (p. 239).

32. Colish, *Peter Lombard*, 149.

33. *Sentences*, preface, no. 5 (p. 4).

34. Ibid. 1, dist. 2, chap. 5, no. 1 (p. 67).

35. Ibid., dist. 4, chap. 2, no. 4 (p. 80).

36. Ibid., dist. 19, chap. 1 (p. 159).

37. Ibid. 2, dist. 2, chap. 1, no. 1 (p. 336). In such *divisiones textus* (to use the term of later commentators on the *Sentences*) Henri Cloes has rightly seen an important element of theological systematization; see "La systématisation théologique pendant la première moitié du XIIe siècle," *Ephemerides theologicae lovanienses* 34 (1958): 277–329, at 325–27.

38. See Ignatius Brady, O.F.M., "The Distinctions of Lombard's *Book of Sentences* and Alexander of Hales," *Franciscan Studies* 25 (1965): 90–116.

39. In Brady's edition, the chapters are subdivided into numbered paragraphs.

40. See Brady, *Prolegomena*, 138*–41*, as well as Ignatius Brady, O.F.M., "The Rubrics of Peter Lombard's *Sentences*," *Pier Lombardo* 6 (1962): 5–25. On the conventions used to transcribe rubrics in Brady's edition, see n. 13 above.

41. See Peter Abailard, *Sic et Non: A Critical Edition*, ed. Blanche B. Boyer and Richard McKeon (Chicago and London: University of Chicago Press, 1976–1977), 89–104. For a recent discussion of Abelard's rules for reconciling authorities, see Cornelia Rizek-Pfister, "Die hermeneutischen Prinzipien in Abaelards *Sic et non*," *Freiburger Zeitschrift für Philosophie und Theologie* 47 (2000): 484–501.

42. *Sentences* 1, dist. 5, chap. 1 (pp. 80–87). For a similar methodological analysis of distinction 46, see Stanley J. Curtis, "Peter Lombard: A Pioneer in Educational Method," in *Miscellanea lombardiana*, 265–73.

43. Peter Lombard misidentifies this quotation, which is to be found in Augustine's own treatise *De fide et symbolo*. The Lombard must have derived the quotation from a secondary source.

44. See Brady, "The Rubrics of Peter Lombard's *Sentences.*"

45. Colish's interpretation, according to which Peter "answer[s] all these questions with a firm 'no' " (*Peter Lombard*, 251), fails to acknowledge Peter's expressly stated doubts and hesitations.

4. THE *SENTENCES*, BOOK I: ON THE MYSTERY OF THE TRINITY

1. Colish's *Peter Lombard* is the most exhaustive and up-to-date example of this approach to the *Sentences*, but Colish's work stands in a tradition that goes back at least to Otto Baltzer, who demonstrated much more briefly how each of the Lombard's ideas is to be situated with regard to his contemporaries, especially Hugh of St. Victor and Abelard. See Otto Baltzer, *Die Sentenzen des Petrus Lombardus: Ihre Quellen und ihre dogmengeschichtliche Bedeutung*, Studien zur Geschichte der Theologie und der Kirche 8:3 (Leipzig: Dieterich, 1902; reprint, Aalen: Scientia, 1987).

2. Except historically! Peter is following the example of Abelard; see Baltzer, *Die Sentenzen des Petrus Lombardus*, 17.

3. *Sentences*, p. 10, l. 25.

4. *Sentences* 1, dist. 2, chap. 1, no. 3 (p. 62).

5. Ibid., chap. 4, no. 2 (p. 64).

6. Ibid., chap. 5, no. 5 (p. 68).

7. Ibid., chap. 3 (p. 63). The phrase is repeated almost literally in chap. 5, no. 5 (p. 68).

8. Ibid.

9. Ibid., dist. 3, chap. 1, no. 1 (p. 68).

10. Ibid., no. 3 (p. 69).

11. Ibid., no. 4 (p. 69).

12. Ibid., no. 5 (p. 70).

13. Colish, *Peter Lombard*, 240. Johannes Schneider's older account of book 1 of the *Sentences*, which also includes material on the reception and transformation of Peter Lombard's doctrine among his pupils, is more reliable. See Johannes Schneider, *Die Lehre vom dreieinigen Gott in der Schule des Petrus Lombardus*, Münchener theologische Studien II, Abteilung 22 (Munich: Hueber, 1961).

14. *Sentences* 1, dist. 3, chap. 1, no. 7 (p. 70).

15. Ibid., no. 9 (p. 71).

16. Ibid., chap. 2, no. 1 (p. 71).

17. Ibid., chap. 2, no. 4 (p. 72).

18. Ibid., chap. 3, no. 1 (p. 75).

19. Ibid., dist. 8, chap. 1, no. 2 (p. 95).

20. Ibid., no. 7 (p. 96).

21. See Ermenegildo Bertola, "Il problema di Dio in Pier Lombardo," *Rivista di filosofia neo-scolastica* 48 (1956): 135–50, esp. 139.

22. *Sentences* 1, dist. 8, chap. 4, no. 2 (p. 99).

23. Ibid., chap. 8, no. 1 (p. 101).

24. Distinctions 35, 36, and 38 have recently become available in French translation, accompanied by a brief introduction; see J.-C. Bardout and O. Boulnois, *Sur la science divine*, Épiméthée (Paris: Presses universitaires de France, 2002), 130–51.

25. *Sentences* 1, dist. 35, chaps. 1–6, no. 2 (p. 255).

26. See ibid., chap. 9, nos. 1 and 2 (pp. 257f.).

27. Ibid., chaps. 1–6, no. 2 (p. 255).

28. I have changed the Douay-Rheims translation here, since it obscures the difference between *ex ipso*, "from him," and *de ipso*, "of him."

29. *Sentences* 1, dist. 36, chap. 2, no. 5 (p. 261).

30. Ibid., dist. 37, chap. 1, no. 2 (pp. 263f.).

31. Ibid., chap. 3, no. 4 (p. 267).

32. Unfortunately, Marcia Colish misinterprets the passage just explained, writing: "He [Peter Lombard] begins by observing that God can be in other things by essence, power, and presence. As for the first, there is one and only one non-divine being with which God unites Himself essentially. This is the man Jesus in the incarnation of Christ.... Peter mentions this exception to get the topic of God's essential union with creatures off the agenda more generally, as a fundamentally inappropriate way of regarding God's presence in the world" (*Peter Lombard*, 266f.). Peter holds unambiguously that God is present to all of creation essentially.

33. *Sentences* 1, dist. 37, chap. 3, no. 5 (p. 268).

34. Ibid., chap. 4, no. 1 (p. 268).

35. Ibid., dist. 6, no. 1 (p. 89).

36. Ibid., no. 3 (p. 90).

37. Ibid., no. 4 (p. 90).

38. Ibid.

39. Ibid., dist. 7, chap. 1, no. 1 (p. 91).

40. Ibid.

41. Ibid. (pp. 91f.).

42. Ibid., no. 3 (p. 93).

43. Ibid., dist. 10, chap. 1, no. 2 (p. 110).

44. See ibid., chap. 2, no. 5, and chap. 3 (p. 113).

45. Ibid., chap. 3, no. 5 (p. 113).

46. See ibid., dist. 13, chap. 3 (pp. 122f.).

47. See ibid., dist. 14, chap. 1 (pp. 126f.).

48. See ibid., dist. 18, chap. 4, no. 1 (p. 157): "Ex praedictis patet quod Spiritus Sanctus sempiterne donum est, et temporaliter datum vel donatum."

49. See ibid., dist. 16, chap. 1 (pp. 138–40).

50. Ibid., dist. 15, chap. 7 (p. 135).

51. Ibid., dist. 17, chap. 1, no. 1 (pp. 141f.).

52. Colish, *Peter Lombard*, 261.

53. *Sentences* 1, dist. 17, chap. 6, no. 8 (pp. 151f.).

54. This point is confirmed by a reading of dist. 23–32 of book 3 of the *Sentences*, which are devoted to faith, hope, and charity. Peter never refers to charity as a virtue, except in three places that have to be interpreted as slips of the pen. See Johann Schupp, *Die Gnadenlehre des Petrus Lombardus*, Freiburger theologische Studien 35 (Freiburg: Herder, 1932), 229 n. 68.

55. See ibid., 224: "Dann sind im Grunde genommen nicht wir die Lie-benden, sondern Gott selbst." Schupp's book contains a detailed treatment on the Lombard's identification of charity with the Holy Spirit (pp. 216–42). Aage Rydstrøm-Poulsen's fine study appeared too late for me to take it into consideration in this chapter: *The Gracious God: Gratia in Augustine and the Twelfth Century* (Copenhagen: Akademisk Forlag, 2002). Pages 380–466 are devoted to Peter Lombard's theory in distinction 17, as well as its earliest followers and critics. For an English translation of, and close commentary on, distinction 17, see my article, "*Fraterna dilectio est Deus*: Peter Lombard's Thesis on Charity as the Holy Spirit," in *Amor amicitiae—On the Love that is Friendship. Essays in Medieval Thought and Beyond in Honor of the Reverend Professor James McEvoy*, ed. Thomas A. F. Kelly and Philipp W. Rosemann, Recherches de théologie et philosophie médiévales, Bibliotheca 6 (Louvain: Peeters, 2004), chap. 21.

56. S. Thomae Aquinatis, *Scriptum super libros Sententiarum Magistri Petri Lombardi*, vol. 1, ed. P. Mandonnet, O.P. (Paris: Lethielleux, 1929), dist. 17, qu. 1, art. 1 (p. 394). Bonaventure's reaction is similar, although he offers a more benevolent interpretation of what he believes the Lombard must have meant; see *Commentaria in IV Libros Sententiarum*, S. Bonaventurae Opera theologica selecta 1 (Quaracchi: Ex typographia Collegii S. Bonaventurae, 1934), dist. 17, pars 1, art. unicus, qu. 1 (pp. 236–40). A good account of the theological implications of the Lombard's position, together with an interpretation of Aquinas's critique, is to be found in Franz Žigon, "Der Begriff der Caritas beim Lombarden, und der hl. Thomas," *Divus Thomas* 4 (1926): 404–24.

57. See Artur Michael Landgraf, *Dogmengeschichte der Frühscholastik*, vol. I/1 (Regensburg: Pustet, 1952), 220–37.

58. Adolf von Harnack, *Lehrbuch der Dogmengeschichte*, 4th ed., vol. 3

(Tübingen: J. C. B. Mohr/Paul Siebeck, 1910; reprint, Darmstadt: Wissenschaftliche Buchgesellschaft, 1964), 620f.

59. See *D. Martin Luthers Werke*, Kritische Gesammtausgabe, vol. 9 (Weimar: Böhlau, 1893; reprint, 1966), 43: "Et videtur Magister non penitus absurdissime loqui." On Luther's reception of the Lombardian teaching on charity, see Paul Vignaux, *Luther commentateur des Sentences (livre I, distinction XVII)*, Études de philosophie médiévale 21 (Paris: Vrin, 1935).

60. *Sentences* 1, dist. 22, chap. 1, no. 1 (p. 178).

61. The treatise on the divine names, with an appendix of related questions, occupies dist. 22–34.

62. See ibid., dist. 23, chap. 1, no. 1 (p. 181).

63. See ibid., chap. 1, no. 3, and chap. 2, no. 1 (pp. 181f.).

64. See ibid., dist. 24 (pp. 187–89).

65. See ibid., dist. 26, chap. 2, no. 1 (p. 197).

66. Ibid., no. 2 (p. 198).

67. Ibid., dist. 33, chap. 1 (pp. 240–43).

68. Ibid., chap. 2, no. 1 (p. 244).

69. See ibid., dist. 30, chap. 1 (pp. 220–22).

70. Ibid., dist. 22, no. 3 (p. 179).

71. See ibid., chap. 4 (p. 179).

72. See ibid., dist. 22, chap. 1, no. 1 (p. 178).

5. THE *SENTENCES*, BOOK II: ON THE CREATION OF THINGS, AND THE FORMATION OF SPIRITUAL AND CORPOREAL ENTITIES, AND MANY OTHER MATTERS PERTAINING TO THESE

1. For the statistics, see Jacqueline Hamesse, *Thesaurus Librorum Sententiarum Petri Lombardi*, series A, *Formae*, Corpus Christianorum, Thesaurus Patrum Latinorum (Turnhout: Brepols, 1991), microfiche 13.

2. *Sentences* 2, preface (p. 329).

3. Ibid., dist. 1, chap. 2 (p. 330). A good account of Peter Lombard's doctrine on creation is to be found in Ermenegildo Bertola, "La dottrina della creazione nel *Liber Sententiarum* di Pier Lombardo," *Pier Lombardo* 1, no. 1 (1957): 27–44.

4. *Sentences* 2, dist. 1, chap. 1, no. 2 (p. 330).

5. Ibid., chap. 3, nos. 4–5 (p. 331).

6. Ibid., chap. 4, no. 4 (p. 332).

7. Ibid., no. 6 (p. 333).

8. Ibid., no. 7 (p. 333).

9. See ibid., chap. 6, no. 6 (pp. 335f.).

10. Ibid., no. 2 (p. 334).

11. Ibid., chap. 6, no. 3 (p. 334).

12. Rob van der Hart, O.P., *The Theology of Angels and Devils*, Theology Today 36 (Notre Dame, Ind.: Fides, 1972), 9.

13. See ibid., 24.

14. Ibid., 17. For an approach to the contemporary interest in angelology from a somewhat different, Thomistic perspective, see Howard P. Kainz, *"Active and Passive Potency" in Thomistic Angelology* (The Hague: Nijhoff, 1972), 1–27.

15. Useful background on the medieval understanding of angels is provided by David Keck, *Angels and Angelology in the Middle Ages* (New York and Oxford: Oxford University Press, 1998). On the development of the theology of angels between c. 1130 and c. 1230, one may consult Marcia L. Colish, "Early Scholastic Angelology," *Recherches de théologie ancienne et médiévale* 62 (1995): 80–109.

16. *Sentences* 2, dist. 2, chap. 1, no. 1 (p. 336). Ermenegildo Bertola provides an overview of Peter Lombard's angelology with particular emphasis on its sources; see "Il problema delle creature angeliche in Pier Lombardo," *Pier Lombardo* 1, no. 2 (1957): 33–54.

17. *Sentences* 2, dist. 2, chap. 4, no. 2 (p. 339).

18. Ibid., dist. 3, chap. 4, no. 10 (p. 347).

19. Ibid., chap. 3 (p. 343).

20. Ibid., chap. 4, no. 7 (p. 345).

21. Ibid., dist. 5, chap. 1 (p. 351).

22. See ibid., dist. 5, chap. 4 (pp. 352f.). On the function of grace in the angelic realm according to Peter Lombard, one may read the excellent account in Johann Schupp, *Die Gnadenlehre des Petrus Lombardus*, Freiburger theologische Studien 35 (Freiburg, Germany: Herder, 1932), 45–56 (esp. 49–52).

23. *Sentences* 2, dist. 8, chap. 2, no. 5 (p. 368).

24. See ibid., chap. 4, no. 1 (p. 369): "daemones, sive corporei sivi incorporei sint."

25. Ibid., dist. 9, chap. 2, no. 2 (p. 371).

26. Ibid.

27. The reflections in this paragraph are inspired by theses that Michel Foucault developed in two of his works, namely, *Madness and Civilization: A History of Insanity in the Age of Reason*, trans. R. Howard (New York: Vintage Books, 1988), and *Discipline and Punish: The Birth of the Prison*, trans. A. Sheridan (New York: Vintage Books, 1995).

28. See Colish, *Peter Lombard*, 303–36.

29. *Sentences* 2, dist. 12, chap. 2 (pp. 384f.).

30. Ibid., chap. 5, no. 4 (p. 388).

31. The four steps are summarized ibid., chap. 6 (pp. 388f.). Another reference to the hidden seeds occurs in dist. 7, chap. 8, no. 2 (p. 363).

32. Ibid., dist. 14, chap. 6 (p. 397).

33. Ibid., dist. 15, chap. 6, nos. 1–2 (p. 403).

34. Ibid., chap. 5, no. 2 (p. 402).

35. Ibid., dist. 16, chap. 3, no. 5 (p. 408).

36. See ibid., chap. 4, no. 1 (p. 409). For a more detailed treatment of the issue of image and likeness in Peter Lombard, see Philipp W. Rosemann, *Omne agens agit sibi simile: A "Repetition" of Scholastic Metaphysics*, Louvain Philosophical Studies 12 (Louvain: Leuven University Press, 1996), chap. 5.

37. See *Sentences* 2, dist. 17, chap. 2, no. 4 (p. 412). According to Colish, Peter admits "that he cannot resolve the question of whether there was a time lag between the creation of Adam's body and the creation of his soul" (*Peter Lombard*, 367), but the text just cited is unambiguous on this point.

38. *Sentences* 2, dist. 17, chap. 3 (pp. 412f.).

39. Ibid., dist. 18, chap. 2 (p. 417).

40. See ibid., dist. 24, chap. 8 (p. 455).

41. Ibid., dist. 19, chap. 1, no. 3 (p. 422).

42. Ibid., dist. 20, chap. 1, no. 3 (p. 428).

43. Ibid., chap. 4, no. 4 (p. 430).

44. See ibid., dist. 19, chap. 1, no. 1 (p. 421).

45. Ibid., dist. 21, chap. 1, no. 1 (p. 433).

46. See ibid., chap. 2 (pp. 433f.).

47. Ibid., dist. 21, chap. 7, no. 1 (p. 437).

48. Ibid., dist. 22, chap. 3, no. 2 (p. 441).

49. Ibid., chap. 4, no. 1 (p. 442).

50. See ibid., chap. 2 (p. 441).

51. Ibid., dist. 24, chap. 7 (p. 455).

52. Marcia Colish interprets this passage as implying that the Lombard meant to "impute greater guilt to Adam" (*Peter Lombard*, 380), thus going back on his earlier opinion according to which Eve was more culpable for the transgression that occurred in original sin. While this interpretation constitutes a legitimate inference, there is no indication that Peter Lombard made such a connection between the historical and the allegorical levels of the Genesis account.

53. *Sentences* 2, dist. 24, chap. 1, no. 2 (pp. 450f.).

54. Ibid., chap. 3, no. 1 (p. 453).

55. Ibid., dist. 25, chap. 7, no. 1 (p. 465).

56. See Schupp, *Die Gnadenlehre*, 64.

57. See *Sentences* 2, dist. 29, chap. 1, no. 2 (p. 492).

58. See Artur Landgraf, *Dogmengeschichte der Frühscholastik*, part 1, *Die Gnadenlehre*, vol. 1 (Regensburg: Pustet, 1952), 95.

59. *Sentences* 2, dist. 28, chap. 1, no. 1 (p. 487).

60. Ibid., dist. 26, chap. 7, no. 2 (p. 477).

61. See ibid., dist. 25, chap. 6 (pp. 464f.).

62. Ibid., chap. 8, no. 2 (p. 466). It is not correct, therefore, that "freedom from any necessity at all was a feature of the human will before the fall. This mode of free will . . . now applies to no one but God" (Colish, *Peter Lombard*, 383).

63. *Sentences* 2, dist. 25, chap. 8, no. 2 (p. 466).

64. See Colish, *Peter Lombard*, 385–93; and Julius Gross, "Abälards Umdeutung des Erbsündendogmas," *Zeitschrift für Religions- und Geistesgeschichte* 15 (1963): 14–33.

65. *Sentences* 2, dist. 30, chap. 6, no. 1 (p. 498).

66. Ibid., chap. 9, no. 1 (p. 500).

67. Ibid., dist. 31, chap. 5, no. 1 (p. 507).

68. Ibid., chap. 4 (p. 506).

69. Ibid., dist. 30, chap. 14, nos. 2–3 (p. 504).

70. See ibid., dist. 35, chap. 1, no. 1 (p. 529), with the commentary by Philippe Delhaye, *Pierre Lombard: Sa vie, ses œuvres, sa morale*, Conférence Albert-le-Grand 1960 (Montreal: Institut d'études médiévales; Paris: Vrin, 1960), 88–93.

71. See *Sentences* 2, dist. 35, chap. 2, no. 3 (p. 531).

72. Colish, *Peter Lombard*, 480.

73. *Sentences* 2, dist. 35, chap. 2, no. 3 (p. 531).

74. Ibid., chap. 5, no. 1 (p. 535f.).

75. On the notion of intellectual practice, see Olga Weijers, *Le maniement du savoir: Pratiques intellectuelles à l'époque des premières universités (XIIIᵉ–XIVᵉ siècles)*, Studia Artistarum, Subsidia (Turnhout: Brepols, 1996).

6. THE *SENTENCES*, BOOK III: ON THE INCARNATION
OF THE WORD

1. *Enchiridion symbolorum definitionum et declarationum de rebus fidei et morum*, ed. Heinrich Denzinger and Adolf Schönmetzer, S.J., 34th ed. (Barcelona: Herder, 1967), no. 749. I am grateful to Dr. Frank Swietek, of the University of Dallas, for discussing the translation of this passage with me.

2. Ibid., no. 750.

3. Ibid., no. 804.

4. J. de Ghellinck, S.J., succinctly summarizes the controversies about the theology of the *Book of Sentences* in his article "Pierre Lombard," *Dictionnaire*

de théologie catholique XII/2 (1935), cols. 1941–2019 (at 2003–11). While these battles lost much of their intensity after the Fourth Council of the Lateran had recognized the orthodoxy of Peter Lombard's Trinitarian theology, they continued to smolder even in the late thirteenth century; on this subject, see the interesting study by Fiona Robb, "A Late Thirteenth-Century Attack on the Fourth Lateran Council: The *Liber contra Lombardum* and Contemporary Debates on the Trinity," *Recherches de théologie ancienne et médiévale* 62 (1995): 110–44.

5. This designation probably originated in Walter of St. Victor's *Contra quatuor labyrinthos Franciae*, which speaks of *nichilianiste*, "nihilianists." See Paul Glorieux, "Le *Contra quatuor labyrinthos Franciae* de Gauthier de Saint-Victor: Édition critique," *Archives d'histoire littéraire et doctrinale du moyen-âge* 19 (1952): 187–335, at 200. For an overview of the main sources of the debate over Christological nihilianism, see Artur Michael Landgraf, *Einführung in die Geschichte der theologischen Literatur der Frühscholastik unter dem Gesichtspunkte der Schulenbildung* (Regensburg: Gregorius-Verlag, 1948), 109–12.

6. Otto Baltzer, *Die Sentenzen des Petrus Lombardus: Ihre Quellen und ihre dogmengeschichtliche Bedeutung*, Studien zur Geschichte der Theologie und der Kirche 8:3 (Leipzig, 1902; reprint, Aalen: Scientia-Verlag, 1987), 99 with n. 4.

7. Certain aspects of this coherence are well seen in Carl Andresen et al., *Die Lehrentwicklung im Rahmen der Katholizität*, Handbuch der Dogmen- und Theologiegeschichte 1 (Göttingen: Vandenhoeck & Ruprecht, 1982), 601–3.

8. Ibid., 602.

9. Ibid., 603.

10. Colish, *Peter Lombard*, 471f. Also see 514–16.

11. *Sentences* 3, dist. 1, intro. (p. 24).

12. Ibid., chap. 3, no. 2 (pp. 26f.).

13. Ibid., chap. 2, no. 1 (p. 29).

14. *Sentences* 2, dist. 31, chap. 5, no. 1 (p. 507).

15. See Alois Stöger, "Flesh," in *Sacramentum Verbi: An Encyclopedia of Biblical Theology*, ed. Johannes B. Bauer (New York: Herder and Herder, 1970), 1:273–78.

16. *Sentences* 3, dist. 3, chap. 1, no. 3 (p. 33).

17. There is no discussion of the virgin birth or of Mary's perpetual virginity in the *Sentences*. Peter Lombard does, however, treat both subjects in one of his sermons, no. 18, "In Annuntiatione B. Mariae" (PL 171: 605B–610D).

18. *Sentences* 3, dist. 5, chap. 1, no. 1 (p. 41).

19. Ibid., chap. 3, no. 1 (p. 47).

20. Ibid., chap. 1, no. 12 (p. 45).

21. Ibid., chap. 2, no. 1 (p. 46).

22. Ibid., dist. 6, chap. 1, no. 1 (pp. 49f.).

23. N. M. Häring, S.A.C., "The Case of Gilbert de la Porrée, Bishop of Poitiers (1142–1154)," *Mediaeval Studies* 13 (1951): 1–40, at 28.

24. See N. M. Häring, S.A.C., ed., "The *Eulogium ad Alexandrum Papam tertium* of John of Cornwall," *Mediaeval Studies* 13 (1951): 253–300. The literature on the three theories as related by Peter Lombard and John of Cornwall is considerable. Apart from the article by Häring cited in the previous note, see Artur Michael Landgraf, *Dogmengeschichte der Frühscholastik*, vol. II/1 (Regensburg: Pustet, 1953), 116–37 (with a response to Häring on pp. 117–20); Robert F. Studeny, S.V.D., *John of Cornwall, an Opponent of Nihilianism: A Study in the Christological Controversies of the Twelfth Century*, Gregorian Univ. diss. (Vienna: St. Gabriel's Mission Press, 1939); and Horacio Santiago-Otero, "El 'nihilianismo' cristológico y las tres opiniones," *Burgense* 10 (1969): 431–43. Unfortunately, it is only after completing this chapter that I discovered Lauge Olaf Nielsen's detailed study of Peter Lombard's theory of the hypostatic union, a study contained in his work, *Theology and Philosophy in the Twelfth Century: A Study of Gilbert Porreta's Thinking and the Theological Explosions of the Doctrine of the Incarnation during the Period 1130–1180*, Acta theologica danica 15 (Leiden: Brill, 1982), 243–79.

25. *Sentences* 3, dist. 6, chap. 2, no. 1 (p. 50).

26. Ibid., chap. 3, no. 1 (p. 52).

27. Ibid., chap. 4, no. 1 (p. 55).

28. John of Cornwall, *Eulogium*, ed. Häring, 265.

29. *Sentences* 3, dist. 7, chap. 1, no. 15 (p. 64). Also see Paul Glorieux, "L'orthodoxie de III Sentences (d. 6, 7 et 10)," in *Miscellanea lombardiana*, 137–47, at 145.

30. *Sentences* 3, dist. 7, chap. 3, no. 3 (p. 66).

31. Ibid.

32. In this question, Paul Glorieux has seen a return to one of the problems formulated at the beginning of distinction 6, namely, whether God was made something else (*aliquid*) or is something else (*aliquid*). Glorieux, of course, interprets *aliquid* as simply "something." In truth, however, distinction 6 addresses a problem concerning the divine nature, whereas distinction 10 is devoted to the personhood of Christ. Thus, it seems to me that 10 is not a "slightly modified" version of 6. The reading of the two distinctions here suggested would explain why the three theories of the hypostatic union are not invoked to resolve the question of distinction 10, a fact that Glorieux finds surprising (see Glorieux, "L'orthodoxie de III Sentences," 139).

33. *Sentences* 3, dist. 10, chap. 1, no. 3 (p. 73).

34. On this point, see Glorieux, "L'orthodoxie de III Sentences," 146f. The true meaning, but also the defects, of Peter Lombard's treatment of Christological nihilianism in the *Sentences* were already well seen more than a hundred years ago, by Julius Kögel in his dissertation, *Petrus Lombardus in seiner Stellung zur Philosophie des Mittelalters* (Greifswald: Julius Abel, 1897), 15 n. 2.

35. See Artur Michael Landgraf, "Schwankungen in der Lehre des Petrus Lombardus," *Scholastik* 31 (1956): 533–44, at 534.

36. The text is quoted in Landgraf, *Dogmengeschichte der Frühscholastik*, vol. II/1, 126 n. 48. For the identification of the student as Peter Comestor (also called "Manducator"), see Ignatius Brady, O.F.M., "Peter Manducator and the Oral Teachings of Peter Lombard," *Antonianum* 41 (1966): 454–90.

37. Landgraf considers the identity of the master uncertain (at least in the *Dogmengeschichte*), while Ignatius Brady believes it is "clear"; see the latter's "Peter Manducator and the Oral Teachings of Peter Lombard," 473 (which includes references to other writings by Landgraf in which he expresses a different opinion).

38. *Sentences* 3, dist. 12, chap. 4 (p. 83).

39. Ibid., dist. 13, no. 8 (pp. 87f.).

40. Ibid., p. 87.

41. Ibid., no. 5 (p. 85).

42. Ibid., dist. 14, chap. 1, no. 3 (p. 90).

43. Ibid.

44. Colish, *Peter Lombard*, 438. Also see 443 and 470.

45. *Sentences* 3, dist. 13, no. 8 (p. 88). Also see ibid., p. 87: "Neque ideo unitas et singularitas personae dividitur." On the problem of Christ's knowledge, see Artur Michael Landgraf, *Dogmengeschichte der Frühscholastik*, vol. II/2 (Regensburg: Pustet, 1954), 44–131, as well as the very precise account in Horacio Santiago-Otero, "Pedro Lombardo: Su tesis acerca del saber de Cristo hombre," in *Miscelánea José Zunzunegui, 1911–1974*, vol. 1, Victoriensia 35 (Vitoria, Spain: Editorial Eset, 1975), 115–25.

46. See *Sentences* 3, dist. 15, chap. 1, no. 1 (p. 93).

47. Ibid., no. 7 (p. 95).

48. See ibid., chap. 2, nos. 2–3 (pp. 98f.). Colish, *Peter Lombard*, 444, misinterprets the distinction between passion and propassion as it applies to Christ's fear and sadness: "In this respect, while men undergo temptation (*passio*) and contemplation of temptation (*propassio*) prior to the consent (*consensus*) which is of the essence in their moral decisions, Christ only experi-

enced the *propassio* and the *consensus*." The word *consensus* does not figure at all in the Lombard's discussion of this matter.

49. *Sentences* 3, dist. 17, chap. 2, no. 2 (p. 106).

50. Ibid., dist. 18, chap. 1, nos. 1–2 (pp. 111f.).

51. Ibid., chap. 2, no. 1 (p. 113).

52. Colish, *Peter Lombard*, 462.

53. *Sentences* 3, dist. 18, chap. 5, no. 1 (p. 116), reading *adopti* for *adepti* in line 20.

54. See ibid., dist. 19, chap. 1, no. 2 (p. 118).

55. Ibid., no. 3 (p. 119).

56. See ibid., dist. 18, chap. 5, no. 2 (pp. 116f.).

57. Ibid., dist. 19, chap. 2 (pp. 120f.). The rights-of-the-devil theory is further developed in dist. 20, chaps. 2–4 (pp. 125–27).

58. This judgment is shared by D. E. De Clerck, "Droits du démon et nécessité de la rédemption: les écoles d'Abélard et de Pierre Lombard," *Recherches de théologie ancienne et médiévale* 14 (1947): 32–64, at 47: "Le Maître des Sentences se contente donc d'amalgamer, sans les réduire à l'unité, les divers éléments que lui fournissent ses prédécesseurs."

59. *Sentences* 3, dist. 23, chap. 1, no. 1 (p. 141).

60. Ibid., chap. 3, no. 3 (p. 143).

61. Ibid., dist. 27, chap. 1, no. 1 (p. 162).

62. Ibid., dist. 23, chap. 9, no. 2 (p. 148).

63. On the virtues in the *Book of Sentences*, see Colish, *Peter Lombard*, 488–516; and Philippe Delhaye, *Pierre Lombard: Sa vie, ses œuvres, sa morale*, Conférence Albert-le-Grand 1960 (Montreal: Institut d'études médiévales; Paris: Vrin, 1961), 52–87.

64. *Sentences* 3, dist. 36, chap. 1, no. 2 (p. 202).

65. Ibid., chap. 2, no. 6 (p. 204).

66. A point well seen by Delhaye, *Pierre Lombard*, 71–73.

67. See, for example, Thomas Aquinas, *Scriptum super Sententiis*, vol. 3, ed. Maria Fabianus Moos, O.P. (Paris: Lethielleux, 1933), dist. 23, qu. 1, art. 4 (pp. 709–16).

68. See ibid., dist. 33, qu. 2, art. 1, sol. 2 (p. 1047).

69. See ibid., dist. 34, qu. 1, art. 1 (p. 1114).

70. Ibid., dist. 37, qu. 2, art. 4, sol. 2 (p. 887).

71. See *Sentences* 2, dist. 41, chap. 2 (p. 564), and Colish, *Peter Lombard*, 515.

72. *Sentences* 3, dist. 37, chap. 6, no. 1 (p. 166).

73. Ibid., dist. 23, chap. 2, no. 1 (p. 141).

74. Ibid., dist. 26, chap. 1 (p. 159).

75. Ibid., chap. 4 (pp. 160f.).

76. On faith and hope, see ibid., dist. 31, chap. 2, nos. 1–2 (pp. 183f.); on the cardinal virtues, see dist. 33, chap. 2 (p. 188); on the gifts of the Spirit, see dist. 34, chap. 2, no. 1 (p. 190).

7. THE *SENTENCES*, BOOK IV, DISTINCTIONS 1–42: ON THE DOCTRINE OF SIGNS

1. *Sentences* 4, dist. 2, chap. 1, no. 2 (p. 240).

2. See ibid., dist. 3, chap. 6 (p. 249). On the connection between Christology and the sacraments in the *Sentences*, see Carl Andresen et al., *Die Lehrentwicklung im Rahmen der Katholizität*, Handbuch der Dogmen- und Theologiegeschichte 1 (Göttingen: Vandenhoeck & Ruprecht, 1982), 603 with n. 158.

3. *Sentences* 4, p. 231.

4. See *Sentences* 2, dist. 35, chap. 4, no. 2 (p. 535).

5. See *Sentences* 4, dist. 1, chap. 1, no. 1 (p. 231).

6. Ibid., chap. 4, no. 2 (p. 233). For a historical elucidation of the elements of this definition, see J. de Ghellinck, S.J., "Un chapitre dans l'histoire de la définition des sacrements au XIIe siècle," in *Mélanges Mandonnet. Études d'histoire littéraire et doctrinale du moyen âge*, Bibliothèque thomiste 14 (Paris: Vrin, 1930), 2:79–96.

7. See de Ghellinck, "Un chapitre," 88.

8. Colish, *Peter Lombard*, 525.

9. See de Ghellinck, "Un chapitre," 91.

10. See *Sentences* 4, dist. 1, chap. 2 (p. 232).

11. Colish, *Peter Lombard*, 531.

12. See *Sentences* 4, dist. 1, chap. 10 (p. 239).

13. For an English translation of distinctions 1 through 26, see Elizabeth Frances Rogers, *Peter Lombard and the Sacramental System*, Columbia Univ. diss. (New York, 1917; reprint, Merrick, N.Y.: Richwood, 1976), 79–246. With a few exceptions, Rogers's translation is faithful and reliable.

14. See *Sentences* 4, dist. 2, chap. 1, no. 1 (p. 240).

15. Ibid., dist. 3, chap. 1, no. 2 (p. 243).

16. Ibid.

17. Ibid., chap. 5, no. 3 (p. 248).

18. Not only has the meaning of *res* changed by comparison with its use in distinction 1; after his treatment of baptism, Peter will also abandon "words" (*verba*) as a significant category for the analysis of the sacraments. On this point, see Rogers, *Peter Lombard and the Sacramental System*, 75.

19. *Sentences* 4, dist. 3, chap. 9, nos. 1–2 (p. 251).

20. See ibid., dist. 7, chap. 3 (p. 278), and chap. 4, no. 1 (p. 279). Colish

claims, "Peter joins Roland of Bologna, Master Simon, and the Porretans in seeing the effect of the sacrament as both the remission of sins and the gift of the Holy Spirit" (*Peter Lombard*, 550). There is nothing in the text of the *Sentences* to suggest that the Lombard considered confirmation to be a means for the remission of sins.

21. Colish (*Peter Lombard*, 551) states that Peter Lombard "joins the majority in disallowing the claim that [confirmation] is more dignified than baptism, arguing that those who make this argument have confused the rank of the minister ... with the effects of the sacrament and its relative necessity for salvation." I do not share Professor Colish's impression that Peter denies the superiority of confirmation over baptism.

22. See Heinrich Weisweiler, "Das Sakrament der Firmung in den systematischen Werken der ersten Frühscholastik," *Scholastik* 8 (1933): 481–523.

23. See *Sentences* 4, dist. 12, chap. 5, no. 1 (p. 308).

24. Ibid., dist. 8, chap. 1 (p. 280).

25. Ibid.

26. Ibid., chap. 3 (p. 281).

27. Ibid., chap. 5, no. 1 (p. 283).

28. Ibid., chap. 4 (p. 282).

29. Ibid., chap. 7, no. 1 (pp. 284f.).

30. Ibid., no. 2 (p. 285).

31. Gary Macy seems to have missed the point of the Lombard's theory of the twofold *res* when he writes, "The *res* of the sacrament is the unity of the Church composed of all the predestined" (*The Theologies of the Eucharist in the Early Scholastic Period: A Study of the Salvific Function of the Sacrament according to the Theologians c. 1080–c. 1220* [Oxford: Clarendon Press, 1984], 122).

32. Again, Macy oversimplifies Peter Lombard's "ecclesiastical approach to the Eucharist" in suggesting, ambiguously, that "anyone who remains in the unity of Christ and the Church spiritually eats Christ" (ibid.). While it is true that unity with the body of Christ is a precondition for receiving the Eucharist spiritually, the spiritual reception presupposes the sacramental one.

33. *Sentences* 4, dist. 9, chap. 2, no. 1 (p. 288).

34. See ibid., dist. 13, chap. 1, no. 4 (p. 312).

35. See Artur Michael Landgraf, *Dogmengeschichte der Frühscholastik*, vol. III/2, *Die Lehre von den Sakramenten* (Regensburg: Pustet, 1955), 207–22. More recently, Gary Macy has studied the literature on this topic in his article "Of Mice and Manna: Quid Mus Sumit as a Pastoral Question," *Recherches de théologie ancienne et médiévale* 58 (1991): 157–66.

36. *Sentences* 4, dist. 13, chap. 1, no. 8 (p. 314).

37. Ludwig Hödl, "Sacramentum und res: Zeichen und Bezeichnetes. Eine begriffsgeschichtliche Arbeit zum frühscholastischen Eucharistietraktat," *Scholastik* 38 (1963): 161–82, at 173.

38. See Henri de Lubac, S.J., *Corpus mysticum. L'Eucharistie et l'Église au moyen âge: Étude historique*, 2d ed., Théologie 3 (Paris: Aubier-Montaigne, 1949).

39. Ibid., 267.

40. Ibid., 117.

41. For an excellent summary and explanation of de Lubac's thesis, see Paul McPartlan, *Sacrament of Salvation: An Introduction to Eucharistic Ecclesiology* (Edinburgh: Clark, 1995), 56–60.

42. De Lubac, *Corpus mysticum*, 9.

43. *Sentences* 4, dist. 10, chap. 1, no. 1 (p. 290).

44. These terms are by no means synonymous, as Ludwig Hödl has convincingly shown in his article, "Der Transsubstantiationsbegriff in der scholastischen Theologie des 12. Jahrhunderts," *Recherches de théologie ancienne et médiévale* 31 (1964): 230–59.

45. *Sentences* 4, dist. 11, chap. 1, no. 1 (p. 296).

46. Ibid., dist. 12, chap. 3, no. 2 (p. 305).

47. Ibid., dist. 11, chap. 3 (p. 299).

48. Ibid., dist. 14, chap. 1, nos. 1–2 (pp. 315f.).

49. Ibid., dist. 22, chap. 2, no. 5 (pp. 389f.). See P. Palmer, "The Theology of *Res* and *Sacramentum* with Particular Emphasis on its Application to Penance," *Proceedings of the Catholic Theological Association of America* 14 (1959): 120–41.

50. See *Sentences* 4, dist. 14, chap. 5 (pp. 322–24).

51. See Paul Anciaux, *The Sacrament of Penance* (New York: Sheed & Ward, 1962), chap. 2, "The History of Penance in the Church" (pp. 46–73).

52. Ibid., 56f.

53. *Sentences* 4, dist. 14, chap. 4, no. 1 (p. 321).

54. Ibid., dist. 17, chap. 1, no. 1 (p. 342).

55. Colish, *Peter Lombard*, 603 and 607, respectively.

56. Ibid., 608.

57. *Sentences* 4, dist. 17, chap. 1, no. 13 (p. 346).

58. Ibid., chap. 3, nos. 1 and 8 (pp. 348 and 350, respectively).

59. Ibid., chap. 4, nos. 1–2 (p. 351).

60. Colish, *Peter Lombard*, 603.

61. *Sentences* 4, dist. 17, chap. 5 (p. 355).

62. Ibid., dist. 18, chap. 5, no. 5, and chap. 6, no. 1 (pp. 360f.).

63. Ibid., chap. 4, no. 6 (p. 358).

64. Marcia Colish points out that "the idea of calling penance a virtue of the mind is not found in any current canonist or scholastic theologian" (*Peter Lombard*, 601).

65. *Sentences* 4, dist. 18, chap. 3 (p. 356).

66. Ibid., dist. 19, chap. 1, no. 3 (p. 365).

67. Ibid., dist. 18, chap. 6, no. 3 (p. 361).

68. Ibid., dist. 17, chap. 4, no. 6 (p. 352).

69. Ibid., dist. 23, chap. 2 (p. 390).

70. Ibid., chap. 4, no. 3 (p. 392).

71. Ibid., chap. 1 (p. 390).

72. See Otto Baltzer, *Die Sentenzen des Petrus Lombardus: Ihre Quellen und ihre dogmengeschichtliche Bedeutung*, Studien zur Geschichte der Theologie und der Kirche, 8:3 (Leipzig, 1902; reprint, Aalen: Scientia-Verlag, 1987), 148.

73. Colish, *Peter Lombard*, 613. Colish reiterates this mistaken interpretation on p. 625.

74. *Sentences* 4, dist. 23, chap. 1 (p. 390).

75. Ibid., chap. 4, no. 5 (p. 392).

76. Ibid., dist. 24, chap. 4, no. 1 (p. 395).

77. Ibid., chap. 9, no. 3 (p. 400).

78. Ibid., chap. 10, no. 2 (pp. 401f.). The epistle read at Mass on each Sunday was drawn from St. Paul.

79. Ibid., chap. 11, no. 3 (pp. 403f.).

80. Ibid., chap. 13, nos. 1–2 (p. 405).

81. Ibid., chap. 16 (p. 406).

82. Plato, *Symposium*, 206C, cited after Plato, vol. III, *Lysis, Symposium, Gorgias*, with an English translation by W. R. M. Lamb, Loeb Classical Library 166 (Cambridge, Mass.: Harvard University Press; London: Heinemann, 1925).

83. Ibid., 207C–208B.

84. For a good analysis of Peter Lombard's theology of marriage, see Hans Zeimentz, *Ehe nach der Lehre der Frühscholastik: Eine moralgeschichtliche Untersuchung zur Anthropologie und Theologie der Ehe in der Schule Anselms von Laon und Wilhelms von Champeaux, bei Hugo von St. Viktor, Walter von Mortagne und Petrus Lombardus* (Düsseldorf: Patmos-Verlag, 1973).

85. *Sentences* 4, dist. 26, chap. 1, no. 1 (p. 416).

86. Ibid., chap. 2, no. 3 (p. 417).

87. Ibid., chap. 3 (p. 418). Peter Lombard evidently does not envisage the increase of the human race as unlimited.

88. Ibid.

89. Ibid., chap. 4 (pp. 418f.): "Et est indulgentia [*Brady*: permissio] in novo

Testamento de minoribus bonis, et de minoribus malis. De minoribus bonis est coniugium, quod non meretur palmam, sed est in remedium. De minoribus malis, id est de venialibus, est coitus qui fit causa incontinentiae. Illud, id est coniugium, indulgetur: id est conceditur; illud vero, id est coitus talis, permittitur: id est toleratur, ita quod non prohibetur." Brady's lection *permissio* does not make sense, which is why I have replaced it with the conjectural *indulgentia*.

90. Ibid., chap. 5, no. 1 (p. 419).

91. Ibid., chap. 5, no. 2 (p. 419).

92. Ibid., dist. 26, chap. 6, no. 1 (pp. 419f.).

93. Ibid., dist. 28, chap. 3, no. 1 (p. 434).

94. Ibid., dist. 27, chap. 6, no. 3 (p. 421).

95. Ibid., dist. 28, chap. 3, no. 2 (p. 435).

96. Ibid., dist. 27, chap. 2 (p. 422).

97. Ibid.

98. Ibid., dist. 28, chap. 4, no. 1 (p. 435): "Quia enim non ancilla vel domina datur."

99. See ibid., dist. 30, chap. 2, no. 3 (p. 440).

100. See Colish, *Peter Lombard*, 695; and Joseph de Ghellinck, S.J., "Pierre Lombard," *Dictionnaire de théologie catholique* XII/2 (1935): 1941–2019, at 2000. De Ghellinck speaks of "sa conception incomplète de la collation de la grâce par le mariage."

101. Colish, *Peter Lombard*, 695.

8. THE *SENTENCES*, BOOK IV, DISTINCTIONS 43–50: ON THE
    RESURRECTION AND THE CIRCUMSTANCES OF JUDGMENT

1. *Sentences* 4, dist. 43, chap. 1, no. 1 (p. 510).

2. See Colish, *Peter Lombard*, 700–703.

3. *Sentences* 4, dist. 43, chap. 1, no. 2 (p. 510).

4. Ibid., dist. 47, chap. 1, no. 1 (p. 537).

5. Ibid., nos. 2–3 (p. 510).

6. Ibid., chap. 3 (p. 512).

7. Ibid., chap. 4, no. 1 (p. 512).

8. Ibid., no. 2 (p. 513).

9. According to Marcia Colish, "facts that occurred openly will be known openly in the next life" (*Peter Lombard*, 711), but there is nothing in the text to support this interpretation.

10. Ibid., chap. 6, no. 5 (p. 515).

11. Ibid., dist. 44, chap. 2, no. 3 (p. 518).

12. Peter does not use the expression "spiritual body" (*corpus spirituale*)

in the eschatology of book 4, although it occurs in book 2 to describe the bodies of the resurrected; see *Sentences* 2, dist. 19, chap. 2, no. 2 (p. 423).

13. *Sentences* 4, dist. 44, chap. 3, no. 2 (p. 519).

14. Ibid., dist. 45, chap. 2, no. 2 (p. 524).

15. Ibid., chap. 4, no. 2 (p. 526).

16. Ibid., chap. 6, no. 3 (p. 527).

17. Ibid., no. 5 (p. 528).

18. Ibid., no. 6 (p. 529).

19. Ibid., dist. 46, chap. 3, nos. 1–2 (pp. 532f.).

20. Ibid., chap. 5, no. 5 (p. 537).

21. Ibid., dist. 47, chap. 2, no. 3 (p. 538).

22. Colish, *Peter Lombard*, 712.

23. *Sentences* 4, dist. 47, chap. 3, no. 2 (p. 539).

24. Ibid.

25. Ibid., no. 3 (p. 539). Colish describes this group as being composed of people "who died with unexpiated but repented sins on their consciences" (*Peter Lombard*, 712). This statement is not borne out by the text of the *Sentences*.

26. *Sentences* 4, dist. 47, chap. 3, no. 3 (p. 539).

27. Ibid., chap. 4, no. 4 (p. 541).

28. Ibid., dist. 48, chap. 1, no. 1 (p. 542).

29. Ibid., chap. 2, no. 3 (p. 544).

30. Ibid., chap. 5, no. 3 (p. 546).

31. Ibid., no. 7 (p. 547).

32. Ibid., dist. 49, chap. 1, no. 5 (p. 549).

33. See Thomas Aquinas, *Scriptum super libros Sententiarum Magistri Petri Lombardi*, book 4, dist. 49, qu. 1, art. 3, quest. 3, resp.

34. *Sentences* 4, dist. 49, chap. 1, no. 7 (p. 550).

35. Ibid., no. 8 (p. 551).

36. Peter Lombard's ideas on the beatific vision are treated, albeit only in passing and in a broader historical context, in Nikolaus Wicki, *Die Lehre von der himmlischen Seligkeit in der mittelalterlichen Scholastik von Petrus Lombardus bis Thomas von Aquin*, Studia friburgensia N.F. 9 (Freiburg, Switzerland: Universitätsverlag, 1954).

37. *Sentences* 4, dist. 49, chap. 1, no. 1 (p. 548).

38. Ibid., nos. 1–2 (p. 548).

39. Ibid., no. 2 (pp. 548f.).

40. Dist. 49, chap. 1, no. 2 (p. 551) speaks, in passing, of people of greater and lesser merit: *aliquis magis meritus . . . aliquis minus meritus*.

41. See Wicki, *Die Lehre von der himmlischen Seligkeit*, 115f. with nn. 10 and 11.

42. *Sentences* 4, dist. 49, chap. 2, no. 2 (p. 551).

43. Ibid., chap. 3, no. 2 (p. 552).

44. Ibid., no. 3 (p. 552).

45. Ibid., dist. 50, chap. 1, no. 4 (p. 554).

46. Ibid., chap. 2, no. 1 (p. 555). The scriptural text underlying this question is Matthew 8:12.

47. Ibid.

48. Colish, *Peter Lombard*, 715.

49. *Sentences* 4, dist. 50, chap. 2, no. 3 (pp. 555f.).

50. Ibid., chap. 7, no. 2 (p. 559).

51. Ibid., explicit (p. 560): "Haec de pedibus Sedentis *super solium excelsum*, quos *Seraphin duabus velis velabant*, scriptori, etsi non auditori, commemorasse sufficit, qui a facie exorsus Sedentis, per media ad pedes usque Via duce pervenit."

52. For an elucidation of the closing sentence, see Ceslao Pera, O.P., "Postilla alla conclusione delle 'Sentenze' di Pietro Lombardo," in *Miscellanea lombardiana*, 103–8. Pera gained inspiration from Aquinas's commentary on the passage.

CONCLUSION

1. Michel Foucault, *The History of Sexuality*, vol. 1, *An Introduction*, trans. Robert Hurley (New York: Vintage Books, 1990), 20.

2. Colish, *Peter Lombard*, 2.

3. In the following pages, I will frequently refer to contributions in the volume entitled *Mediaeval Commentaries on the* Sentences *of Peter Lombard: Current Research*, vol. 1, ed. G. R. Evans (Leiden/Boston/Cologne: Brill, 2002). Moreover, a good selection of literature on the history of commentaries on the *Sentences* is available in John Van Dyk, "Thirty Years since Stegmüller: A Bibliographical Guide to the Study of the Medieval Sentence Commentaries since the Publication of Stegmüller's *Repertorium commentariorum in Sententias Petri Lombardi* (1947)," *Franciscan Studies* 39 (1979): 255–315.

4. Many of Landgraf's and other scholars' studies on the earliest reception of the *Sentences* are listed in Artur Michael Landgraf, *Einführung in die Geschichte der theologischen Literatur der Frühscholastik unter dem Gesichtspunkte der Schulenbildung* (Regensburg: Gregorius-Verlag, 1948), 96–109.

5. See John Marenbon, "Medieval Latin Commentaries and Glosses on Aristotelian Logical Texts, before c. 1150 A.D.," in idem, *Aristotelian Logic, Platonism and the Context of Early Medieval Philosophy in the West*, Variorum Collected Studies Series CS 696 (Aldershot, Hamps., and Burlington, Vt.: Ashgate, 2000), article 2.

6. Ibid., 80.

7. Ibid., 88.

8. Ibid., 96.

9. See ibid., 93.

10. See Olga Weijers, *Le maniement du savoir: Pratiques intellectuelles à l'époque des premières universités (XIIIᵉ–XIVᵉ siècles)*, Studia Artistarum, Subsidia (Turnhout: Brepols, 1996).

11. See Raymond-M. Martin, O.P., "*Filia Magistri*: Un abrégé des *Sentences* de Pierre Lombard," *Bulletin of the John Rylands Library* 2 (1915): 370–79, esp. 373–75.

12. See Martin Grabmann, *Die Geschichte der scholastischen Methode*, vol. 2, *Die scholastische Methode im 12. und beginnenden 13. Jahrhundert* (Freiburg, Germany: Herder, 1911; reprint, Berlin: Akademie-Verlag, 1988), 389.

13. Artur Landgraf has partially edited an abbreviation from the 1180s in his article "Frühscholastische Abkürzungen der Sentenzen des Lombarden," in *Studia mediaevalia in honorem admodum Reverendi Patris Raymundi Josephi Martin* (Bruges: De Tempel, 1948), 171–99.

14. See Martin, "*Filia Magistri*," 372.

15. Hugh of St. Cher's authorship of the *Filia Magistri* is established in Artur Landgraf, "Mitteilungen zum Sentenzenkommentar Hugos a S. Charo," *Zeitschrift für katholische Theologie* 58 (1934): 391–400, at 392f.

16. See Artur Landgraf, "Problèmes relatifs aux premières Gloses des Sentences," *Recherches de théologie ancienne et médiévale* 3 (1931): 140–57, esp. 142f. Also see the same author's "Sentenzenglossen des beginnenden 13. Jahrhunderts," *Recherches de théologie ancienne et médiévale* 10 (1938): 36–55, esp. 54f. (which has a slightly different taxonomy of the *Sentences* glosses).

17. See Joseph de Ghellinck, S.J., "Les notes marginales du *Liber sententiarum*," *Revue d'histoire ecclésiastique* 14 (1913): 511–36 and 705–19.

18. Ibid., 717.

19. See Artur Landgraf, "Drei Zweige der Pseudo-Poitiers-Glosse zu den Sentenzen des Lombarden," *Recherches de théologie ancienne et médiévale* 9 (1937): 167–204.

20. See O. Lottin, O.S.B., "Le prologue des Gloses sur les Sentences attribuées à Pierre de Poitiers," *Recherches de théologie ancienne et médiévale* 7 (1935): 70–73. Also see the detailed discussion in Philip S. Moore, C.S.C., *The Works of Peter of Poitiers, Master in Theology and Chancellor of Paris (1193–1205)* (Washington, D.C.: Catholic University of America, 1936), 145–64.

21. See Raymond-M. Martin, O.P., "Notes sur l'œuvre littéraire de Pierre le Mangeur," *Recherches de théologie ancienne et médiévale* 3 (1931): 54–66, esp. 60–64. On pp. 63f. of this article, Père Martin has edited the prologue of the Pseudo-Poitiers gloss. An additional section of the prologue was subsequently

discovered and edited by Dom Lottin (see the article cited in the preceding note). In addition, Ludwig Hödl has recently edited the glosses on *Sentences* 1, dist. 25, chap. 3; see his article "Die Sentenzen des Petrus Lombardus in der Diskussion seiner Schule," in *Mediaeval Commentaries on the* Sentences *of Peter Lombard*, 25–40, at 37–40.

22. A curious literary genre that came into existence in the early stages of the reception of the *Sentences* is exemplified by Master Udo's *Summa super sententias*, a text dating from around 1160–1165. Neither an abbreviation nor a gloss of the Master's work, the *Summa* follows the arrangement of topics, and sometimes even the words, found in the *Book of Sentences*, without however intending to serve as a tool for the study of the Lombard. In fact, the *Summa super sententias* seems to have been conceived as an independent theology. See O. Lottin, O.S.B., "Le premier commentaire connu des Sentences de Pierre Lombard," *Recherches de théologie ancienne et médiévale* 11 (1939): 64–71.

23. See Artur Landgraf, "The First Sentence Commentary of Early Scholasticism," *The New Scholasticism* 13 (1939): 101–32, esp. 119f. Similar remarks occur in the preface to Landgraf's edition of the work: *Der Sentenzenkommentar des Kardinals Stephan Langton*, Beiträge zur Geschichte der Philosophie und Theologie des Mittelalters 37:1 (Münster: Aschendorff, 1952), xxxvii.

24. Landgraf, *Der Sentenzenkommentar des Kardinals Stephan Langton*, 18.

25. See *Magistri Alexandri de Hales Glossa in quatuor libros Sententiarum Petri Lombardi*, vol. 1, *In librum primum*, Bibliotheca Franciscana Scholastica Medii Aevi 12 (Quaracci and Florence: Typographia Collogii S. Bonaventurae, 1951).

26. See Ignatius Brady, O.F.M., "The Distinctions of Lombard's *Book of Sentences* and Alexander of Hales," *Franciscan Studies* 25 (1965): 90–116.

27. See, for instance, *Magistri Alexandri de Hales Glossa*, lib. 1, dist. 3, nos. 54–55 (pp. 73–74).

28. One such exception occurs right at the beginning of the commentary on the prologue; see ibid., expositio prologi, no. 1 (p. 5).

29. See *S. Bonaventurae Commentaria in quattuor libros Sententiarum Magistri Petri Lombardi*, vol. 1, *In primum librum Sententiarum*, S. Bonaventurae Opera Omnia 1 (Quaracchi: Typographia Collegii S. Bonaventurae, 1882).

30. See Philipp W. Rosemann, "What Is an Author? Bonaventure and Foucault on the Meaning of Authorship," *Fealsúnacht: A Journal of the Dialectical Tradition* (Belfast) 2 (2001–2002): 23–45.

31. See Russell L. Friedman, "The *Sentences* Commentary, 1250–1320: General Trends, the Impact of the Religious Orders, and the Test Case of Predestination," in *Mediaeval Commentaries on the* Sentences *of Peter Lombard*, 41–128, esp. 84–100.

32. See S. Thomae Aquinatis *Scriptum super libros Sententiarum Magistri Petri Lombardi*, ed. P. Mandonnet, O.P., vol. 1 (Paris: Lethielleux, 1929).

33. See Martin Grabmann, *Die Werke des hl. Thomas von Aquin: eine literarhistorische Untersuchung und Einführung*, reprint of the 3d ed., Beiträge zur Geschichte der Philosophie und Theologie des Mittelalters 22, 1/2 (Münster: Aschendorff, 1967), 289.

34. On the composition of the *Ordinatio*, see C. Balić, *Les commentaires de Jean Duns Scot sur les quatre livres des Sentences*, Bibliothèque de la Revue d'histoire ecclésiastique 1 (Louvain: Bureaux de la Revue, 1927). Balić summarizes his findings on pp. 239–46. Several aspects of his account have been challenged by Vladimir Richter, S.J., *Studien zum literarischen Werk von Johannes Duns Scotus*, Veröffentlichungen der Kommission für die Herausgabe ungedruckter Texte aus der mittelalterlichen Geisteswelt 14 (Munich: Verlag der Bayerischen Akademie der Wissenschaften, 1988).

35. See Ioannis Duns Scoti *Ordinatio—Prologus*, Opera Omnia, ed. C. Balić, vol. 1 (Vatican City: Typis Polyglottis Vaticanis, 1950).

36. See Friedman, "The *Sentences* Commentary, 1250–1320," 92.

37. See Ioannis Duns Scoti *Ordinatio—Liber primus: Distinctio prima et secunda*, Opera Omnia, ed. C. Balić, vol. 2 (Vatican City: Typis Polyglottis Vaticanis, 1950), dist. 1, pars 3, qu. 5 (p. 124, ll. 11–15).

38. Ioannis Duns Scoti *Ordinatio—Prologus*, ed. Balić, Introductio, p. 165*.

39. See Guillelmi de Ockham *Scriptum in primum Sententiarum—Ordinatio: Prologus et distinctio prima*, ed. G. Gál, O.F.M., and Stephen Brown, O.F.M., Guillelmi de Ockham Opera philosophica et theologica, Opera theologica 1 (St. Bonaventure, N.Y.: Franciscan Institute, 1967).

40. See Maarten J. F. M. Hoenen, "The Commentary on the *Sentences* of Marsilius of Inghen," in *Mediaeval Commentaries on the* Sentences *of Peter Lombard*, 465–506, esp. 466.

41. See Paul J. J. M. Bakker and Chris Schabel, "*Sentences* Commentaries of the Later Fourteenth Century," in *Mediaeval Commentaries on the* Sentences *of Peter Lombard*, 425–64, esp. 428.

42. See Marsilius von Inghen, *Quaestiones super quattuor libros Sententiarum*, vol. 1, *Super primum, Quaestiones 1–7*, ed. Manuel Santos Noya, Studies in the History of Christian Thought 87 (Leiden: Brill, 2000), xxvii–xxviii. Hoenen presents a table that shows the correlation between Peter Lombard's distinctions and Marsilius's *quaestiones;* see Hoenen, "The Commentary on the *Sentences* of Marsilius of Inghen," 495.

43. Hoenen, "The Commentary on the *Sentences* of Marsilius of Inghen," 496.

44. See Marsilius von Inghen, *Quaestiones super quattuor libros Sententiarum*, vol. 1, ed. Santos Noya, xxvii n. 55.

45. John Van Dyk, "The Sentence Commentary: A Vehicle in the Intellectual Transition of the Fifteenth Century," in *Fifteenth-Century Studies*, vol. 8, ed. G. R. Mermier and E. E. DuBruck (Detroit, Mich.: Fifteenth-Century Symposium, 1983), 227–38, at 230.

46. See ibid., 234.

47. Ibid., 232.

48. See Martin Grabmann, "Johannes Capreolus, O.P., der 'Princeps Thomistarum' († 1444), und seine Stellung in der Geschichte der Thomistenschule," in idem, *Mittelalterliches Geistesleben*, vol. 3 (Munich: Hueber, 1956), 370–410.

49. See *D. Martin Luthers Werke: Kritische Gesammtausgabe*, vol. 9 (Weimar: Böhlau, 1893), 28–94.

50. Apart from several articles, there are three monographs devoted to Luther as commentator on the *Sentences*: Paul Vignaux, *Luther, Commentateur des Sentences (Livre I, distinction XVII)*, Études de philosophie médiévale 21 (Paris: Vrin, 1935); Lawrence F. Murphy, S.J., *Martin Luther, commentator on the Sentences of Peter Lombard: Theological Method and Selected Theological Problems*, Marquette Univ. diss. (Ann Arbor, Mich.: UMI Dissertation Services, 1970); and Josef Wieneke, *Luther und Petrus Lombardus: Martin Luthers Notizen anläßlich seiner Vorlesung über die Sentenzen des Petrus Lombardus, Erfurt 1509/11*, Dissertationen, Theologische Reihe 71 (St. Ottilien: EOS Verlag, 1994). Parts of Father Murphy's excellent study later appeared in article form.

51. *D. Martin Luthers Werke*, 9:30.

52. *Sentences* 3, dist. 22, chap. 1, no. 3 (p. 136).

53. *D. Martin Luthers Werke*, 9:29. The translation is Murphy's, with some slight modifications (Murphy, *Martin Luther, Commentator on the Sentences of Peter Lombard*, 77f.). The last sentence of the quotation is difficult to translate. The Latin reads: "Dilige ergo integros et fideles purosque authores aut saltem (si ita fieri sit necesse) populari fac sint tibi familiaritate conjuncti, philosophos inquam i.e. opiniosos dubitatores." Murphy, in his detailed commentary on the prologue, conjectures that it could be "a hastily written sentence" (ibid., 98 n. 34).

SELECT BIBLIOGRAPHY

EDITIONS OF PETER LOMBARD'S WORKS

Gloss on the Psalter. PL 191: 55A–1296B.

Gloss on the Pauline Epistles. PL 191: 1297A–1696C and PL 192: 9A–520A.

The Book of Sentences. Magistri Petri Lombardi *Sententiae in IV libris distinctae*, ed. Ignatius Brady, O.F.M., 2 vols., Spicilegium Bonaventurianum 4–5 (Grottaferrata: Editiones Collegii S. Bonaventurae Ad Claras Aquas, 1971–1981). For an English translation of book 4, dist. 1 through 26, see Elizabeth Frances Rogers, *Peter Lombard and the Sacramental System*, Columbia Univ. diss. (New York, 1917; reprint, Merrick, N.Y.: Richwood, 1976). Rogers's translation, prepared on the basis of an older edition of the *Sentences*, is reliable, though with a few exceptions.

Sermons. Most of Peter Lombard's sermons are printed among the works of Hildebert of Lavardin, in PL 171: 370C–376B (no. 1 in Brady's *Prolegomena*); 376B–381C (no. 2); 381D–388B (no. 4); 715B–720D (no. 5); 723A–727D (no. 6); 394A–401D (no. 7); 401D–409C (no. 8); 615C–623B (no. 9); 623C–627B (no. 10); 845D–853B (no. 11); 443B–451A (no. 12); 451B–456C (no. 13); 853C–864A (no. 14); 456C–463C (no. 15); 491B–502C (no. 16); 605B–610D (no. 18); 510A–524C (no. 19); 524D–530D (no. 20); 796C–806C (no. 21); 685D–695D (no. 22); 556A–564A (no. 23); 352C–363D (no. 24); 871C–873C (no. 25); 567D–572A (no. 26); 432C–439D (no. 27); 368A–370C (no. 34; of dubious authenticity).

COLLECTIVE VOLUME AND JOURNAL

Miscellanea lombardiana (Novara: Istituto geografico de Agostini, 1957). Proceedings of a colloquium organized by the Pontificio Ateneo Salesiano of Turin. The thirty-three contributions are of unequal value, but include several items that have become part of the canon of standard literature on Peter Lombard.

Pier Lombardo. Journal of Lombard studies, published in only four volumes between 1957 and 1960. Very few libraries in the United States (and presumably elsewhere) own copies of *Pier Lombardo*, but it is possible to order individual articles through the interlibrary loan system.

SECONDARY LITERATURE ON PETER LOMBARD'S LIFE AND WORKS

Brady's *Prolegomena* to his edition are the most comprehensive and authoritative source of information: Magistri Petri Lombardi *Sententiae in IV libris distinctae*, ed. Ignatius Brady, O.F.M., vol. 1, part 1, Spicilegium Bonaventurianum 4 (Grottaferrata: Editiones Collegii S. Bonaventurae Ad Claras Aquas, 1971). Important additions are to be found in vol. 2 of the same edition, also prepared by Brady: *Sententiae in IV libris distinctae*, vol. 2, Spicilegium Bonaventurianum 5 (Grottaferrata: Editiones Collegii S. Bonaventurae Ad Claras Aquas, 1981), 7*–100*. Further precisions in Ignatius Brady, O.F.M., "Pierre Lombard," in *Dictionnaire de spiritualité* 12 (1986): 1604–12.

Other Important Contributions by Father Brady

Brady, Ignatius, O.F.M. "Peter Lombard: Canon of Notre Dame," *Recherches de théologie ancienne et médiévale* 32 (1965): 277–95.
———. "Peter Manducator and the Oral Teachings of Peter Lombard," *Antonianum* 41 (1966): 454–90.

Other Literature relating to Peter Lombard's Life and Works

de Ghellinck, Joseph, S.J. "Pierre Lombard," *Dictionnaire de théologie catholique* XII/2 (1935): 1941–2019. A classic general introduction to Peter Lombard, dated in parts, but still instructive.

de Hamel, C. F. R. *Glossed Books of the Bible and the Origins of the Paris Booktrade* (Woodbridge, Suffolk: Brewer, 1984). On Peter Lombard's role in the revision of the *Glossa ordinaria*.

Protois, Félix. *Pierre Lombard, évêque de Paris, dit le Maître des Sentences. Son époque, sa vie, ses écrits, son influence* (Paris: Société générale de librairie catholique, 1881), 123–48. Still the best available treatment of the Lombard's sermons, with several excerpts.

Stirnemann, Patricia. "Histoire tripartite: un inventaire des livres de Pierre Lombard, un exemplaire de ses *Sentences* et le destinataire du Psautier de Copenhague," in *Du copiste au collectionneur: Mélanges d'histoire des textes et des bibliothèques en l'honneur d'André Vernet*, ed. Donatella Nebbiai-Dalla Guarda and Jean-François Genest, Bibliologia 18 (Turnhout: Brepols, 1998), 301–33. New findings on MS. *Troyes, Bibliothèque municipale 900*, one of the principal manuscript witnesses of the *Sentences*.

LITERATURE ON THE *BOOK OF SENTENCES*

Baltzer, Otto. *Die Sentenzen des Petrus Lombardus. Ihre Quellen und ihre dogmengeschichtliche Bedeutung*, Studien zur Geschichte der Theologie und der Kirche, 8:3 (Leipzig, 1902; reprint, Aalen: Scientia-Verlag, 1987). An older work, still useful as a summary of the *Sentences'* main theses and as a basic introduction to its sources.

Colish, Marcia L. *Peter Lombard*, 2 vols., Brill's Studies in Intellectual History 41 (Leiden/New York/Cologne: Brill, 1994). Magisterial study by the most widely published contemporary Lombard scholar. Not all of Colish's interpretations, however, are beyond dispute.

Word Index

Hamesse, Jacqueline. *Thesaurus Librorum Sententiarum Petri Lombardi*, series A, *Formae*, Corpus Christianorum, Thesaurus Patrum Latinorum (Turnhout: Brepols, 1991). The index is published on microfiche.

Sources of the Book of Sentences

Bougerol, Jacques-Guy. "The Church Fathers and the *Sentences* of Peter Lombard," in *The Reception of the Church Fathers in the West: From the Carolingians to the Maurists*, ed. Irena Backus (Leiden/New York/Cologne: Brill, 1997), 113–64.

Cavallera, Ferdinand. "Saint Augustin et le *Livre des Sentences* de Pierre Lombard," *Archives de philosophie* 7, no. 2 (1930): 186–99 = [438]–[451].

Gastaldelli, Ferruccio. "La *Summa sententiarum* di Ottone da Lucca: Conclusione di un dibattito secolare," *Salesianum* 42 (1980): 537–46. Identifies the *Summa sententiarium*, one of the Lombard's principal contemporary sources, as a work by Master Otto of Lucca.

Wicki, Nikolaus. "Das *Prognosticon futuri saeculi* Julians von Toledo als Quellenwerk der Sentenzen des Petrus Lombardus," *Divus Thomas* (Fribourg) 31 (1953): 349–60.

Studies on Specific Aspects of the Theology of the
Book of Sentences, *Arranged Systematically*

Schneider, Johannes. *Die Lehre vom dreieinigen Gott in der Schule des Petrus Lombardus,* Münchener theologische Studien II, Abteilung 22 (Munich: Hueber, 1961). Reliable study of the Lombard's understanding of the divine essence and the Trinity, although perhaps slightly too historical in its comparative approach, for which Peter Lombard represents nothing more than a particular step in the gradual perfection of theological doctrine.

Bertola, Ermenegildo. "Il problema di Dio in Pier Lombardo," *Rivista di filosofia neo-scolastica* 48 (1956): 135–50.

———. "La dottrina della creazione nel *Liber Sententiarum* di Pier Lombardo," *Pier Lombardo* 1, no. 1 (1957): 27–44.

———. "Il problema delle creature angeliche in Pier Lombardo," *Pier Lombardo* 1, no. 2 (1957): 33–54. Bertola's articles provide helpful summaries of certain aspects of the *Book of Sentences*, usually with an emphasis on the sources of Peter Lombard's teachings.

Schupp, Johann. *Die Gnadenlehre des Petrus Lombardus,* Freiburger theologische Studien 35 (Freiburg, Switzerland: Herder, 1932). A fine book, with a detailed treatment of the Lombard's identification of charity with the Holy Spirit.

Žigon, Franz. "Der Begriff der Caritas beim Lombarden, und der hl. Thomas," *Divus Thomas* 4 (1926): 404–24.

Rydstrøm-Poulsen, Aage. *The Gracious God: Gratia in Augustine and the Twelfth Century* (Copenhagen: Akademisk Forlag, 2002), 343–466. This important new study places the Lombard's teachings on charity in the larger context of his conception of grace, both in the *Sentences* and in other works (pp. 343–91). Moreover, Rydstrøm-Poulsen offers a detailed discussion of the earliest reception of Peter's identification of charity with the Holy Spirit, by masters sympathetic to (pp. 392–434) and critical of it (pp. 435–66). This book appeared after I had completed my own chapter 4.

Landgraf, Artur Michael. *Dogmengeschichte der Frühscholastik,* vol. I/1 (Regensburg: Pustet, 1952), 220–37. Historical background on the Lombard's doctrine on charity.

Rosemann, Philipp W. *Omne agens agit sibi simile: A "Repetition" of Scholastic Metaphysics,* Louvain Philosophical Studies 12 (Louvain: Leuven University Press, 1996), 143–57. Discussion of the metaphysical implications of Peter Lombard's teachings on man as the image and likeness of God.

Nielsen, Lauge Olaf. *Theology and Philosophy in the Twelfth Century: A Study of Gilbert Porreta's Thinking and Theological Expositions of the Doctrine of the Incarnation during the Period 1130–1180,* Acta theologica danica 15 (Leiden: Brill, 1982), 243–79. Synthetic discussion of Peter Lombard's understanding of the Incarnation, arguing that Peter was an adherent of the *habitus* theory.

Glorieux, Paul. "L'orthodoxie de III Sentences (d. 6, 7 et 10)," in *Miscellanea lombardiana,* 137–47. Argues convincingly that Peter Lombard did not defend the doctrine of Christological nihilianism, at least in the *Sentences.*

Santiago-Otero, Horacio. "El 'nihilianismo' cristológico y las tres opiniones," *Burgense* 10 (1969): 431–43.

Häring, Nikolaus M., S.A.C. "The Case of Gilbert de la Porrée, Bishop of Poitiers (1142–1154)," *Mediaeval Studies* 13 (1951): 1–40. Contains a valuable interpretation of Peter Lombard's three theories of the hypostatic union.

Häring, Nikolaus M., ed. "The *Eulogium ad Alexandrum Papam tertium* of John of Cornwall," *Mediaeval Studies* 13 (1951): 253–300. Edition of John of Cornwall's famous commentary on the three theories.

Santiago-Otero, Horacio. "Pedro Lombardo: su tesis acerca del saber de Cristo hombre," in *Miscelánea José Zunzunegui, 1911–1974,* vol. 1, Victoriensia 35 (Vitoria: Editorial Eset, 1975), 115–25. Incisive discussion of the knowledge that Christ possessed qua human being.

Delhaye, Philippe. *Pierre Lombard: sa vie, ses œuvres, sa morale,* Conférence Albert-le-Grand 1960 (Montreal: Institut d'études médiévales; Paris: Vrin, 1960). Synthetic introduction to Peter Lombard's ethics.

de Ghellinck, Joseph, S.J. "Un chapitre dans l'histoire de la définition des sacrements au XIIᵉ siècle," in *Mélanges Mandonnet. Études d'histoire littéraire et doctrinale du moyen âge,* Bibliothèque thomiste 14 (Paris: Vrin, 1930), 2:79–96.

Hödl, Ludwig. "Sacramentum und res—Zeichen und Bezeichnetes: Eine begriffsgeschichtliche Arbeit zum frühscholastischen Eucharistietraktat," *Scholastik* 38 (1963): 161–82.

de Lubac, Henri, S.J. *Corpus mysticum. L'Eucharistie et l'Église au moyen âge. Étude historique,* 2d ed., Théologie 3 (Paris: Aubier-Montaigne, 1949).

258   SELECT BIBLIOGRAPHY

Celebrated and controversial study, indispensable for an understanding of Peter Lombard's place in the development of the doctrine on the Eucharist.

Zeimentz, Hans. *Ehe nach der Lehre der Frühscholastik: eine moralgeschichtliche Untersuchung zur Anthropologie und Theologie der Ehe in der Schule Anselms von Laon und Wilhelms von Champeaux, bei Hugo von St. Viktor, Walter von Mortagne und Petrus Lombardus* (Düsseldorf: Patmos-Verlag, 1973).

Wicki, Nikolaus. *Die Lehre von der himmlischen Seligkeit in der mittelalterlichen Scholastik von Petrus Lombardus bis Thomas von Aquin*, Studia friburgensia N.F. 9 (Freiburg, Switzerland: Universitätsverlag, 1954). Contains useful remarks concerning the Lombard's conception of beatitude.

STUDIES ON THE TRADITION OF COMMENTARIES
ON THE *SENTENCES*

Mediaeval Commentaries on the Sentences *of Peter Lombard: Current Research,* vol. 1, ed. G. R. Evans (Leiden/Boston/Cologne: Brill, 2002). Collective work presenting important new research on the tradition of *Sentences* commentaries. A second volume is planned to fill gaps in the areas treated in the first. Most notably, the first volume does not contain a contribution on the earliest reception of the *Sentences*.

Landgraf, Artur Michael. *Einführung in die Geschichte der theologischen Literatur der Frühscholastik unter dem Gesichtspunkte der Schulenbildung* (Regensburg: Gregorius-Verlag, 1948), 96–109. Provides references to important older literature on the reception of the *Sentences* in the twelfth and early thirteenth centuries.

Stegmüller, Friedrich. *Repertorium commentariorum in Sententias Petri Lombardi,* 2 vols. (Würzburg: Schöningh, 1947). As the title indicates, this book offers a list of glosses and commentaries of the *Sentences*. The list comprises 1,407 entries, reflecting the state of research in the late 1940s. Several updates have appeared; for a complete bibliography see Steven J. Livesey, "*Lombardus electronicus*: A Biographical Database of Medieval Commentators on Peter Lombard's *Sentences*," in *Mediaeval Commentaries on the* Sentences *of Peter Lombard: Current Research*, vol. 1, ed. G. R. Evans (Leiden/Boston/Cologne: Brill, 2002), 1–23 (on p. 2).

Van Dyk, John. "Thirty Years since Stegmüller: A Bibliographical Guide to the Study of the Medieval Sentence Commentaries since the Publication of Stegmüller's *Repertorium commentariorum in Sententias Petri Lombardi* (1947)," *Franciscan Studies* 39 (1979): 255–315. Good bibliography, though not comprehensive.

SCRIPTURE REFERENCES

NAME INDEX

SUBJECT INDEX

adoptionism, 133–34

angels: their aversion (Fall) and conversion, 98–100, 108–9; creation of, 97–98; guardian angels, 102; intercession by, 183–85; mediating between nature and grace, 102; orders of, 101–2; properties, 98, 100–101; as servants to human being, 95. *See also* demons

Arianism, 134

authority, 8, 18, 21, 47–48, 60, 63, 66–70. *See also* Scholastic method; tradition

beatific vision, 189–91

body, mystical, 152–56, 175–77

body, spiritual, 101, 245–46

Book of Sentences (Peter Lombard): abbreviations of, 202; commentaries upon, 203–10; consultation aids in, 64–65; date of composition, 55; division into distinctions, 64–65, 204, 207; glosses upon, 202–3; literal interpretation of Scripture in, 103–5, 110, 117; its merits and shortcomings, 195–98; method, 61–70, 105; rubrics in, 65; sources, 55–57; structure, 57–62, 144, 193; Gloss on the Pauline Epistles, 44–48, 50–53, 225–26; Gloss on the Psalms, 43–44, 50–53, 225; sermons, 49, 226–27, 237. *See also* theological topics

canon law, 21–23, 149, 159, 173

canons regular, 57

celibacy, 171

Chalcedon, Council of, 16

charity, 85, 87–90, 99, 138–44, 165–66, 175, 177–78, 187, 189–90, 197–98

Chartres, school of, 94

Christology: Christ's passion, 136–39; Christ's twofold will, 136; Christ's twofold wisdom, 134–35; Christ's virtues, 139–43; hypostatic union, 124–30, 195, 238; nihilianism, 118–19, 131–33, 195, 237–39; structure of Peter Lombard's, 119–21; and Trinitarian theology, 121–22; two